D1566696

THEORY OF PUBLIC CHOICE

Theory
of
Public Choice

Political Applications of Economics

edited by

James M. Buchanan and Robert D. Tollison

Ann Arbor
The University of Michigan Press

Contents

v

I
INTRODUCTION

1

Involved Social Analysis

Robert D. Tollison

Modern social science has emerged as an involved and relevant field of inquiry. Recent times have seen a wide engagement of the social scientist in government activity. This is especially true of economists who have become essential staff members at high levels in public bureaucracies. Areas of involvement have ranged from stabilization policy to application of price theory tools in public investment projects and in budgetary reform. There is a point, however, to raising questions about the involvement of the economist in democratic process. The rationale for such a discussion is pertinent because the political involvement of economists leaves them open to the charge of participation as partisans rather than scientists in their application of economic analysis. The application of economic tools can be a strong positive influence in the political adversary process. Much of the internal work of economists in government is of this character (forecasting for example). This is a valuable role for the economist. But in the more purely partisan behavior of the economist in government, it is clear that there are definite boundaries between what is *bona fide* political economy and what is pure political behavior. In a "public choice" frame of reference the search for consensus under the guideline of Pareto optimality defines the proper role of the economist in public proceedings. This does not rule out the advocacy of particular policies. Much of the innovation in public policy that we see proposed today came initially from economists. Would we be better off without the policy proposals of Friedman or Heller or other well-known political economists? Indeed there is clear incentive in the political adversary process for positive propositions about public policy to be segregated from purely ideological arguments. Questions may be raised about the strength of this adversary process and about the ability

3

of the press to discern such matters correctly. But we are not quarreling here with the distinctly positive contributions of economists to public policy debates, as such. Our purpose is to suggest, however, a different method of social analysis that has been found useful. We think that this method merits more attention from students of the public sector than heretofore.

Modern welfare economics has long focused on the inadequacy of neoclassical methodology, particularly on the inappropriateness of interpersonal comparisons of utility as a part of analysis which claims to be scientific. The values of the economist are neither more nor less interesting than those of other participants in democratic proceedings. The role of the economist is to stress his positive analysis, and if he advocates a proposal, to seek consensus. Under such a procedure the involvement of the economist in political activity can be unambiguously welfare increasing. The question becomes that of determining what kind of involvement the methodology of modern welfare economics leaves for the economist *qua* scientist. The writers in this volume basically adopt a modified Pareto-Wicksell framework in their approach to social analysis. The reason is simple—we do not wish to make interpersonal utility comparisons; we are unwilling to play God. Given this constraint, we are forced to look at the revealed choice behavior of individuals as the basic informational inputs in determining "goodness" or "badness" of social policy. This methodology is consistent in describing the work in this volume. We do not, however, seek to impose this methodology on others (since this would, in itself, be an interpersonal comparison). Our objective is simply to make our own position explicit and in the process (we hope) to indicate the potential attractiveness of this approach to other scholars. Under the modified Paretian framework, the striving for universal acceptance of analytical propositions based on adequate testing becomes the key priority for the economist. Consensus is the only standard by which "rightness" can be discerned under this approach. The application of nonuniversal principles to social problems is just another form of a social welfare judgment. The involvement and relevance of the economist under the Paretian-Wicksellian guidelines is based on an unbiased application of intelligence and analytical skills to deduce generally acceptable solutions to social problems.

The modified Paretian-Wicksellian framework implies that the social scientist must be prepared to accept the status quo when analysis indicates that tractable "solutions" to social problems are not possible. In the absence of possible agreement on change among broad segments of the citizenry, the social scientist has no means of saying that change is or is not desirable. He accepts what is for the simple reason that this is where he starts. An example may be provided in the case of the absence of emerging markets where apparent spillovers or externalities exist. As has been repeatedly pointed out, this phenomenon may reflect the irrelevance of the apparent spillover effects (the costs may exceed the gains to be achieved from internalization). The correct social policy in this case is one of allowing the apparent problem to persist until new technology is available. In other words, the discovery of market failure by itself is not sufficient to invoke an unexamined alternative (government). Government is also a major producer of externalities. This is not, of course, to argue that the possibility that the status quo is optimal should rule out attempts to measure the costs and gains of comparative institutional arrangements or to search for new alternatives. The examination of invoked alternatives and the search for new solutions to social problems is a primary responsibility of the involved social scientist. But reform is always advanced as presumed Pareto-optimal only, and proposals are always subject to validation by collective consensus. Reform is achieved through search for consensus which often emerges slowly over time.

The involved and relevant social scientist must believe in his science, as such. The Marxist view that economic science is relative to a historical period and that it provides a rationale for the ruling interests must be thoroughly rejected. The Paretian framework is not consistent with the Marxian position because genuine consensus under constitutional rules does not imply a class basis for social change. The Paretian construction, because of the unanimity sanction, implies a truly participatory basis for social change. In this approach public policy is not something legislated by or for powerful lobbies or the wealthy capitalists; either everyone agrees or there is no change.

This volume embodies the elements of what we feel is a valid methodological and operational involvement of social science in democratic process. Part II consists of an essay by James M. Buchanan in which he discusses the methodological deficiency of "open" social analysis. He argues, quite simply, that the behavioral network for all choice be closed, that "public choice" as well as "private choice" be analyzed.

Parts III and IV contain papers which are illustrative of how closed social analysis offers explanations of many murky regions in political economy. For the most part the papers of Part III rely on the device of a median or representative man to generalize results to the social setting. Buchanan's papers on the quite different subjects of medical care and fiscal policy, both written initially for publication in England, explain why the orthodox predictions—prescriptions in these two policy areas—remain unconfirmed and unheeded in the real world of democratic politics. His papers on the earmarking of taxes and public utility pricing demonstrate the severe limitations of the orthodox analysis with an open behavioral system. Lindsay shows that the introduction of a sharing variable to the individual's utility function can explain the origin and continuing support of the National Health Service in Great Britain. The papers by Goetz and by Pauly and Johnson show how a "public choice" approach modifies important and well-established theorems in public finance. Wagner's paper on debt limitation provides a new perspective on the role of public debt limitation in state and local fiscal organization. His paper on the draft and military choice examines the relations between conscription, democratic warfare decisions, and the size of the military budget in a collective choice framework.

By contrast with the papers of Part III, those of Part IV derive their results because analysis of individual choice cannot be directly generalized when social choices are genuinely collective. Buchanan's paper on the Pigovian margins represents a straightforward extension of orthodox welfare economics to a discussion of "political externalities." Stubblebine and Pauly examine important practical questions involved in the institutional organization of the educational system in the political-private interaction context. The two papers by Charles Goetz, one on earmarking and the other on grants (with Charles McKnew), show how group choice inconsistencies may produce apparently paradoxical social outcomes. Greene discusses the transfer of collective functions to federal authorities under a federalist system where these functions could be performed just as efficiently on the state-local level. Davis and Meyer challenge Downs's familiar hypothesis about budget size in a democracy. Buchanan and Tullock and Buchanan and Pauly show respectively how accepted views about monopoly and tax deductions are modified in a closed behavioral analysis. Tollison discusses a proposal to eliminate the draft in favor of voluntarism through a special public debt issue.

Part V contains a concluding essay by Gordon Tullock in which he discusses the reasons why social science has been increasingly colonized by economic methodology. Tullock also presents a proposal for the reform of social science inquiry.

Of the total of twenty-three papers, five have not been previously published. Of the eighteen that have been published, only a small number have appeared in journals readily accessible to the practicing social scientist in the United States.

Four of the papers were published initially in *Public Choice*, a relatively new journal which is edited by Gordon Tullock and which is issued for the Public Choice Society by the Center for the Study of Public Choice at Virginia Polytechnic Institute and State University. The Center, the journal, and the approach are new, and as the papers in this volume indicate, new insights are offered on age-old issues of social policy. The "theory of public choice" remains on the threshold of development, but to those who seek both "realism" and "relevance" in their science, who seek informed and impartial "involvements," these preliminary essays may be suggestive of the extensive scope for research in a subdiscipline that will remain open-ended.

II

METHODOLOGY OF THE
THEORY OF PUBLIC CHOICE

2

Toward Analysis of
Closed Behavioral Systems

James M. Buchanan

This book contains several applications of the "theory of public choice." This theory represents an attempt to close up the analysis of social interaction systems. In this respect it may be compared and contrasted with the familiar "open" system analyzed in traditional economic theory. The latter is a highly developed theory of market interaction. Beyond the limits of market behavior, however, analysis is left "open." The "public choices" that define the constraints within which market behavior is allowed to take place are assumed to be made externally or exogenously, presumably by others than those who participate in market transactions and whose behavior is subjected to the theory's examination. The limitation of analysis to open behavioral systems can be helpful if the objective itself is comparably restricted to that of making predictions about a few variables. If the behavioral elements that are neglected remain genuinely external, little can be gained by closing the system analytically. As applied to orthodox economic theory, this would suggest that the formation of "public choice" may be left out of account, provided that the objective of the theory is limited to making positive predictions about market structure and nothing more. Such a limitation would, of course, greatly restrict the usefulness that economic theory might have in policy discussion. Political economy or welfare economics could not represent a natural extension of the positive theory in this context.

The observed behavior of economists does not conform to such a consistent and narrowly restricted role for their discipline. Many economists have examined the complexities of market structure on the assumption that economic motivation is pervasive. Utilizing such results, they have isolated and identified market failure. Much of modern welfare economics owes its origin to Pigou, whose primary contribution involved an emphasis on the possible divergence between private and social marginal product (cost). Almost without pause, Pigou and the economists who have followed him assumed that the behaving individuals in market process are motivated exclusively by private values, defined economically, and that social effects of their actions are neglected. This procedure represents a consistent extension of the behavioral assumption that is implicit in standard theory. Criticism becomes justified only when the "failures" of market process identified in this way are presumed to be correctable by political or governmental regulation and control. This last step represents an arbitrary and nonscientific closure of the behavioral system and, as such, cannot be legitimate. The critically important bridge between the behavior of persons who act in the marketplace and the behavior of persons who act in political process must be analyzed. The "theory of public choice" can be interpreted as the construction of such a bridge. The approach requires only the simple assumption that the same individuals act in both relationships. Political decisions are not handed down from on high by omniscient beings who cannot err. Individuals behave in market interactions, in political-governmental interactions, in cooperative-nongovernmental interactions, and in other arrangements. Closure of the behavioral system, as I am using the term, means only that analysis must be extended to the actions of persons in their several separate capacities.

I. *The Elitist Model: An Open Behavioral System*

Economists who have talked about "market failure" under the assumption that persons behave as automatons in market interaction have blithely, indeed almost blissfully, seemed willing to turn things over to the corrective devices of the politician-bureaucrat. What is the reason for this? Have the welfare economists assumed that persons are so much influenced by their institutional-environmental setting as to make ordinary men "socially conscious" when they take on political or bureaucratic roles? Some of the socialist romantics may have reflected this attitude, but this is not characteristic of those who have participated actively in sophisticated policy discussion. The practicing (and preaching) welfare economist does not really consider crossing the bridge. He does not think of the man who behaves in the marketplace, and whose behavior he examines, as the same person who either does or should make collective or public decisions for the whole community. This explains my usage of the term "open system." The implicit assumption has been that someone else, someone other than the participants in the marketplace, lays down the rules for collective order.

This limited and essentially open behavioral model can be made logically consistent and self-contained. The classical Italian scholars in public finance, such men as De Viti de Marco, Puviani, Einaudi, and Fasiani,[1] deserve credit for recognizing the necessity of defining specifically their assumed models of political order. Several of these scholars, and notably De Viti de Marco and Fasiani, developed parallel structures of analysis. On the one hand, fiscal phenomena were examined in a model where the producers-suppliers of collective-governmental "goods" are simultaneously consumers-demanders. This closure of the behavioral system is equivalent to that which "the theory of public choice," as presented in this book, embodies. Merely to define this interaction system (which was called "democratic," "cooperative," or "individualistic" by different writers) forces analysis of behavior of persons in separate capacities. On the other hand, and in sharp contrast, fiscal phenomena were examined in a model where collective-governmental decisions, effective for the all-inclusive community, are made by an elite or ruling group (members of a winning majority coalition, a party hierarchy, an aristocracy, an "establishment," a ruling central committee, a dictator). This model concentrates attention on the behavioral reactions of persons in the larger community, reactions to the set of collective decisions that are imposed externally upon them. To make this model complete, however, the behavior of the members of the elite in choosing the decision set must be analyzed. Different persons act in different roles. As I have suggested, this is a consistent model and it contains implications that can be tested.

The criticism that may be lodged against those who have worked in the tradition of modern welfare economics is not that they have employed this ruling class or elitist model of analysis. Quite the contrary; had they done so, or had they expressed a willingness to do so, their work would have exhibited an internal coherence that has been largely absent. This lack of coherence warrants the legitimate criticism that the "theory of public choice" implies, whether directly or indirectly. The social theorist remains and should remain free to select his own model, and this selection should be informed by those aspects of reality which the theorist expects to explain

1. For a general discussion of the contributions of these scholars, along with appropriate bibliographical references, see the essay, "The Italian Tradition in Fiscal Theory," in my *Fiscal Theory and Political Economy* (Chapel Hill, 1960).

more adequately. What the theorist should not be allowed to do is to work uncritically without being forced to look at the internal behavioral structure of his model. If the individual actors in the economic process are assumed to be divorced from the decision-making structure that defines the constraints on their behavior, the openness of the system must be acknowledged. A "science" that is limited to an analysis of reaction patterns can, of course, be constructed. This may be of value to those who do participate in rule-making. It is unacceptable, however, for the practitioner of this "reaction science" to infer "failure" or "inefficiency" if the latter are measured against criteria that are themselves derived from the valuation of the individuals who are reacting, and then to imply that such "failure" either will be, can be, or should be removed by some change in the behavior of others, namely those who participate in the establishment of the constraints. Before this can be done, a plausible "theory" of the behavior of the members of the ruling elite must be developed. Until midcentury, such a theory was almost wholly neglected by social scientists, with the Italian public-finance scholars again providing a notable exception. Some of the elements of such a theory are now emerging, and important contributions have been made by some of the same scholars who have worked in the theory of public choice.[2] The development of an acceptable theory of bureaucratic behavior can be interpreted as bridging the gap through an explicit recognition of dual decision structures.

11. *Public Choice and Private Choice*

The "theory of public choice" rests instead on a single decision structure. It involves the explicit introduction of a "democratic" model, one in which the rulers are also the ruled. The theory examines the behavior of persons as they participate variously in the formation of public or collective choices, by which is meant choices from among mutually exclusive alternative constraints which, once selected, must apply to all members of the community. In acting or behaving as a "public choice" participant, the individual is presumed to be aware that he is, in part, selecting results which affect others than himself. He is making decisions for a public, of which he forms a part.

2. I refer to such works as: Anthony Downs, *Inside Bureaucracy* (Boston, 1967); Gordon Tullock, *The Politics of Bureaucracy* (Washington, D.C., 1965).

This characteristic feature of "public choice" distinguishes it sharply from "private choice." We may typify the latter by individual behavior in an idealized market setting: If a person acts, say, as a buyer or seller in a fully competitive market, he has no sensation that his own behavior modifies the environment of other persons. He acts as if he generates changes in his "private" economy only. Despite the analyst's recognition that each economic act influences, even if infinitesimally, the conditions confronted by all market participants, the participant himself is not cognizant of this.

It is precisely in the domain of welfare economics that this idealized behavior which I have called "private choice" becomes impossible. When a person is able to modify the economic environment of others through his own behavior, and when he can recognize this, the welfare economist refers to "externality." This is formally equivalent to the divergence between marginal private and marginal social cost or product, mentioned earlier. It is clear that when personal behavior generates externality, whether this be positive or negative, it must take on characteristics of "public choice," even if the actor does not explicitly acknowledge his role as a decision-maker for the relevant community of persons (small or large) that are affected. In one sense, individual behavior in an externality relationship may be interpreted as a sort of halfway house between the idealized "private choice" typified by buying and selling in competitive markets and the idealized "public choice" typified by voting in purely democratic referenda. It is not surprising, therefore, that several of the contributors of essays in this book have approached their subject matter through the technical analysis of externalities. By contrast, it remains surprising that Pigovian welfare economists, in general, have failed to sense the internal contradiction between their models of economic interaction where external costs and benefits become criteria for market failure and their models of political behavior where such externalities are presumed to be corrected.

There is, of course, a difference in the institutional-environmental setting for personal behavior in the market and in the political process. The individual whose private economic behavior pollutes the air and imposes external costs on others in his community (a classic example of an external diseconomy) may be partially unaware of the effects of his actions on others. Even if he is aware of these effects, he may treat as "his own property" the atmosphere elements (air) that others claim in common, implicitly or explicitly. By comparison, consider the individual who votes in a political referendum and who, say, supports the imposition of taxes on all persons in a well-defined political community. He is exerting an external diseconomy on others, and he may be fully aware that he is affecting their potential economic positions. But the voter claims no "property right" in the selection of the tax system, as such. His behavior may be tempered by his understanding that, in subsequent referenda on taxes and on other contraints, he will find himself in losing rather than winning political coalitions. On some such grounds as this, a plausible case can be made out that "political pollution" is subject to somewhat more intensive internal behavioral constraints than "economic pollution." The implications of such an argument should, however, be kept in mind. Once the welfare economist accepts such a defense of his orthodoxy, he is already partially in the "public choice" camp. He is, willy-nilly, being forced to close up his behavioral system.

At the current stage of development in social and behavioral science, this would represent significant progress. Whether or not and to what extent men behave differently under varied institutional-environmental constraints deserves much more inquiry and investigation. Some research along these lines will be carried out in due course. But the bridge has been crossed once it is so much as acknowledged that the same men are involved in the several decision processes.

III. *The Economic Model of Behavior*

This section introduces both the main strength and the main limitation of the "theory of public choice," as developed and applied in the papers in this book and by scholars elsewhere. This theory has been developed almost exclusively by scholars who are professional economists. As Gordon Tullock discusses in his essay in this book, the theory of public choice might be taken to reflect economic imperialism, interpreted as efforts by economists to expand the boundaries of their own discipline so as to make it applicable to more and more aspects of human behavior. As they have done so, it should have been expected that the explanatory potential of the strictly economic model of behavior would be gradually eroded, as indeed most of its users will readily acknowledge. The model has been demonstrated to retain surprising strength, however, even when applied to behavior that might initially have seemed to be almost wholly noneconomic. Methodologically, the economic model remains singular in its ability to generate conceptually refutable hypotheses regardless of its particular application.

The economic model of behavior is based on the motivational postulate of individual utility maximization. This postulate, in itself, remains empirically empty until further restrictions are imposed on the definition of utility or, technically, on the utility function. Once this step is taken, once the "goods" that the individual (in some average or representative sense) values are identified, the way is open for the derivation of hypotheses that can be tested against observations. The economic model is almost entirely predictive in content rather than prescriptive. The actors who behave "economically" choose "more rather than less," with more and less being measured in units of goods that are independently identified and defined. This becomes a prediction about behavior in the real world that the economist carries with him as a working professional scientist. As such, the economist neither condemns nor condones the behavior of those whose behavior he examines. He has no business to lay down norms of behavior for the consumer, producer, voter, or for anyone else. In its pure sense, economic theory is devoid of valuation at this normative level.

Failure to understand the descriptive and predictive content of economic theory along with a proclivity to interpret all social "science" in prescriptive terms has caused many critics to deplore the "dismal science" and to rail against the "crass materialism" that economic behavior allegedly represents. The appropriate response of the economist to such criticism should be (but perhaps too rarely has been) that he is wholly unconcerned, as a professional scientist, about the ethically relevant characteristics of the behavior that he examines. To the extent that men behave as his model predicts, the economist can explain uniformities in social order. To the extent that men behave differently, his predictions are falsified. It is as simple as that.

The criticisms of the economic model of behavior, and of the science that embodies this model, have been long-continuing and pervasive even when the model has been limited in application only to the behavior of persons in well-defined market processes. These criticisms need not concern us here. But it should be apparent that when attempts are made to stretch the central predictive model beyond these confines, when the economic approach is extended to "public choice," the criticisms stemming from nonpredictive and nonscientific sources should be intensified. For precisely to the extent that the model loses some of its predictive content, its use to the nonscientist seems to become more and more suspect in some prescriptively relevant sense. A single example illustrates this point. The nonscientist may accept the use of an economic model of behavior, and he may acknowledge its explanatory power in relation to the price-making and price-taking by buyers and sellers of groceries. He may not condemn the economist out of hand for advancing the prediction that buyers will purchase more beans when they are cheapened relative to potatoes. By contrast, the same non-scientist may object, and strenuously, if the economist expands his horizons and uses essentially the same behavioral model to predict that the bureaucrat will increase his awards of public contracts to the prospect that sweetens the personal package of emoluments allowable within the legal constraints. Here the bureaucrat is, like the buyer at the corner grocery store, predicted to demand more of that "good" that is relatively cheapened in price. Because of the predictive-prescriptive confusion, however, the economist becomes suspect; he is interpreted as replacing the "is" by the "ought" in circumstances where prevailing moral principles make strict economic behavior partially or wholly unacceptable.

IV. *Noneconomic Models of Behavior*

Because of the predictive-prescriptive confusion, however, along with its subsequent creation of reluctance in noneconomist social scientists to undertake rigorous positive examination of behavior patterns, the extension of orthodox economic models to nonmarket behavior seems to fill an awesome gap in social analysis. Precisely because other approaches than the economic have been prescriptive, the latter appears initially to be more important in yielding predictive hypotheses about nonmarket behavior than it would be were alternative models also used in a positive or predictive manner. This latter would require that the noneconomic models be transformed. The traditional prescriptive norms *for* personal behavior would have to be converted into predictive hypotheses *about* personal behavior. The "ought" would have to be replaced by the "is." If this transformation can be effected, noneconomic models can be extended to many aspects of behavior, including an invasion of the domain traditionally commanded by the economists. If the theory of public choice and related work represents "economic imperialism," the way is surely open for the noneconomists to turn the tables and extend behavioral models of their own into the realm of market interactions. All social scientists should applaud the emergence of competing means of closing up the analyses of behavioral systems. And, even in the strictly defined market process, there are surely important unexplained residues that may be examined against alternative behavioral hypotheses.

Consider first, and briefly, the dominant ethical system in the history of the West, Christianity. This system has been almost exclusively discussed and elaborated as a set of prescriptive norms for personal behavior, a set of "shoulds," "commandments," "precepts."

Nonetheless, it is possible to convert this ethical system into hypotheses about behavior. We may do so by beginning with individual utility functions as methodologically helpful starting points even if they remain empirically empty. In its starkest form, Christianity is represented by an individual utility function in which "goods" attributed to others are valued equally with "goods" attributed to the person whose function is being defined. Furthermore, there can be no discrimination among the large set of "others" in the pure predictive model of Christianity. For predictions to be made, "goods" must be identified, but, once this is done, hypotheses may be derived and subjected to observation. Do individuals in some average or representative sense behave as the Christian model predicts? Casual empiricism alone suggests that the central hypothesis has at least some explanatory potential. We do observe individuals giving up "goods" to others, including the set of "others" where the individual units remain unidentified to the donor and wholly outside meaningfully drawn boundaries of personal relationship (funds are freely given for the feeding of starving children in Biafra). Research should be extended and carried forward to determine the explanatory limits of this strict Christian hypothesis. In this respect and at this point, the efforts of Kenneth Boulding should be especially noted. Almost alone among social scientists, and once again from a professional background in economics, Boulding has drawn attention to the explanatory potential of what he called the "integrative" system of interaction, which is essentially his version of what I have called here the Christian hypothesis. Other scholars, many of whom have also worked in the theory of public choice, have joined Boulding in developing an "economics of charity." Such men as William Vickrey, Gordon Tullock, Earl Thompson, David B. Johnson, and Thomas Ireland have made contributions in this obvious attempt to include all forms of human behavior in a framework of positive analysis.[3]

3. See Kenneth Boulding, "Notes on a Theory of Philanthropy," *Philanthropy and Public Policy*, ed. by Frank G. Dickinson (New York, 1962); William Vickrey, "One Economist's View of Philanthropy," *Philanthropy and Public Policy, op cit.*; Gordon Tullock, "Information Without Profit," *Papers on Non-Market Decision-Making*, Vol. II (Charlottesville, Virginia, 1967); Thomas Ireland, "Charity Budgeting" (Unpublished Ph.D. Dissertation, Alderman Library, University of Virginia, 1968); David B. Johnson, "The Fundamental Economics of the Charity Market" (Unpublished Ph.D. Dissertation, Alderman Library, University of Virginia, 1968); Earl Thompson, "Do Competitive Markets Misallocate Charity," *Public Choice*, IV (1968), 67–74.

Conversion of the prescriptive norm of Christianity into a predictive hypothesis in its pure or pristine form immediately suggests an intermediate approach, one in which the utility function attributes positive values to the "goods" of others, but where the "others" are personally identified, either as individuals or as members of groups embodying certain descriptive characteristics. This approach yields a whole set of possible behavioral hypotheses, the working out and testing of which may be summarized in such various rubrics as "the economics of the family," "the economics of marriage," "the economics of clubs," "the economics of ethnic groups," and so forth. In each case, the word "economics" suggests only that the positive analyses in each case remain largely in the hands of professionally trained economists. But my point of emphasis here is only that work in each of these areas reflects an attempt to accomplish what I have called here the closing of the whole behavioral system.

v. *The Kantian Generalization Principle Treated*
As an Explanatory Hypothesis

A more interesting approach, and one that seems hardly to have been explored at all, lies in converting the prescriptive norm of Kantian ethics into a predictive hypothesis about individual behavior. Like the more restricted but comparable Christian hypothesis, this could be treated as a complete model which may have more or less explanatory potential under different behavioral environments. Prescriptively, the Kantian principle instructs a person to consider as a duty that form of behavior that will, when generalized to the whole community of persons, generate results that are desired in some noninstrumental sense. Predictively, the Kantian hypothesis states that when behavior is recognized to affect others, these effects will be taken into account and behavior adjusted as appropriate. The interests of others than the actor are included, however, not out of "love" as in the Christian ethic, but out of a form of enlightened self-interest which is based on a generalized recognition of the reciprocity of social interaction. Translated into utility-function terms, the "goods" that are positively valued by the individual are those attributed to or assigned to himself and not to others. The utilities of others, generally or specifically, do not enter the utility function in any directly interdependent fashion. The interdependence that seems to be inferred from the results arises because the "goods" that the individual values are more inclusive and less instrumental than those upon which the orthodox economic models have concentrated attention.

Clearly, something akin to the Kantian hypothesis describes many aspects of human behavior. Large areas of social life are, and must be, organized essentially on anarchistic principles. Individual property rights are not well-defined, yet "pollution" is kept within reasonably tolerable limits by self-imposed constraints on behavior which can only reflect adherence to something like a generalization principle. And, indeed, this hypothesis offers some prospect for methodological reconciliation between the economist's analysis of market behavior and the noneconomist's analysis of nonmarket behavior. It may be plausibly argued that the Kantian hypothesis would yield predictions about market behavior that are identical to those produced by the more restrictive models of economic theory. The individual buyer or seller in a fully competitive market does not influence the position of others than himself. Hence, he may behave in strict accordance with Kantian precepts when he acts as the automaton of economic theory.

The two hypotheses may diverge only when externalities characterize the economic interaction process. If the Kantian hypothesis should be dominant, there may be no need for policy makers to express concern about environmental or atmospheric pollution or erosion arising from personal behavior, and there might be no inefficient congestion of available publicly used facilities. Similarly, there should be little concern about the narrow and possibly self-seeking behavior of political representatives and bureaucrats. If the Kantian hypothesis about individual behavior should be generally corroborated, individuals who participate in "public choice" would be acting in the genuine "public interest," as defined by the widespread adherence to the generalization principle.[4]

It should be apparent that what is needed is considerably more research to ascertain the explanatory power of competing behavioral hypotheses, any one or any combination of which will allow a closure of the social interaction system. One result of such research will surely be that the relative applicability of the competing hypotheses will vary from one institutional-environmental setting to another. And indeed a central part of the research may be the identification of those institutional characteristics that seem to exert an influence

---

4. Individuals may, of course, disagree as to what the "public interest" is, and conflicts may arise even when each and every person behaves in accordance with Kantian precepts. Resolution of such conflicts raises interesting problems, but the source of conflicts here would be quite different from the more familiar private interest-public interest dichotomy.

on personal behavior. In a paper that is not included in this volume,[5] I examined the possible influence of the sheer size of the interacting group on the individual's willingness to behave in accordance with the Kantian precepts. Charles Goetz has responded to my challenge, and he has demonstrated that, under certain conditions that involve the joint sharing of a collectively provided "good," the directional influence of numbers may be more than offset by the change in payoff differentials consequent on changing sizes of the group.[6] There are other apparent, and less "economic," characteristics of interaction settings that may be examined for their influence on personal behavior patterns. The influence of the family, the tribe, the church, the local community, the political party, the civic club, the team, . . . all of these and more can be important and can affect overall social stability. Effective research seems only in its very early stages.

v i. *We Cannot Have It Both Ways*

In conclusion, I should emphasize the relevance of seeking closure of the behavioral systems in our analyses by returning to the comparison and contrast between the position taken by the post-Pigovian welfare economists and that taken by those who have contributed to the "theory of public choice," as represented variously in this book. Neither group should be allowed to operate in an open system of analysis. As I have stressed earlier, the post-Pigovian should not be allowed to generate excitement and ultimately to modify social policy by his alleged discoveries of "market failures" without, and at the same time, acknowledging the comparable "failures" of his proposed political-governmental correctives. The discovery of market failures is normally based on the usage of a narrowly constrained utility function which describes individual market behavior in terms of narrow self-interest. If, in fact, individuals behave in such a manner in the marketplace, the inference should be that they will also act similarly in other and nonmarket behavioral settings. The burden of proof must rest on the discoverer of market failure as he demonstrates that the behavioral shift into a nonmarket setting involves a dramatic widening of personal horizons.

5. "Ethical Rules, Expected Values, and Large Numbers," *Ethics*, LXXVI (October 1965), 1–13.
6. Charles J. Goetz, "Group-Size and the Voluntary Provision of Public Goods," Working Paper 24 (Blacksburg, Virginia, November 1968).

The same restrictions should be imposed on those of us who have tried to extend the economists' model into nonmarket spheres of behavior. We should not be allowed to discover "political failures" because we have succeeded in isolating the self-seeking behavior of politicians and bureaucrats and, at the same time, be unconcerned about the "market failures" that show up because of externalities. Both the post-Pigovian welfare economists and the public choice economists should be required to work within broadly consistent analytical models. Both groups work essentially with an economic model; neither group should be allowed to slip into its own version of some Kantian-like hypothesis when and if this suits ideological prejudices.

The post-Pigovian may rescue himself from contradiction by either one of two routes. He may, as indeed several eminent welfare economists have done, join the ranks of the public-choice theorists and look critically at "government failures" alongside market failures. The result will be the emergence of some ideologically neutral grounds upon which both the public-choice theorists and the reformed Pigovians can evaluate alternative institutional arrangements on what must be a case-by-case comparative analysis.

The second escape from contradiction lies in the explicit extension of some variant of the Kantian hypothesis to market as well as to nonmarket behavior. The social scientist who sees bureaucracy as something other than the self-seeking of individuals within their own career hierarchy can also begin to look on market behavior and on the workings of markets differently. And indeed there are indications that some analysts are taking this route; witness the increasing attention that has been given to the so-called "social responsibility" of business.

The "theory of public choice" is only one step in the direction of an internally consistent social science. It should be interpreted as such by its proponents as well as by its critics. Its explanatory power varies greatly from application to application, but the number and the variety of these that are contained in this book alone should be sufficient to suggest both the generality of the theory and the promise of continued work.

III

INDIVIDUALS AS PUBLIC CHOOSERS

3

The Inconsistencies of the National Health Service

James M. Buchanan

To a detached observer in 1965, Great Britain's 17-year experiment in providing "free" health services exhibits many signs of failure. In July 1965, an overwhelming majority of the delegates to the Swansea meeting of the British Medical Association supported a resolution calling for the introduction of privately collected fees from patients, recoverable from the state, to be included as one method of remuneration in the "doctors' charter" at present under negotiation with the Minister of Health. Even before this unpredicted and unexpected expression of professional opposition, the Association held the undated resignations of nearly 18,000 family doctors (out of a total of 23,000) pending the outcome of negotiations on many points with the Minister. Relatively fewer numbers are entering the medical profession each year, and the emigration of British-trained doctors continues.[1] The number of practicing doctors declined by 300 from October 1963 to October 1964, in the face of a substantial net increase in population. Resident staff in British hospitals has come increasingly to be composed of immigrants, mostly from India and Pakistan. Hospital facilities are overcrowded, and long delays in securing treatment, save for strictly emergency cases, are universally noted.

What are the reasons for these apparent failures in the system for which so much was hoped in 1948? Why do the ideals of the late 1940's remain so far out of reach, even after 17 years? Some such understanding is essential if anything other than gimcrack reforms

Reprinted by permission of the publisher from The Institute of Economic Affairs, *Occasional Paper 7*, November 1965.

1. See J. R. Seale, "Medical Emigration: A Study in the Inadequacy of Official Statistics," in *Lessons from Central Forecasting*, Easton Paper 6, IEA, October 1965.

are to be introduced. Recent events in the United States and in Canada make it additionally important to evaluate and interpret British experience correctly. In 1965, also in July, the United States embarked upon its own program of national government financing of medical care for the aged. The Canadian government is actively considering proposals to provide major federal aid to provincial health-service systems. Can similar failures be predicted in these two cases?

There are three possible explanations of the apparent failure of the National Health Service. Are the undesirable features observed in the British system due to mistakes in administering the health services, mistakes that "wiser" men or parties could have avoided? Are these difficulties due to the very structure of the institutions through which health services are provided, and which could, therefore, be removed only after major reforms in this institutional structure? Or, finally, are these difficulties inherent in the nature of the health services themselves? Can services that are privately valued by individuals—"personal" services—be provided "free" by governments?

I shall argue that only the second of these questions needs to be answered affirmatively. The observed failures of the NHS can be explained by the *structure of the institutions*. This suggests that, at best, improvements in administration can provide only short-term palliatives. Explanations are not to be found in either wrong-headed decisions by ministers or short-sighted policies of political parties. Governments that remain broadly democratic can be successful in providing "free" services, but only if they do so within institutions that promote general consistency in the social decision-making process. In models that approximate to the British structure, I shall explain the observed results by showing that in their *private or individual choice* behavior as potential users or demanders of health-medical services, individuals are inconsistent with their *public or collective choice* behavior as voters-taxpayers who make decisions on supplying these same services. The individuals who are the demanders and those who are the suppliers are, of course, basically the same persons acting in two separate roles, and the facts themselves suggest the inconsistency. My central point is that this inconsistency does not in any way reflect irrationality on the part of individual decision-makers, but that it arises exclusively from the institutional setting for choice on the two sides of the account. Once this relatively simple point is recognised and accepted, the directions for possible constructive reforms become clear.

My discussion is limited to institutional theory. I shall not discuss either the historical development of the NHS or its descriptive characteristics at present. This discussion is also positive; I shall not be concerned here with the normative question as to how health services "should" be organised, privately or publicly. In what follows, I shall first review briefly the traditional principle of neoclassical predictions and the British experience. The reasons for the refutation of these predictions are shown to lie in economists' failure to analyse political choice-processes. The individual and the collective settings for individual choice behavior are examined in some detail, and models that seem to typify the British example will be presented. Finally, brief attention will be given to alternative institutional arrangements that might eliminate the fundamental inconsistencies.

I. *The Elasticity Principle*

If the price elasticity of individual demand, i.e., the responsiveness to a (small) change in price, is significantly higher than zero over the applicable range, governments cannot efficiently "give away" goods or services. This is one of the most widely accepted principles in the theory of public finance. It is found in most modern textbooks, but it also finds authority in such respected neoclassical writers as Pigou and Wicksell.[2] Within its traditional setting, the principle is valid. If government tries to supply goods or services that are privately divisible among separate persons at zero prices to users, the quantity demanded by all individuals in the aggregate will be significantly larger than the quantity that would be demanded at prices set by (marginal) cost, except where the price elasticity approaches zero.

For some goods and services this required elasticity condition is satisfied. For example, the government could, without undue losses in efficiency, provide "free" funeral services, for the very simple reason that each person dies only once; a zero price does not produce a larger demand for funerals than a high (or even a low) price. For other goods and services, "free" provision would obviously be impossible, for example, beefsteaks, motor cars, and minks. Between such extremes as these, various goods and services may be arrayed in terms of predicted elasticity coefficients over the relevant range of prices. Education, for example, can within limits be made avail-

2. A. C. Pigou, *A Study in Public Finance* (London, 1928); Knut Wicksell, *Finanztheoretische Untersuchungen* (Jena, 1896).

able free of direct user charges because each child can "demand" only one year's quantity of service per year.[3] Medical-health services clearly fall somewhere along the spectrum between education and motor cars. For certain types of medical care, price elasticity may be low indeed; there should be approximately the same number of broken legs treated under zero and under marginal-cost prices. For other types of health service, however, price elasticity may be relatively high. The British experience suggests that the demands for drugs[4] and for consultation by general practitioners, and possibly for hospital care, fall into this category. For medical-health services taken as an undifferentiated whole, individuals will be led to demand significantly larger quantities at zero-user prices than they would demand at positive prices.[5] This part of the neoclassical principle amounts to nothing more than a straightforward application of the first law of demand.

But there is more to be said about the principle. It states that governments cannot *efficiently* give away goods and services that do not satisfy the required elasticity condition. In this form, the principle says nothing at all about the manner in which the inefficiencies will be generated when this condition is not met, or about the final incidence of such inefficiences. Economists have normally assumed that these inefficiences would take the form of relatively excessive investment in supplying the services in question. This assumption represents a simple extension of consumer-sovereignty models in which supply is expected always to adjust to demand over the long run. The presumption has been that, should governments try to give away services that fail to meet the required elasticity condition, they will find it necessary to extend supply to meet expressed demand, even at the expense of relative over-investment in the services. In

3. For such services as funerals and education, individual demands for improvements in *quality* under zero user-pricing replace, to some extent, the more direct individual adjustments in *quantity* that are possible with goods and services falling along the opposite end of the array suggested. At best, however, these demands for quality improvements become pressures upon governments for change; they cannot, in themselves, consume resources.

4. Since the 2s. charge for prescriptions dispensed under the NHS was abolished on February 1, 1965, Ministry of Health figures show that prescriptions have risen 20 percent in number and 28 percent in cost compared with the same period in 1964; by comparison, certified sickness rose by only 7 percent.

5. This is the economic theory behind the vague allusions by some sociologists to a "price-barrier."—Editor.

responding to "needs" criteria at zero-user prices, governments would have been predicted to devote relatively too much public outlay to the provision of such divisible, personal services as medical care, "too much" being measured against the standard criteria for allocating resource use of consumer preferences as expressed in the market. The alternative response that governments might make in such situations seems rarely to have been considered. They may make decisions on the supply of the service independently of the demands for the service, and on the basis of quite different considerations. As a result, the inefficiencies may take the form of deterioration in the quality of the services themselves, including congestion of available facilities.

11. *External Economies*

A second and, to some extent, independent principle has emerged from theoretical economics, and finds its origin in Pigou's discussion of external economies and diseconomies.[6] When an activity generates significant external economies, individual or private organisation has been held to generate relative under-investment. The standard Pigovian inference is that a lower-than-optimal amount of the activity will take place. Medical-health services have been classified by many economists as being such that private or individual organisation produces significant external economies. This is, of course, the argument that has been thought to provide the economic rationale for a shift from private organisation to public or collective organisation. Under the latter, presumably, the relevant external effects can be internalised in the collective-decision process. The orthodox Pigovian prediction would be that such a shift in organisation, from private to public, would result in substantial increases in outlay on providing the services.[7]

6. A. C. Pigou, *The Economics of Welfare* (3d. ed. London, 1929).

7. In a paper previously published, Milton Kafoglis and I examined this hypothesis within the standard model of post-Pigovian welfare economics. We showed that total investment in supplying a service may not be increased by a shift from private to public organisation, even when the presence of relevant external economies is acknowledged. Our discussion centered on the necessity to distinguish inputs and outputs. We demonstrated that under certain assumptions about the substitutability between private and public provision in individuals' utility functions, overall efficiency might be increased without expansion in investment, even on the presumption that government decisions are fully correct. See James M. Buchanan and Milton Z. Kafoglis, "A Note on Public Goods

III. *The Neoclassical Prediction*

The two strands of economic analysis sketched above become mutually reinforcing when prediction is made concerning the direction of change in the total resources used in medical services that would result from substituting a socialised or nationalised service for a privately organised service, in whole or in part. The welfare economist, concentrating his attention on the predicted presence of external economies and ignoring problems of collective decision-making, predicts that such a change in organisation will increase the resources invested from suboptimal to optimal levels. The traditional public finance theorist might agree with the welfare economist, but, being somewhat more sophisticated as regards attention to political decisions, and recognising the elasticity conditions, he predicts that governments will tend to expand investment *beyond* optimal limits. In trying to meet expressed "needs" for or demands on the available facilities, substantial over-investment might take place. The sophisticated neoclassical economist, taking both of these considerations into account, would have seemed on quite safe grounds in predicting that, after 1948, total outlay on health-medical services in Great Britain would increase substantially *relative to that which would have been made under the alternatives.*

Experience in Great Britain so far does not corroborate such neoclassical predictions that might have been, and were, made.[8] Since 1948, total outlay on medical-health care has increased less in Great Britain than in the United States, where it is supplied largely in the market, even after all of the appropriate statistical adjustments for income-wealth levels, population, etc., are made.[9] The task before us becomes that of "explaining" why these predictions failed. For this purpose, it is not necessary to discuss further the theory of external economies and its possible application to the organisation of medical-health services. Such discussion becomes relevant to the normative question concerning the efficient method of organising the services and to the comparative results of alterna-

---

Supply," *American Economic Review,* June 1963, pp. 403–14. The argument developed in this earlier paper and its relationship to the discussion in the present *Paper* is summarized in the Appendix, pp. 20–22.

8. For example, Seymour Harris, "The British Health Experiment: The First Two Years of the National Health Service," *American Economic Review,* May 1951, pp. 652–66.

9. See John and Sylvia Jewkes, *The Genesis of the British National Health Service* (Oxford, 1961).

tive structures. The aim here is much more limited; we seek only to understand the broad pattern of results that are observed under the British experiment of collectivising the health services, results that are at variance with the neoclassical predictions. We can do this by concentrating on elementary analysis.

The central part of the elasticity principle seems to be corroborated. At zero levels of user price, individuals are observed to demand relatively large quantities of health services, and we may presume that these quantities would be substantially reduced upon the establishment of positive charges. (Experience with drug fees alone suggests this result.) The neoclassical prediction relating to *individual* or *private* responses to the provision of "free" health services does not therefore seem to be challenged by the evidence.

It is in relation to the *public* or *collective* responses to these demands that predictions seem to have gone astray. Responsible *collective*, i.e., governmental, decision-makers have not expanded investment in supplying health services to the levels of expressed *individual* demands. The inefficiencies that have arisen are clearly not in the form of excessive total outlay on the health services. The British experience strongly suggests that, rather than responding to "needs" through increases in aggregate supply, governments have chosen to allow the quality of services to deteriorate rapidly, both in some appropriate, physically measurable sense[10] and in terms of congestion costs imposed on prospective consumers.

The failures of the National Health Service are not exhibited by a disproportionately large fraction of British resources being drained away through investment in supplying it; the failures are exhibited by breakdown in the quality of the services themselves due to the disparity between the facilities supplied and the demands made upon them.

IV. *Democratic Choice Process*

Could this combination of results have been predicted by a more satisfactory model of choice behaviour? Can the observed pattern of results be explained? I shall show that explanation becomes possible when a plausible model for democratic choice process is added.

---

10. Physical measurement of quality is, of course, difficult in any setting, and notably so when research advances are as rapid as in medical care. Nevertheless it seems clear that quality of service, for example in British hospitals, has been allowed to deteriorate, relative to that which would have been predicted to be present under a nationalised scheme.

We must extend the standard theory so that we can say something about the predicted responses of individuals in their capacities as participants in *collective* or group decisions. Only when this step is taken can we make some elementary predictions about the reactions of governments to privately expressed demands on health facilities and services.

The evidence suggests that the neoclassical inference that governments respond straightforwardly to "needs" is invalid. Economists have not examined either this inference or that of theoretical welfare economics (that governments act "optimally") carefully because analysis of the political-choice mechanism has been held to be outside their range of competence. Institutional and policy analysis in both neoclassical and Keynesian economics has suffered because of this implicit refusal to extend the model of individual choice behaviour. The result has been a sharp distinction between the choice behaviour of the individual in market processes and his behaviour in political processes. Implicitly, analysis has presumed that governmental decisions are divorced from the preferences of individual citizens. The first requirement for a more sophisticated explanation of observed experience is an explicit construction of a model for the political-decision process.

In any system that is properly described by the much-abused word "democratic," political decisions must ultimately be made by the individuals who hold membership in the politically, or collectively, organised group. Individuals make choices in two separate capacities, as buyers-sellers in ordinary markets for *private* goods and services, and as buyers-sellers of *public* goods and services in the political process. Only within recent years has rigorous analysis come to be applied to the second type of individual choice behaviour. An economic theory of collective decision-making remains in its infancy, but, even with the rudimentary models that are available, significant advances in an understanding of the general results of democratic political systems can be made.

At any general level, analysis of political process must take some account of the rules and the institutions through which separate individual choices, whether directly or indirectly expressed, are combined so as to produce results that, once selected, are uniformly imposed on all members of the political unit. Obviously, different rules can produce decisively different results, even should the underlying structure of individual preferences remain unchanged. Economy in explanation at the very beginning of analysis, however, may be gained by neglecting the necessarily complex examination of alternative rules. Such an examination should not be introduced until the explanatory potential of simpler models has been exhausted. In certain cases it may be possible to explain phenomena of the real world satisfactorily through reliance on single-person models, that is, through an analysis limited to the choice behaviour of a single, isolated individual as he participates in political process. If such an analysis works there is no need to resort to more complicated interactions under collective-decision rules, despite the possible emergence of additional explanatory potential.

I hope to show that the observed experience of the NHS can be satisfactorily explained by analysing the behaviour of the individual citizen, as a demander of health services on the one hand and as a potential voter on the other. Considerations of the way in which his preferences are translated into government policy in the political process are not needed. In other words, the results are those that would emerge from the rational calculus of the individual as private or individual demander and as public or collective supplier of health services. For clarity, the model to be discussed could be assumed one in which all individuals are identical to the single person, or, alternatively, one in which the single person is genuinely "representative" of the whole community.

Consider now a single individual. He participates in both market decisions and political decisions. In the former he chooses the quantities of private goods and services he will buy or sell, demand or supply. He will do so individualistically and privately, and the divisibility of the goods and services ensures that he can act separately and independently from other persons. The individual can select his own most preferred level of consumption of, say, beer, without in any way deciding or even affecting what any one, or all, of his fellow citizens shall consume. In the second capacity, as a participant in the political process, the individual also chooses the quantities of public goods and services that he will demand and supply. But here he will do so as a member of a group. Although his own preferences will determine the manner of his voting, the outcomes must be applied to *all* members of the group. A choice implies, therefore, a willingness to finance stated quantities of a good or service for all members of the group through appropriately chosen taxes also levied on all members.

Nothing more than a cursory examination of the institutions of the NHS is required to recognise that an individual is placed in the position of demanding medical-health services in a market-like choosing capacity. The "market" he confronts presents him with opportunities of selecting preferred quantities of services at zero prices. He chooses individualistically and privately, and, on the *demand* side, "free" health services are treated in much the same way as "free" beer, that is, the demand would swell more or less rapidly. At the same time, however, the individual as a participant in collective-political choice, as a voter-taxpayer-beneficiary, must indicate his decision on the aggregate quantity of medical-health services to be supplied to the community as a whole. In this capacity he cannot select an outcome for himself that will not also be applicable for everyone else. On the *supply* side, medical-health services are not "free" in any sense of the word; on the contrary, they are severely limited by consideration of all the other alternatives—more schools, better housing, larger pensions—that would have to be sacrificed if they were expanded solely in response to demand at zero prices.

Once this essential splitting of the individual's decision is recognised, the inconsistency in results is not at all strange. Indeed, this inconsistency is precisely what careful analysis would lead us to predict.

v. *The Individual as Private Demander and Public Supplier*

Why will the individual demand more services privately than he will supply publicly? This is the kernel of the internal conflict in the National Health Service.

We may first concentrate on his behaviour in demanding services made available to him by the community at zero-user prices. What will determine the quantity demanded? One of the first lessons in elementary economics provides the answer. The rational person will extend his demands on such services to the point at which the marginal utility becomes zero: that is, so long as additional services promise to yield positive benefits, there will be no incentive for the individual to restrict his "purchases." But, one may say, this sort of behaviour will be "malingering," the word commonly heard in 1965 British comments on the health service. Should not the individual consumer, or prospective consumer, recognise that, when he extends his own private demands to such limits, he uses up resources that are valuable to the community and for which the community must pay?

The individual who is well informed may well recognise that his own behaviour in this respect will commit valuable resources.[11]

11. Survey data indicate that individuals tend to be grossly uninformed about the costs of publicly-supplied medical services in Great Britain, and that there is a consistent tendency to underestimate these costs. This direction of error tends to accentuate the behavioral incon-

This point is not in question, and our explanation does not depend on ignorance to explain the observed results. Accurate recognition and measurement of the social costs of health-medical services will in no way modify the behaviour of the individual in demanding such services. Faced with no direct-user charges, he will not find it personally advantageous to restrict his own demands, although he may fully appreciate that the value of these services to him is less than the cost imposed on the whole community in supplying them. The individual's behaviour in this case is precisely equivalent to that of the person who refuses to contribute voluntarily to the financing of a mutually desired purely public or purely collective good (the "free-rider" who benefits whether he pays or not).[12]

In either of these two situations, the individual, indeed each and every individual, may recognise full well that he, along with *all* of his fellows, would be better off if *everyone*, in practice, behaved differently. But there is nothing he is able to do, individually and voluntarily, to affect the way in which others behave.[13] If he decides, privately and personally, to reduce his own demands on the services, for reasons of "social conscience," he will be acting irrationally. But since his behaviour will not, in itself, modify the behaviour of others in the aggregate, he will be foregoing opportunities for personal gains, however slight, without benefiting others to any measurable extent. Under choice conditions such as these, it is not at all surprising that what is called "malingering" is widely observed.

Let us now shift our attention to the behaviour of the same individual, who is assumed to be both informed and rational, as he participates directly or indirectly in the political-choice process. We may consider his participation in decisions on the supply of health services independently from his participation in decisions on other issues for collective action. He must indicate his preferences, in some voting or quasi-voting process, among alternative health-

---

sistency discussed in this *Paper*. By contrast, there seems to be a consistent tendency for individuals to overestimate the costs of publicly-supplied education. See *Choice in Welfare*, IEA, 1963. *Choice in Welfare*, 1965, also indicates the degrees of knowledge or ignorance of the taxes paid and social benefits received by households of varying income and size.

12. In the modern theory of public finance, the individual behaviour in this situation is discussed at length as the "free-rider problem."

13. He finds himself caught in an n-person analogue to the familiar prisoners' dilemma, much discussed in modern game theory. See R. Duncan Luce and Howard Raiffa, *Games and Decisions* (New York, 1958) pp. 94–102.

service budgets, each of which embodies a specific quantity of services to be made available for the whole community, and each of which, in turn, embodies an implied levy of taxes sufficient to finance the matching quantity. How much taxation will the individual prefer in combination with how much total outlay on the health services?

To the extent that he is well informed, the individual can make some reasonably accurate translation between the tax or cost side and the level of health-service benefits that may be provided. He will know, roughly, what level of tax rates will be required to finance each level of health-service budget and, in turn, what quantity of aggregate services each budget will supply. But what will determine his own choice among budgets? The individual's own preferences will be controlling here as they are in private choice, but here he cannot choose between positions for himself independently from or in isolation from the positions of all others in the political group. Here choice involves indicating a preference for one *group* outcome over the others, even though this choice may be largely determined by the individual's own position in this outcome. Each alternative for choice embodies results not only for the participating or "voting" individual but also for all others. Each budget defines a specific expected level of services along with a specific expected level of taxation, along with a distribution in both cases.

This is a choice setting that is categorically different from that which characterises the demand side. In his capacity as a participant in collective choice, the individual must *balance costs against benefits*. He will try, as best he can, to estimate the tax costs that various levels of service will impose on him and he will weigh these against estimates of benefits that he will secure from these various levels. Clearly any choice on the individual's part here to extend supply to the point where the marginal utility from the services becomes zero would be foolish because the sacrifice of alternatives would be relatively enormous. The individual will quite rationally indicate a preference for an aggregate supply of services that falls below such satiation levels. His choice, in a political-decision context, will be for a quantity of gross investment in health services much lower than that which would be required by a policy of providing constant-quality services to the extent indicated by privately expressed "needs."[14]

14. In this second choice situation, the individual is not in the n-person analogue to the prisoners' dilemma at all. Here the analogue would

v i. *Application to British Experience*

I suggest that the observed breakdown in the NHS can at least be partly explained by the theory of institutional choice outlined above. The politicians who have made the decisions on investment in the health services have been simply responding to the preferences of individual citizens. The observed results are precisely those that the theory would have enabled us to predict. Alternative hypotheses concerning the behavior of politicians can, of course, be advanced, and some of them might be of explanatory value. My emphasis is on the point that no supplemental hypotheses are required; the experience can be explained by postulating that politicians behave "as if" they transmit the preferences of citizens into political outcomes.

As indicated at several places, the first half of the theory is a straightforward application of one of the most elementary of economic principles, about which there will surely be little or no debate. The novelty or innovation in this analysis lies in its extension of what is essentially economic reasoning to political decisions. This economic theory of politics remains unfamiliar territory, but we are fortunate here in that no complex models seem to be needed to explain satisfactorily the health-service experience. There has been no need to resort to models of majority rule, of parliamentary systems of government, of political parties, of political leadership. This is not to deny that some such models might provide equally satisfactory explanations of real-world results. One of the fundamental methodological principles for all science, however, is that of accepting the simplest hypothesis when a genuine choice among explanations is possible. All that has been necessary here is a simple acknowledgement that individual preferences are influential in determining political outcomes. The results suggest that the transmission of these preferences into outcomes does take place, quite independently of the particular way in which this process operates.

This is merely another way of stating that the British political order is assumed to be effectively "democratic." The theory can-

---

be the individual prisoner's voting choice for a standard "policy for confessing" to be applied for all prisoners. The difference in the two choice situations for the individual creates inconsistency in results. There is no need for us to extend the analysis beyond the level of the single individual. We need not call upon the more complex models of group-choice for explanation.

not be used simultaneously to explain the results from a democratic political model and to prove that the system is, in fact, democratic. If a *dirigiste*, nondemocratic political structure is postulated, explanation of the observed results would necessarily be different.

VII. *Directions for Reform*

If the explanation advanced in the *Paper* is accepted, the directions for reform in the institutions of the NHS are indicated. The inconsistency between demand-choice and supply-choice must be eliminated, and the individual, as the ultimate chooser, must be placed in a position where the two parts of what is really a single decision are not arbitrarily separated. This can be accomplished only if an explicit decision on demand is allowed to call forth or to imply a specific supply response, or if an explicit decision on supply embodies a specific demand response. The splitting into two parts of what must be, in the final analysis, a single decision must be removed.

To illustrate that any arbitrary splitting of the demand-supply decision will create inconsistency, we may examine the various alternatives other than the one found in practice. Suppose, as our first example, that an attempt should be made to provide health services "free," as currently, but that, also, an attempt should be made to cover the costs of these services through "free" contributions, without the imposition of coercive taxes. In this situation, individuals would have health services freely made available to them but they would also be allowed freely to make whatever contributions they choose toward financing them. Predicted results of this institutional combination are obvious. Relatively little would be collected in contributions, since all individuals would be placed in "free-rider" positions. The system would be characterised by gross under-supply and gross over-demand, with resulting deterioration in quality in all respects. The institutional combination in being embodies only one-half of this worst possible system.

As a second illustrative example of a split-decision structure, let us suppose that, as in the preceding case, individuals are asked to make voluntary contributions but that, on the demand side, decisions are made publicly, not privately. The government would, in this situation, place restrictive limits on the use of the health services, but there would be no collective decision on the total amount to be supplied. This structure need not exhibit quality deterioration due to excessive individual demand, but the aggregate quantity of health services would be grossly inadequate and much below that quantity which would satisfy criteria for the optimal use of resources. This institutional combination is mentioned here only because it represents the exact reverse of that which is in being; here there would be public or collective demand decisions and private or individual supply decisions. The inefficiencies would take a dramatically different form from those currently observed.

Any reasonably workable set of institutions must bring demand decisions and supply decisions into the same framework for individual choice. There are only two alternatives here. The first is to allow individuals to make both demand decisions and supply decisions privately. This amounts to treating medical-health services as private and allowing the ordinary institutions of the market to operate. Individuals would be allowed, as they now are, to adjust demands privately and independently, but not at zero prices. Instead, prices would be set by competitive forces and the services finally made available would be determined not through a collective-political decision but by the private decisions of many suppliers responding to expressed demands. This structure would be an efficient one in the restricted sense that no apparent shortages or surpluses would be observed.

Market organisation may not, however, take adequate account of the external economies in certain types of medical-health services. In addition, the distributive results of market organisation may not prove broadly acceptable and direct transfers of income-wealth to mitigate them may not be feasible. For either or both these reasons, or others, the market organisation of health services based on the distribution of income that emerges from a market economy may be rejected.

The alternative institutional structure is one in which both the demand side and the supply side are joined in a collective or public choice process. If the market solution is rejected, this becomes the only avenue of reform. The institutions through which individuals are allowed to adjust demands, privately and individually, to zero-price health services must be eliminated, and a specific collective decision on aggregate supply or quantity of services must be made to embody a specific quality of final services distributed in a specific manner among individuals. This means that the government must decide, collectively, how much health services each member of the group shall have available to him. There must be some determinate allocation of final services among persons, either in physical quantity units or in more flexible units of general purchasing power. In the first case, each individual would be allowed to utilise specific maximum quantities per year: x visits to the surgery; y minor oper-

ations; z days in a hospital. In the second case, each individual
would be allowed to utilise a total "value" of service of P pounds
per year as he chooses among the various health services. This
scheme would allow for a somewhat wider individual range of
choice among health-service facilities, but it would require, of
course, the assigning of specific "shadow prices" to the different
services made available. Either of these two schemes would, however, eliminate the institutional inefficiencies that are currently
observed. There need be no congestion of available facilities and
no continuing deterioration in service standards. The allowable demand on the facilities would be limited by the supply decision, and
that would be that.

The objections to these modifications in existing institutions
stem from the failure to allow for individuals who may desire,
privately and personally, to utilise more health-medical services
than any collective or political determination of allowable limits
would provide. Such a desire, or need, may be due to fortuitous
circumstances, and it may be largely independent of user price in
many instances. If a collective limit of 30 days in hospital is imposed, what about the person whose illness requires 60 days?

Considerable improvements may be made in overcoming such
objections if the many separate categories of health services are
differentiated and treated separately. In general terms, however,
this genuine problem of above-limit demands under any publicly
financed system of health services can only be met by allowing for
a market or market-like set of institutions to emerge which supplements the publicly financed, publicly supplied facilities. The advantages of such a system are that there need be no limits placed
on the total amount of health services to be utilised by any single
person or family; the necessity for limits applies only to the total
amount of health services that shall be *publicly* financed and/or
publicly supplied for him. Over and beyond these limits, the individual may be allowed to choose as much or as little as he desires,
and for any reason.

Any detailed discussion of the particular features of the combined institutional structure that seems indicated as relatively
efficient would require a second paper. One implication of the argument may be noted. Consideration should be given to an institutional structure that replaces, in whole or in part, direct public or
governmental supply and operation by *public financing* of privately
organised operation. This structure would allow for greater flexibility in individual adjustments while, at the same time, it would
facilitate bringing the demand side and the supply side more closely

into co-ordination, in both public and private choices. On the basis of externality, equity, or other arguments, a political or collective decision can be made on the aggregate quantity of health services that will be *publicly financed*, and this decision can include a set of maximum limits, defined in purchasing power units, that will be made available to each person. These need not, of course, be equal among separate persons and groups. Individuals could be provided with vouchers for these indicated limits, which they could then utilise in purchasing health services as they chose. To the extent that their demands exceeded the amounts that could be purchased for such limits, individuals would be able to extend utilisation by privately financed supplements, these being financed directly by paying fees or charges or through various possible private insurance schemes.

My concern is not with recommending the institutional structure that Great Britain "should" adopt. The various institutional reforms above are mentioned to illustrate that an efficient NHS *can be organised* once the inconsistencies are recognised. Under a continuation of the existing structure the observed inefficiencies are likely to become more and more serious over time.

Appendix

Criteria for Aggregate Investment in Health Services

There are two distinct elements of the British experience that seem to refute the normative implications of neoclassical welfare economics. These are the failures of total investment in health services to rise demonstrably above that which would have been forthcoming under private organisation, and the willingness of governments to allow apparent quality deterioration including increasing congestion of available facilities. This *Paper* has been limited to an explanation of the second of these elements.

In a paper published in 1963, written jointly with Milton Kafoglis of the University of Florida, an hypothesis was advanced that can partly "explain" the first of these two characteristic elements of the British experience. National Health Service data were cited as illustrative of the more general argument. It may be helpful here to summarise the argument of the Buchanan-Kafoglis paper and to relate it to that which this *Paper* advances.

The Buchanan-Kafoglis analysis was concerned with comparing total outlay on a service under private and under public organisation when, at the margin of private extension, there are significant ex-

ternal economies. Whether or not such external economies characterise medical care in general need not be discussed in detail here.
Some types of services, notably prevention of communicable dis-
eases, seem clearly to exhibit such external economies, and, if necessary, the argument can be restricted in application to them. The
orthodox Pigovian and post-Pigovian theorems about the divergence
between marginal private and marginal social products suggest that
an organisational shift from the private sector to the public sector
would result in an increase in total resource commitment to the
service in question. Implicitly, the whole analysis assumes that collective decision-makers would invest "optimally." The Buchanan-
Kafoglis argument did not modify this implied assumption about collective decision-making. The argument showed, however, that a
distinction between resource inputs and consumption output is required. The presence of significant external economies implies that
outputs should be increased but, if "efficiencies" in utilising inputs
are produced by a shift from private to public organisation, total
resource commitment may not be increased by this shift from a suboptimal to an optimal position.

The argument was illustrated by a medical-care example. Consider the case of a highly communicable disease the spread of which
can be prevented only by improved sanitation measures. In this situation, the community may find that collectivisation of the service,
with the component change in *distribution* of total resource investment, provides for a greater than one-for-one substitute for individuals' previously undertaken outlays. The superior efficiencies
may be such that the optimally distributed investment generates
optimal outputs with less resources than private investment. This
result need not, of course, be present, but the analysis suggests that
organisational-institutional changes that effectively internalise external economies need not imply expanded overall resource commitment.

What does this analysis signify for the experience of the NHS?
It suggests that the relatively limited total outlay on the provision of
medical-health facilities since 1948 does not, in itself, imply that the
aggregate investment is suboptimal. To the extent that external
economies characterised the pre-1948 organisation of the services,
the change in distributional efficiency achieved under general collectivisation may have been sufficient to guarantee optimal supplies
at observed levels of outlay. On the other hand, to the extent that
relevant external economies did not characterise pre-1948 experience, no such increased distributional efficiency should have taken
place. But, in this case, there is no economic argument, as such, for
collectivisation and the private or market organisation tends to gen-

erate optimal levels of supply. The analysis suggests, therefore, that, regardless of the extent to which relevant external economies might have been present under private organisation, no implication can be drawn concerning relative levels of outlay required for "optimality."

If comparative levels of overall investment in medical-health care since 1948 tell us nothing at all about the attainment of the socially desired or optimal provision, how can the "wisdom" of collective decision-makers after 1948 be evaluated? Here we resort to the second element that is observed, namely, congestion on the available facilities. Does this congestion, in itself, tell us anything? Does it suggest that total investment is suboptimal? No such inference is possible. The congestion that is observed indicates only that the supply of medical-health services at a standard quality is not sufficient to meet demand at zero user prices. But, since zero-user prices are not demonstrably optimal in themselves, there is no implication that the supply of standard-quality services sufficient to meet all demands at these prices would produce optimal levels of investment.

Therefore, if we look at the experience of the NHS in the framework of theoretical welfare economics, we can infer nothing at all concerning the "correctness" or "incorrectness" of the collective decisions that have been made as regards overall or aggregate levels of provision. The observed facts are consistent with either nonoptimal or optimal levels of investment since 1948.

The distribution of the services made available must be sharply distinguished from the aggregate levels of supply. It seems highly unlikely, of course, that this distribution has been "efficient" or "optimal" since, as the analysis of the present *Paper* shows, the results depend on the private adjustments of many separate persons. The collectivisation of demand decisions might or might not involve a larger resource commitment; it would almost certainly involve a modified pattern of distributing the services that are made available.

Applied to the economics of health services, the emphasis of the earlier Buchanan-Kafoglis paper was on the question: What do the observed facts tell us about the level of total resource usage as measured in terms of the standard criteria of theoretical welfare economics? The answer is: Nothing at all.

The emphasis of the present *Paper* has been quite different and is on the question: Can the observed facts be explained satisfactorily in terms of simple models of private and public choice?

The dominant weakness of the NHS is not the inefficiencies of public or collective decisions. It is rather the inconsistency between these decisions and the private or individual decisions on the demand side.

4

Medical Care and the Economics of Sharing

Cotton M. Lindsay[1]

This paper provides an economic explanation of the observed wide-spread support of direct public provision of medical care. It is based on a characteristic of the relevant market different from character-istics which underlie various arguments in support of public pro-vision. Thus Arrow has resorted to particular uncertainty elements in the demand and supply of medical services to justify government intervention.[2] Weisbrod has developed the implications of an option demand characteristic which indicates that purely private provision of health facilities may be "suboptimal."[3] Pauly has explored the role of externalities of consumption in the demand for medical care.[4]

Each of the characteristics noted has its own implications for the required adjustment in the structure of the medical market. There remains, however, an aspect of demand bearing similar implications for the medical market which has received scant attention from economists. That aspect is the apparently universal desire and will-ingness to share. It is the attitude often expressed that everyone should have "equal access" to the medical resources available; that

Reprinted by permission of the author and publisher from *Economica*, November 1969.

1. The writer is grateful for the generous advice and criticism given by Professor James M. Buchanan in the preparation of this study. A NATO Post-doctoral Fellowship provided financial support for research at the London School of Economics and Political Science.

2. Kenneth J. Arrow, "Uncertainty and the Welfare Economics of Medical Care," *American Economic Review*, LIII (1963), 941–73.

3. Burton A. Weisbrod, "Collective–Consumption Services of Indi-vidual–Consumption Goods," *Quarterly Journal of Economics*, LXXVIII (1964), 471–77.

4. Mark V. Pauly provides a rigorous analysis of the implications of externalities of consumption for the organization of medical care provision in his doctoral dissertation, "Efficiency in Public Provision of Medical Care," Department of Economics, University of Virginia, 1967.

medical need and not economic status should determine eligibility for medical care; that high income or wealth should not entitle one to better or more care. This argument runs throughout the literature of medical economics, but it has never to my knowledge been examined formally for its economic as opposed to its normative content. This paper attempts to fill this void.

i. *A Theory of Sharing*

For simplicity in introducing the model it will be assumed initially that everyone has the same "medical needs," whatever that may mean. The egalitarian attitude under discussion holds that the amount of care made available to anyone should be based strictly on "medical need" and not on "economic status." We may therefore infer from this that what is desired among individuals demonstrating the same "medical need" is *more equal* treatment. Such a desire might be formalized into a utility function with the following characteristics:

$$(1) \qquad U^j = U^j(x_1^j, x_2^j, \ldots, x_n^j, e_1)$$

$$\text{where } e_1 = -\sum_{i=1}^{s} \left| x_1 - x_1^i \right|^5$$

In other words the individual would value, in addition to quantities of the n private goods available, the degree of equality with which one of these goods (i.e. medical care) is distributed. He would obtain positive satisfaction from a redistribution in shares which reduced the dispersion in individual holdings.[6] This may be seen more clearly with the aid of Figure 1 which assumes (*a*) a community of two persons of differing incomes, (*b*) where demand for the good in question is normal, and (*c*) where the supply is perfectly elastic.

Schedules D_1 and D_2 are individual demand schedules of the poorer and the richer man respectively yielding consumption quantities OA

5. The expression defining e_1 is given a negative sign simply to facilitate discussion. It is convenient to use e_1 to describe the degree of equality of given shares. Thus as the absolute value of e_1 falls, and the dispersion in shares lessens, we may describe the process interchangeably as an "increase in equality" or a "rise in e_1."

6. The degree of equality in shares (the e_1 term) may, of course, be measured a number of ways. A good intuitive case might be made for choosing the standard deviation which weights extreme values more heavily. The method chosen was selected arbitrarily for expositional convenience in the analysis which follows.

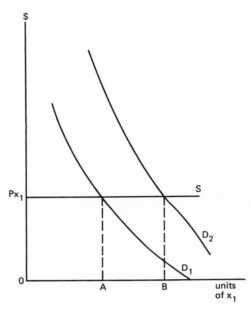

Figure 1

and OB. The value of the e_1 term in this case is clearly AB by our definition. If the wealthy individual has a utility function as described in (1), he will positively value a reduction of AB (an increase in e_1). Similarly in the large number case the individual would value a reduction in the total variation in consumption shares.[7]

7. This approach is similar to that developed by James M. Buchanan in his "An Economic Theory of Clubs," *Economica*, XXXII (February 1965), 1-14, where separate utility function arguments were employed representing the size of the group consuming each item. This approach also bears a similarity to though remains fundamentally different from that found in the studies of Harvey Leibenstein, "Bandwagon, Snob, and Veblen Effects in the Theory of Consumers' Demand," *The Quarterly Journal of Economics*, LXIV (May 1950), 183–207; James Duesenberry, *Income, Saving, and the Theory of Consumer Behavior*, Cambridge, Mass., 1949, Chapter IV; and William J. Baumol, *Welfare Economics and the Theory of the State* (London, 1952), 88–94. These treat the case in which the quantity demanded of a particular good is affected by the quantities consumed by others. As will become clear, this approach is unnecessarily restrictive.

It might be argued that separate treatment of this aspect of demand is unnecessary since it seems to concern only the parameters governing the wealthy individual's valuation of the good itself. To include these considerations as a separate argument in the utility function may seem redundant. For example, consumers prefer apples with flavor. Yet it is not necessary to include flavor as a separate argument in the utility function. It is a characteristic governing the value placed on apples themselves. This argument does not apply to the current example for two reasons: (*a*) The provision of greater equality itself yields external economies, and (*b*) there are means of obtaining a rise in the value of the e_1 term (i.e. a subsidy) which are completely independent of the quantity of the good desired or purchased privately.

The nature of the external economies which arise in the provision of greater equality may be noted by referring again to the simplified model used above. As long as only one individual in the community has the altruistic attitude described in (1), no problem is created. The individual may proceed to adjust to his own evaluation of greater equality by producing the private equilibrium amount.[8] The amount thus produced will satisfy Paretian optimality conditions. If, however, more than one such individual exhibits these egalitarian preferences, private adjustment will not lead to the welfare frontier. Individual unilateral activity to promote greater equality provides external economies to others who value equality. The familiar "free-rider" effect is present. One individual's activity to increase his own e_1 value provides a "free" extension of equality to all others. Only collective action to promote greater equality will permit extension of this activity to the optimum level.

It appears then that this externality characteristic in the provision of greater consumption equality may provide an argument for some possible government intervention in the allocation of medical resources. Given a widespread incidence of these egalitarian preferences, government promotion of equality in shares of the fund of medical resources would indeed be called for. In order to determine the nature of the intervention required, however, we must examine the activity of sharing itself.

11. *The Means of Sharing*

This leads to an examination of the second exceptional characteristics of the demand for equality noted above. There are indeed

8. The methods by which greater equality may be produced are reviewed below.

several methods which might be alternatively or jointly employed to produce the desired extension of equality in consumption of the good in question. These may be illustrated with reference to Figure 1. The inequality in shares consumed may clearly be reduced by either inducing the poor individual to consume more than OA or by inducing the wealthy individual to consume less than OB. So far as the e_1 term in the utility function alone is considered, the means chosen is a matter of indifference. It is simply equality as such that is desired. Further examination reveals, however, that the options available for inducing either are broader still. There are four alternatives which a wealthy individual might employ to promote the desired extension of equality:

1. The burnt-offering method. The wealthy individual might purchase the full amount OB which his private demand dictates and simply destroy (or at least not use) a portion of this amount. Insofar as the amount he actually consumed was nearer OA, greater equality in consumption would have been served.[9, 10]

2. The gift method. Greater consumption equality could be achieved if the wealthier individual purchased the full amount OB and transferred a portion directly to the poor.[11] Clearly this method would attack the existing inequalities from "both ends."

3. The abstention method. The wealthy individual might achieve greater equality in distribution of the good by simply refraining from purchasing the full amount OB in the market.

4. The subsidy method. Finally the wealthy individual might promote greater equality in consumption of the good by continuing to consume at his private level OB while offering a subsidy to promote extended consumption by the poor.

9. Though this method may seem trivial, it is certainly not without historical (even Biblical) precedent.

10. It may be objected here that having done so, the wealthy individual would reenter the market to purchase more of the good bringing his holding back up toward his original private consumption level. The final reduction in his holding would then result only from the income effect of this loss. This objection is invalid. It ignores the fact that this reduction results from his demand for equality and would leave him at private adjustment equilibrium.

11. It is assumed here that some means is found to prevent the poor from readjusting their holdings in response to this transfer. Such a readjustment would reduce the second half of the result of the transfer to its income effect proportions.

As noted above, an individual responding to the preferences described would be indifferent among units of equality produced via any of the four methods listed. This does not imply, however, that he would employ the methods indifferently. On the contrary, acting rationally, he would seek to promote equality to the point where his marginal evaluation of a unit of equality was equal to the marginal subjective cost of that unit. In so doing he would, of course, strive to employ the least cost methods of producing that quantity. In examining the individual decision calculus regarding how much equality he would produce as well as which methods he would elect to employ, it is therefore necessary to specify clearly the cost implicit in each method.

iii. *The Costs of Sharing*

The subjective cost of promoting consumption equality is simply the value to the individual doing the promoting of the item or activity surrendered in the process.[12] The difficulty of identifying this cost is in defining a unit of equality. As noted above, the selection of the definition adopted here was arbitrary. The complete analysis to follow may be rejected on the grounds that this definition is not acceptable. In that case, however, at least the guidelines for the applicable analysis are established in the following. One need only plug in the preferred definition.

The definition chosen does have certain convenient properties which recommend it. For example, it is clear that in a group of any size, the sacrifice of one unit of the good in question via the burnt-offering method will produce a single corresponding unit of equality for the individual concerned.[13] All subsequent sacrifices, as well, produce equality on a similar one for one basis. It is therefore quite simple to construct a marginal cost schedule for producing equality via this method utilizing Figures 1 and 2. The cost to the individual concerned of the first and subsequent units of equality produced is the value of the corresponding unit of the good in question which is sacrificed. Assuming he has originally purchased his full private demand quota OB, the cost of the first unit will be p_{x_1}, the market

12. It will facilitate discussion to focus attention originally on the *primary* effects of this activity. As noted above, individual unilateral promotion of consumption equality results in external economies to others who value it. These secondary effects will be brought into the discussion at a later point.

13. The external effect of his activity on others is ignored for the moment, as noted.

price of the commodity. Furthermore, the marginal cost schedule will simply be a reflection of the leftward portion of the demand curve. This is shown in Figure 2 as schedule S_1.

The cost functions of the remaining three methods may be derived in a similar fashion. The marginal cost function of method 2, the gift method, differs from that of method 1 in only one respect. In giving the good to a poor man rather than destroying it, the individual makes a double incursion in inequality. He increases the size of a poor man's holding while at the same time reducing the size of his own. The transfer of one unit of the good in this fashion produces twice as much equality (increasing the value of e_1 by two). The cost of producing equality via this method is therefore exactly half the cost of the burnt-offering method. The marginal cost schedule for the gift method is thus shown in Figure 2 as S_2, having exactly half the slope of S_1 and a y-intercept of $p_{x_1}/2$.

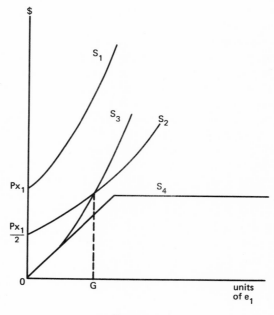

Figure 2

The derivation of the cost of the abstention method must be approached somewhat differently. Although it produces equality in the same "one for one" proportions as method 1, the cost of this method is clearly less. The individual who restrains his consumption in this manner has not actually devoted resources to goods he cannot use. He has free income which he may devote to other uses. The cost of producing a unit of equality in this manner is therefore only the consumer surplus sacrificed in the failure to consume the item. This is represented in Figure 1 by the area under the demand curve D_2 above the market price p_{x_1}. Clearly then the individual's marginal cost schedule for producing equality via the abstention method is identical to S_1 but shifted downward by the value of the constant p_{x_1}. This is shown in Figure 2 as schedule S_3.

The cost of producing equality via the subsidy method is the cost of inducing a poor individual to purchase more of the good.[14] Each unit of the good he is thus influenced to add to his normal consumption increases e_1 by one unit. Since we have assumed a perfectly elastic supply of medical care at price p_{x_1}, the marginal cost of producing equality can never rise above this amount.[15] There is reason to believe, however, that over some range of output the cost may indeed be less. This may be illustrated with reference once again to Figure 1. Conceptually, at least, in the two person case a wealthy individual might induce a poor individual to consume additional units by offering to bear the portion of the price of the marginal units which exceeded the poor individual's evaluation of them. In other words, given the poor individual's demand schedule D_1, the subsidy required would be the amount represented by the area between supply schedule S and D_1.[16]

The analysis becomes a good deal more complicated as the number of individuals involved is increased above the basic two person situation. The slope of this marginal cost curve may be steeper or flatter depending on the relative proportions of those subsidizing and being subsidized. It is really unnecessary to deal with these complications, however, as the essential characteristics for our purpose still appear manifest. Whatever the number, insofar as one additional unit of consumption produces one unit of equality, the maximum marginal cost of producing equality via the subsidy method will remain p_{x_1}, the price of a unit of the good itself. Fur-

14. Or alternatively of inducing some other wealthy individual to purchase less. This possibility is arbitrarily ignored.

15. It is further assumed that the good in question is never supplied in such quantity to the poor that it takes on a nuisance value.

16. The actual administration of such a subsidy scheme might prove more costly than a flat-rate subsidy over the full range of consumption of the good. For this reason costs may be significantly higher than depicted. For a thorough analysis of these problems see Mark V. Pauly, "The Theory of Consumption Subsidies" (forthcoming).

thermore, even in a large number setting, the marginal cost of inducing the first units of increased consumption is likely to be quite small. The marginal cost schedule for the subsidy method of achieving consumption equality would therefore resemble S_4 in Figure 2. It rises from a point near the origin to a plateau at the rightward extremity.

We now have cost schedules for each method of individual unilateral promotion of equality of consumption. Before we may proceed to a discussion of the decision calculus used in selecting among these methods, however, two additional factors must be considered. We must examine the implications of a nonseparability characteristic in some of the methods of producing equality, and we have yet to consider the external effects generated by this activity.

It will be recalled from the earlier discussion that inequality may be attacked from two sides. The large holdings may be reduced, or the small holdings extended. We have considered three methods, however, methods 1, 2 and 3 which all involve a reduction of the large holding. It is clear that one may not give up the same unit to be simultaneously (1) destroyed, (2) given to the poor, and (3) not purchased at all. One may not therefore operate simultaneously on the lowest portions of two of these three cost curves. Efforts to combine the various methods in least cost proportions must be wary of this. If, for example, a significant quantity of the good has been sacrificed via the burnt-offering method, the cost of producing one unit of equality via the gift method is no longer only $p_{x_1}/2$ but something more. The individual concerned must therefore choose among these three discrete methods rather than attempt to combine them.

The second factor remaining to be examined is the effect of the external economies generated in the process. This interaction of private and collective adjustments where such effects are present has been examined exhaustively by Buchanan.[17] He shows that by moving an activity which produces external effects from the private sector to the collective sector, individual production frontiers are shifted. This can be shown as follows. Any individual acting alone who produces one unit of the good provides a windfall gain to all others who value it. These others will then adjust their own production downward in response to this windfall yielding a net output to the original individual of less than one. On the other hand, if

17. James M. Buchanan, *The Demand and Supply of Public Goods* (Chicago, 1968), Chap. 2.

these production decisions are made collectively, the result is reversed. One individual agrees to produce one unit only if all others produce some amount as well. By incurring the same cost as in the individual production case above, the individual in effect produces a net output of many times more than one unit via the collective process.[18] He will clearly be led to extend his activity when it is "collectivised."

The essential characteristic of this process for the selection of least cost methods of producing equality is that this increase in productivity will apply equally to all methods. Given our assumption of community indifference among methods, the manner in which the individual agrees to produce equality in the collective process will be irrelevant to the decisions of others regarding the quantity they agree to produce. The effect of the external economies produced is therefore that of a scalar applied to the production functions (or cost functions) of the various methods available. In Figure 2 this will have the effect of reducing the slopes of the marginal cost functions by a uniform factor. The overall effect will therefore be identical to a change in the scale of the horizontal axis. Insofar as the *relative* positions of the marginal cost schedules are unaffected by the externality aspect, the analysis may proceed. We need only assume that the required adjustment in the scale of the horizontal axis has been made.

IV. *The Selection Process*

Having established the effects of the external economies generated in the production of equality, we may now observe the process of selecting the least cost techniques for producing the desired level. Since the introduction of externalities has altered nothing essential here, Figure 2 may still be used for this exposition. The most obvious step in this selection is the elimination of the burnt-offering method as an economical method for producing equality. Clearly it would be less costly to extend production via the subsidy method S_4 to *any level* than to produce even one unit via the former. It is also obvious that the subsidy method will be employed to some extent. Since the marginal cost schedule for this method extends from near the origin, it follows that at least some portion of the total will likely be produced via this approach.

18. This discussion ignores the possibility of strategic behavior in the collective decision process. Such behavior is deemed to be unlikely in a large-number political setting.

Whether method 2 or 3 is combined with method 4 to produce the desired level requires closer scrutiny. The decision between the two appears ambiguous. We recall that the nonseparable property of these two methods dictates that only one be employed. Yet the two schedules intersect, seemingly indicating that the method selected may depend on the quantity desired. Small quantities appear less costly via the abstention method while production of large quantities appears more economical via the gift method.

This ambiguity is removed by noting the location of the intersection itself. It is easily shown that it lies at precisely the point where both schedules reach the market price of the good in question.[19] It will never pay to produce a quantity of equality greater than OC via either of these methods, since marginal additional units are always available at cost p_{x_1} via the subsidy method. The chooser will therefore select the method which produces quantities less than OC with the lower average cost.[20] Since S_3 intersects S_2 from below at OC, it is clear that S_3 will be chosen. The least cost "package" of methods will therefore be a combination of subsidy with restraint on the size of individual shares, i.e., rationing.[21] The proportions in which the two methods would be combined are illustrated in Figure 3.

19. This is shown by recalling the relationships between the marginal cost functions. From our definitions we note the following:

$$(2) \qquad S_1(e_1) = 2S_2(e_1) \quad \text{and} \quad (3) \quad S_1(e_1) = S_3(e_1) + p_{x_1}.$$

Substituting (3) in (2) and rearranging terms, we get

$$(4) \qquad\qquad\qquad S_3(e_1) = 2S_2(e_1) - p_{x_1}.$$

At the point of intersection $S_2(e_1)$ will equal $S_3(e_1)$. Thus subtracting $S_2(e_1)$ from both sides and setting the results equal to zero, we get

$$(5) \qquad\qquad S_3(e_1) - S_2(e_1) = S_2(e_1) - p_{x_1} = 0,$$

which simplifies to

$$(6) \qquad\qquad\qquad S_3(e_1) = S_2(e_1) = p_{x_1}.$$

20. The actual decision processes are complicated by the necessity to choose a discrete system to be combined and adjusted marginally with a third. This requires that the chooser be governed by both marginal and average cost values in this decision. The ultimate quantity produced via the method selected is determined by marginal considerations while the choice between the two methods themselves must be decided on average cost grounds.

21. It is interesting to note that this analysis confirms speculations of James Tobin made well over a decade ago in which he suggested that

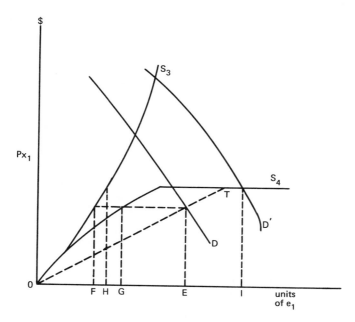

Figure 3

Figure 3 is a diagram containing the marginal cost schedules for the two selected methods facing a "typical voter" in the political process. It is assumed that the scalars resulting from external effects have been applied to these marginal cost curves. This means that the quantities reflected as produced at the various marginal cost levels are the total quantities which the collectivity would produce subject to general agreement. The dotted schedule OT, the horizontal sum of the two marginal cost curves, represents the locus of least cost combinations. Assuming that the voter's marginal evaluation curve for consumption equality is D, he would favor a program producing OE equality. Such a program would entail a subsidy measure which produced amount OG and a rationing measure which

---

rationing might be justified by "egalitarian" preferences where "the arguments in the consumers' utility functions were not absolute physical quantities but . . . were amounts relative to the consumption of others." James Tobin, "A Survey of the Theory of Rationing," *Econometrica,* 20 (October 1952), 549.

produced OF.[22] Alternatively, if his marginal evaluation schedule were D′, then he would favor a total program of OI of which OH was produced through rationing and HI was produced via a subsidy.

v. *Selecting the System*

The basic analysis to this point has suggested a two-pronged attack on the inequality of shares of the commodity which results from market distribution. On the one hand, tax supported subsidies to the poor are to be made to promote an extension of their consumption increasing the degree of equality "from below." At the same time restraint on the level of consumption is to be applied via rationing, extending equality "from the top." Before the final step toward drawing conclusions relevant to the real world may be taken, however, two remaining considerations must be dealt with. The costs of administrative overhead implicit in the two systems must be considered, and more importantly, the convenient assumption of equal "medical need" must be relaxed.

The relaxation of the equal "medical need" assumption poses no problems analytically. We may simply increase the number of e_1 terms in expression (1) to include all the relevant states of health. The individual as a member of the collectivity is then assumed to face a trade-off situation with regard to the degree of equality he wishes to produce among the various states. The actual choice calculus involved in this process seems completely straightforward. The difficulty arises in conjunction with the second consideration raised above. The costs of administering either a subsidy or a rationing system along the lines suggested may severely constrain the actual options open in this regard. The mere tasks of defining clinically identical states or of identifying individuals in such states appears a practical impossibility. Coupled with the fact that individuals would almost daily be shifting from one state to another, this would seem to rule out either the standard rationing or subsidy approach keyed to this characteristic. Resort to some second-best alternative program is clearly suggested.

Among the alternatives which might be considered is a single-source program on the order of Britain's National Health Service.

22. It is quite essential to note that while he would favor this level in the context of the political decision process, he privately is motivated by "free rider" incentives to reduce his own activity below the level shown. The necessity to employ the coercive powers of the state for enforcing restraint on consumption (rationing) and levying taxes to support the subsidy program is therefore evident.

It is surprising how well this system seems tailored to the essential requirements derived from the analysis above. Clearly it attacks the problem of unequal consumption from "both ends." On the one hand, since it is financed almost totally from general revenues which in turn are obtained through progressive taxation, the element of subsidy to the poor is retained. On the other hand, since virtually all citizens are participants in the National Health Service program which is required to administer "equally" to all, the ability of the wealthy to purchase extraordinary amounts of care is clearly circumscribed. The physicians themselves are charged with the responsibility of dispensing care in accordance with their own appraisals of "medical need."

It might be argued that individuals are free to purchase any quantity of private medicine in Great Britain, hence there is no real restraint on consumption, but closer examination will prove the contrary. Private medicine, though it was not forbidden by the National Health Service Act, was isolated by insuring that its use was a substitute for rather than a complement of state medicine.[23] The individual desiring care is therefore effectively forced to choose either public or private medicine. By offering Health Service medicine at virtually no cost, the *relative price* of private medicine is made much more costly. This increase in relative price clearly acts as a restraining factor on the private purchase of medicine.

It is difficult in fact to conceive of another practical means of introducing the required restraint into the distribution of medical care. As noted above, a rationing scheme is not practical here. There is no restraint characteristic in the subsidized national health insurance schemes found in America and other countries, and it is difficult to conceive of one being introduced. Therefore, in communities and nations where egalitarian feeling is strong and a spirit of national sharing is general, a National Health Service may indeed be the most efficient means of satisfying these wants. Aneurin Bevan, the principal architect of and first Minister of Health under the National Health Service may indeed have had keen vision in 1948 at the advent of the new experiment when he remarked:[24]

> The picture I have always visualized is one, not of "panel doctoring" for the less well off, nor of anything charitable or demeaning, but

23. For example, private patients of general practitioners are not entitled to prescription drugs at nominal cost as are Health Service patients. Private patients of consultants must pay the full cost of their hospitalization.

24. Aneurin Bevan, letter to *Lancet*, July 3, 1948, p. 24.

rather of a nation deciding to make health-care easier and more effective by pooling its resources—each sharing the cost as he can through regular taxation and otherwise while he is well, and each able to use the resulting resources if and when he is ill.

v i. *Conclusion*

The foregoing has provided a possible theoretical foundation upon which the institutional characteristics and structure of the British National Health Service *may* be justified. No attempt has been made to analyse the structure itself to determine whether the desired results predicted of the program are in fact achieved. Such an examination might reveal factors not considered here which act to thwart the egalitarian aims of the Health Service. For example, to a certain extent medical care is clearly rationed among individuals on the basis of the opportunity cost of the time spent "waiting" for service rather than on the basis of the doctor's evaluations of the relative "medical needs" of competing patients. Furthermore, the ability of doctors to make consistent evaluations of "medical need"—indeed, the ability of the profession to establish abstract guidelines for the use of individual physicians in rendering the decisions—seems questionable. These are operational issues, however, which may only be resolved satisfactorily by examining the performance of the system in being.

A more fundamental question regarding the appropriateness of the structure of the National Health Service is whether the British people do in fact have preferences similar to those described above which are sufficiently intense to justify the approach suggested. Only if a large segment of society believes that medical care should be distributed equally among men of all stations, and is willing to bear the costs of implementing these beliefs, is such a program justified. No attempt has been made in this study to quantify or test for the existence of such preferences. Indeed the results of any such attempt would likely be of limited value. All of the problems associated with the measurement of demand functions for public goods are present here.[25] This may well be one of those situations in which the politi-

25. For a systematic review of these and related problems see James M. Buchanan, *Public Finance in Democratic Process* (Chapel Hill, 1967), Part I.

Information obtained through opinion surveys in 1963 and 1965 sponsored by the Institute of Economic Affairs casts some doubt on the dominance of the egalitarian attitude among the population at large. Well over half of those participating in the survey felt that universal state pro-

cian's sensitive ear may better read the preferences of his constituents than the econometrician with his computer. In any case, the politician has made his reading and acted accordingly. He apparently feels that the provision of medical care is indeed a special case calling for unique treatment by governments. In view of the foregoing, it would appear that the *onus probandi* has fallen to the economist to prove him wrong.

---

vision of medical care should be discontinued. On the other hand, more than two-thirds of those questioned stated that they would prefer the current National Health Service regime to state distribution of vouchers worth 70 per cent of the cost of comprehensive private insurance coverage. See Arthur Seldon, *After the N. H. S.*, Occasional Paper 21, Institute of Economic Affairs, 1968, pp. 13–19.

5

Easy Budgets and Tight Money

James M. Buchanan

Despite the old saying, taking candy from the baby is more difficult than not, and governments, even more than ordinary mortals, are delighted by smiles and fearful of screams. As between monetary policy and fiscal policy there is, as the Radcliffe Committee put it, "always a choice," but the alternatives may not be equally pleasant to the chooser. The factors influencing such a choice are worthy of more attention than has been given them, by the Committee and by others, especially when governments are recognized for what they are and must be in any real world.

I propose to discuss here the choice among *instruments* of stabilization policy. I want to leave out of account, so far as possible, discussion of the choice among *objectives* for economic policy. There is also a "line of least resistance" in the choice of objectives for policy. I shall not discuss this problem, however, for three reasons: First, the political pressures impinging on choices among objectives have been more widely recognized than those similarly impinging on choice among instruments. Second, governments do not explicitly choose objectives; they choose instruments. Finally, and more importantly, only by unscrambling these two parts of stabilization policy can we make sense out of either of them.

For my purpose, we may assume that a particular objective or set of objectives has been selected. There remains the choice among instruments, and, broadly speaking, there are two instruments of stabilization policy, *fiscal* and *monetary*. There is little direct connection between the choice of these two means of implementing policy and the objective to be pursued. Fiscal policy may be utilized primarily to achieve a surplus in the international balance of payments, or monetary policy may be used to promote full employment and rapid economic growth. In the most likely case, a mix

Reprinted by permission of the publisher from *Lloyds Bank Review*, April 1962.

of instruments will be used, more or less successfully, to achieve a mix of objectives. I shall assume, without arguing the point here, that either of these two instruments, properly employed, can be equally successful in achieving the objectives selected.

There is a "theory" of choice here, but practice seems at odds with it. Many economists argue, for example, that fiscal policy should be relied on as the primary instrument of stabilization. And the Treasury, in its evidence given to the Radcliffe Committee, paid lip service to this predominance of fiscal policy as the primary stabilizing device in the modern economy. As the Committee noted, in its review of the experience, however, easy budgets have been presented against the backstop of a "flexible monetary policy" which can, if need be, be relied on to keep inflationary pressures in check.

The clearest statement of the practice, as opposed to the theory, was made by Professor Frank Paish, who, in *The Statist* for November 10, 1961, said:

> It is important that the measures taken to control the economy should be symmetrical. In recent years the measures to expand demand have taken the form mainly of tax reductions, while the main burden of restricting demand has been placed on monetary policy and higher interest rates. A continuation of this policy could raise interest rates without limit.

This observed asymmetry in the practical application of fiscal policy and monetary policy over the different phases of the cycle merits attention. Most reasonably well-informed persons will recognize this asymmetry as being broadly characteristic of the policy experience of Great Britain and the United States, as well as other Western countries, in the years since the second world war, and especially during the decade of the 1950s. It has come to be more or less accepted that the budget provides the major weapons for stimulating spending (public and private), while monetary policy comes into its own only in periods of threatened or actual inflation. Only very recently, as reflected in the statement by Professor Paish, or in an October speech by Lord Cromer, has concern come to be expressed about the fundamental disproportion that such a policy structure must involve.

Few will quarrel with the facts of the matter. But few go beyond these to the interesting questions. Why has the asymmetry in the choice of instruments come about? Could this have been predicted to occur? Can it be expected to continue? I shall try to show that some elementary considerations for political realities will, in fact, suggest that the observed facts could readily have been predicted. If this is accepted, however, I shall show that the implications for the theory or principle of public debt are highly damaging to the ideas of "modern" economists.

Familiar explanations for the emphasis on fiscal policy in expanding demand and on monetary policy in restricting it may be found. For one thing, such a policy combination might seem to be just the ticket after a reading of almost any of the standard textbooks in elementary economics. These books, all written within the framework of the so-called Keynesian theory, will usually refer to that deceptively simple analogy "you can't push on a string." This analogy has probably had more influence on ordinary thinking than any of the more complicated, because more qualified, analytical models. In any case, the impact on thought is that monetary policy is of quite limited usefulness in stimulating demand, since people are not necessarily induced to spend by the mere availability of funds. Hence, so the argument goes, fiscal policy, the deliberate use of the budget for stabilization purposes, must become the primary antirecession weapon. And, since some symmetry seems better than none, cyclical "balance" between fiscal and monetary measures is secured by employing the latter to restrict demand when needed. This crudely simple policy model is widely accepted today, by economists and informed politicians alike, despite the ratchet effect on the interest rate noted by Paish, the implications for budgetary balance, and the demonstrated effectiveness of monetary policy in stimulating as well as restricting demand.

1. The Bias of Fiscal Policy

A second explanation is considerably more sophisticated, but still familiar. If political reality is recognized at all (and it seldom is by academic scribblers), surely it suggests the strong bias of fiscal policy toward the creation of budget deficits rather than budget surpluses. Governments, that is to say, politicians, faced with any sort of responsive citizenry or electorate, are surely cognizant of two powerful and ever-present forces. Constant pressure is exerted upon them to reduce (not to increase) the level of taxes, and, at the same time, to expand (not to reduce) both the range and the extent of the various public services. As the Plowden Committee quite properly noted, the third pressure for budgetary economy, so strong in former times, no longer exists as an effective counterforce comparable in strength to the other two.

Both of the dominant pressure groups, the tax reducers and the expenditure expanders, direct their fire at the politicians, who must, other things equal, respond (otherwise, they will not remain politicians for long). These pressures assume especial importance in an economy where tax rates are already prohibitively high in the view of many people, and where ever-expanding public spending programmes have been firmly "built in" to the structure of expectations. Governments will, quite predictably, seize on any opportunity or excuse for deficit creation offered to them by the economists, as is the case during modern recessions. Deficit financing enables both of these groups to be satisfied simultaneously—the politicians' dream world come true.

The situation during booms is exactly the reverse. To carry out effective stabilization measures through the budget then requires that both of these pressure groups be countered. Tax rates must be maintained or increased, and public spending programmes curtailed or at any rate not expanded. The experience in Great Britain during recent months suggests that the latter is especially difficult, even when an explicit curtailment objective is announced in advance. And, if the Chancellor presents a "tough" budget in April, this will be the exception that proves the rule. Can anyone express serious surprise that budget surpluses have so rarely occurred, except by accident, since fiscal policy has "matured," so to speak, while budget deficits have been the order of the day?

11. *The Independence of the Monetary Authorities*

The suggested bias in fiscal policy is, however, only one half of the story. It may be that fiscal policy will tend to be used only to expand demand but as yet nothing has been said to indicate that there is an offsetting bias in the use of monetary policy. Is monetary policy biased toward restriction?

There is an argument that attempts an answer here, although, as I shall indicate, I do not think it need be accepted. It is sometimes advanced, however, that because of the nature of the institutions, monetary policy instruments can be, and are, relatively divorced from current "political" pressures. The monetary authorities are presumed to remain considerably more free than their Treasury counterparts from day-to-day, week-to-week influences of public opinion which, in this argument, are inherently "evil." Because of this relative freedom, these authorities can safely take "unpopular" steps that the politicians dare not take. The comparative isolation places the task of restricting demand on these authorities almost by default. Being the wise and good men they are, they must pick up the dirty linen left over by the one-sidedness of fiscal policy and, to a degree, redress the balance.

This argument is a persuasive one, especially in a superficial sense, and especially in application to the United States, where the Federal Reserve Board is, to a large but undetermined and unpredictable extent, independent of Treasury authority and control. It is less persuasive in a British context, where the central bank is, officially, within the public sector. Thus the Radcliffe Report points out that Bank of England witnesses sometimes drew a distinction between the activities of the Bank as agent of the Treasury and "the affairs of the Bank" in which it is supposed to have a wider measure of autonomy. "During this decade," the Committee comments, "this distinction has had no practical force, and we therefore do not propose to complicate our description of the Bank's activities by further reference to it."

III. *A Simpler Explanation*

Elements of both the explanations sketched above are, no doubt, helpful in understanding the policy asymmetry with which we are concerned. We can, however, explain the asymmetry more simply. And as I recall, one principle of scientific method, attributed usually to William of Occam, tells us that we should always choose the simplest explanation of phenomena when alternative explanations are possible.

We do not need to assume that the monetary authorities have relatively greater autonomy, nor to posit the existence of a bias in fiscal policy in its crudest form. It is possible to explain our asymmetry between the use of fiscal policy and monetary policy over the course of the cycle on the assumption that these instruments are, to the same degree, influenced by "politics." This is a less restricted approach which is, at the same time, somewhat more realistic for the institutions of democratic societies when these are considered generally and over long periods.

I assume only that governments will, when faced with a choice between these two policy instruments, tend to choose the one that creates the lesser disturbance and that generates the less violent reaction on the part of the citizenry. This is all that is required to show that during recessions governments will implement stabilization objectives through fiscal policy measures instead of monetary policy measures and that, conversely, during periods of threatened or actual inflation, they will resort primarily to monetary methods of control. I do not, of course, suggest that governments will always act in this way, or that the asymmetry is an inevitable result of democratic decision-making. I shall show only that, in the present state of thinking about fiscal-monetary institutions, this behaviour on the part of governments seems predictable, and, as noted, the limited facts available to us do support this prediction.

Note also that governments may or may not be successful in achieving the stabilization that they aim to achieve. Success or failure in this respect is not relevant to the discussion here, which attempts only to explain governments' choices between the *instruments* of policy.

IV. An "Ideal Type" Fiscal Policy

Before proceeding, it will be useful to reduce each of the broad policy alternatives to one simple variant, to one stylized model, or "ideal type," so to speak. For fiscal policy, I propose to mean the deliberate unbalancing of the cash budget of the national government (with budget defined in an overall or inclusive sense) to promote stabilization purposes, whether these be defined in terms of employment, growth, price-levels, or balances of payments. In unbalancing the budget, I assume that changes will be made in the rate of taxation, rather than in the rate of government spending. Finally, I assume that a budget deficit, when created, is financed wholly by the issue of *new currency*, or, in its modern institutional context, by "borrowing" from the central bank. Conversely, I shall assume that a budgetary surplus, when and if created, is disposed of by some effective neutralization of the excess revenues collected: for example, by building up government's cash balance or by retiring national debt held by the central bank.

This idealization of fiscal policy allows us to discuss a whole set of related instruments in terms of a single simple policy action. It eliminates confusion by ruling out of account the operation of the automatic fiscal stabilizers. Perhaps more importantly, it removes the complexities that arise when budget deficits are financed by the issue of genuine public debt rather than new currency.

v. An "Ideal Type" Monetary Policy

More objections may be raised to my idealization of monetary policy. I shall use this term to refer to the purchase and sale of government securities in the open market by the central bank and/or the monetary authorities, with the objective, of course, of furthering economic stabilization. In other words, the open-market weapon becomes the model here for analysing any and all types of monetary action. When deflation or unemployment threatens, corrective monetary policy consists in the purchase of government securities (bonds) from the public with newly created funds, that is, commercial bank reserves. When inflation threatens, corrective monetary policy consists in the sale of government securities in the open market, thereby reducing the cash reserves of the banking system. In the first instance, the public ends up with more cash and fewer government securities, quite apart from any secondary effects stemming from the operation of the deposit multiplier. In the second instance, the public ends up with more bonds and less cash. Monetary policy in this "ideal type" amounts to a modification in the asset structure of individuals and firms, with central bank purchases adding to overall liquidity during periods of recession and sales subtracting from overall liquidity during periods of inflation.

Note that, in this model of monetary policy, interest rate changes, in themselves, are *not* considered the instruments of monetary policy. Interest rates change only as a result of changes in the demand for and the supply of bonds. This is, I think, a legitimate model, and all monetary policy can be reduced to what might be called an "open-market equivalent." Interest rates, as prices, cannot be changed arbitrarily without some changes in the underlying demand-supply conditions, unless excess demand or excess supply is to be produced. If this is allowed to happen, problems of credit rationing or surplus credit arise. It seems preferable, and more realistic, to remain in an equilibrium model, which is, of course, present when the authorities take action to initiate or to follow up Bank Rate changes by accompanying open-market action which may include an exchange of long-term and short-term national debt.

Considerable authoritative support for this model is to be found in the testimony of the Chief Cashier of the Bank of England before the Radcliffe Committee. He suggested that changes in Bank Rate are made effective only because, through open-market action, the discount houses are forced to borrow at that rate. Many modern discussions of monetary policy (including those of the Radcliffe Committee) have gone astray precisely because of an undue concentration on changes in interest rates to the neglect of the underlying demand-supply changes in securities and money markets that implement the rate changes.

There is purpose in adopting this "ideal type" for monetary policy. Note that, here, monetary policy consists in increases and decreases in interest-bearing national debt held outside the central bank.

v i. *Debt Issue Versus Taxation*

The intent of introducing these two "ideal types" can now be made clear. I can, through this device, present the fiscal policy and the monetary policy alternatives quite starkly, and in such a way that the distinctions between the two are openly revealed. Fiscal policy reduces to changes upwards and downwards in tax rates. Monetary policy reduces to changes upwards and downwards in interest-bearing national debt held outside the public sector. In comparing these two instruments we may, therefore, examine the differences between increasing taxes and increasing debt on the one hand, and, on the other, between decreasing taxes and retiring national debt.[1]

Again, let us look at the simple politics of the matter. Governments are assumed to be responsive to the desires of the electorate and to seek either to minimize citizenry displeasure or to maximize citizenry satisfaction through their choices of policy instruments. Given that assumption, it takes no sophisticated analysis to indicate that public debt will be issued in lieu of increasing taxes and, for the same reason, on the down side taxes will be reduced in preference to debt retirement.

This rather simple explanation of the asymmetry seems "plausible" and "realistic." I propose, however, to bring this plausibility out into the clean and open air, for the underlying analysis requires explicit discussion. When this step is taken, it will be seen that the "theory" or "principle" of public debt that emerges is wholly at odds with that which dominates modern economic orthodoxy. Indirectly, therefore, the observed asymmetry in the choice of fiscal and monetary policy instruments over the cycle provides some positive evidence that the "classical" or "old-fashioned" notions about public debt remain correct after all, and despite the onslaught of the post-Keynesians. This allows me to bring up yet another defence of these classical principles of public debt, additional to those already presented in my recent book, *Public Principles of Public Debt* (1958).

v i i. *Classical Principles of National Debt*

If our simple model has any relevance, it suggests that there is less intensive public reaction against restrictive monetary policy (i.e., the

1. I am concerned with *primary* effects here. Both instruments will generate *secondary* effects, through the multiplying effects on deposits generated by changes in bank reserves. Nevertheless, if the same degree of expansion or contraction is assumed to be achieved by fiscal or by monetary means, these secondary effects can be roughly identical as between the two instruments.

issue of public debt) than there is against restrictive fiscal policy (tax increases). And, on the other side of the cycle, that there is more intensive "relief" provided through tax reduction (expansive fiscal policy) than there is through debt retirement (expansive monetary policy). This seems certainly to be true, but I want to ask why. Why does an increase in interest-bearing debt arouse less antagonism on the part of the public than a tax increase designed to accomplish roughly the same objectives?

The answer is, I submit, a very old and a very simple one and one that has been understood by sensible men for centuries. The issue of national debt allows the real costs of the restrictive measures to be postponed in time, to be shifted to individual taxpayers in future accounting periods. Actually, there should be little point in discussing this elementary principle of debt, public or private, were it not that the great weight of modern intellectual opinion comes down heavily on the side that denies its validity.

If this basic classical principle of public debt is accepted, the explanation we seek has been located. Those who must pay current taxes are members of the electorate at the moment when the policy action is taken. These taxpayers exist in the here and now, and their opposition to increases in tax rates can be heard. By contrast, who can arise to oppose an increase in tax rates in future periods, which an issue of public debt must embody? Current taxpayers will, of course, offer some reaction in anticipation of their expected future liabilities, but, when confronted with any choice between these and current tax increases their preferences are not hard to predict. By and large, and with few exceptions, modern governments will find debt issue less unpopular than taxation.

VIII. *The Modern Theory of Public Debt*

As I have noted above, however, this line of reasoning depends on an acceptance of the classical principle of public debt. If, instead of this, the dominant modern theory of national debt is substituted, we are left without such an explanation of the policy asymmetry which does, after all, seem so plausible. What is this modern theory of national debt which, in its current version, stems from an aftermath of the Keynesian revolution in economic thought? The heart of the argument consists in a denial of the central point of the classical theory. It is asserted that an internal public or national debt cannot involve a shifting of real costs forward in time. So long as the citizens within the economy purchase the securities sold by the government there can be no postponement of real costs, so the argument goes, because current purchasing power is given up when the debt is issued. Insofar as the national debt is internal, the method of financing cannot affect the location of real costs in time. As with taxation, all real costs are imposed immediately on the decision to borrow. The issue of public debt is, in this conception, not generically different from taxation.

Since no actual resources, in the net, are "used up" in an attempt to mop up excess liquidity during inflationary periods, either through tax increases or through the open-market sale of securities, the implication of the modern theory of debt would seem to be that no "real costs" are involved in either case. But even the most naive approach to the political process reveals the fallacy here. Surely governments that are responsible for implementing stabilization policy would be surprised to learn from the economist that tax increases, at any time and for any purpose, impose no real costs on taxpayers.

The point is that, for governmental decisions, thinking in terms of social aggregates and not in terms of individuals as specific taxpayers has been, and is, grossly misleading. Let us accept the weakness in the modern conception here, however, and go on to examine a second implication of this argument. Since public debt can shift no burden or cost to future periods, it is, as we have said, equivalent to taxation. Hence, there should, on the average, be no greater resistance to tax increases than to increases in the size of outstanding national debt, or so the argument implies.

At this point the theory examined here requires a closer look. With tax increases, there is no difficulty in appreciating the fact that, relatively speaking, the costs that must be involved are placed squarely on those persons who are subjected to the increased rates. Even if the sole purpose of the tax increase is that of mopping up excess liquidity, those paying the additional taxes "suffer" relative to those in the group who, presumably, gain from having an effective anti-inflationary policy introduced. But where are the equivalent costs when the alternative policy instrument—national debt issue—is employed for the same purpose?

Recall that, in this modern view that we are discussing here, these costs cannot be shifted forward to taxpayers in future periods. Suppose that the excess liquidity is mopped up by open-market sales of government securities. Who suffers the effects of this restriction in the primary sense, in the same way that the taxpayer suffers? Clearly, it is not the persons who purchase the securities, since they make a simple, voluntary, market transaction. Yet these are the only persons who, directly, give up current purchasing power—liquidity —in the whole process. They do so, however, because they are provided with a promised interest return in future periods; their sacrifice of current command over resources is a voluntary one. But, since theirs is the liquidity that is mopped up, no other members of the social group suffer any direct "stabilization burden" comparable to that imposed on the taxpayer. Under this theory, therefore, it is to be wondered that governments ever impose taxes at all, since public debt is wholly burdenless.

The theory is, of course, nonsense; it may be, quite legitimately, called the modern economists' version of the perpetual motion machine. The difficult thing to explain is the dominance that it has achieved over good minds. Any careful consideration of the elementary logic of decision-making leads inexorably to an acceptance of the classical principles of public finance, at least in their broad essentials. The difference between taxation and public debt is that the first imposes current period costs, the second postpones these costs to future periods.

I X.   *Some Necessary Qualifications*

As is usual in such discussions as these, certain qualifications in the argument must be introduced lest critics pounce. In the commentary above, I do not imply the complete absence of cost or burden when restrictive monetary policy is implemented. Interest rates, generally, will rise, and prices of old bonds will fall. Potential borrowers will be disappointed, and potential lenders gratified. These effects are essentially *secondary,* and they are similar to the secondary effects that would be produced by a similarly restrictive policy, implemented by the alternative method of raising taxes. In addition, such effects as these are *indirect,* and to a large extent the gainers balance off against the losers so that no net impact on the decision process could readily be predicted.

Also, as noted above, given the fractional reserve basis for deposits in commercial banks, either restrictive fiscal or restrictive monetary policy will work itself out through the operation of the deposit multiplier. A contraction in bank reserves will generate a multiple contraction in deposits, and, in the process, some borrowers will suffer a real burden. This particular effect should, however, be essentially the same whether it is due to a tax increase or to open-market sales, provided that the same degree of net liquidity is taken out of the system in each case.

These second-order effects could be discussed in some detail, but such discussion may have been, in itself, a source of confusion. Too much concentration on second-order and indirect effects tends to conceal from view the sharp distinction between the *primary* impact of the two policy alternatives. And it is these primary effects that I emphasize here.

x. *Tax Reduction Versus Debt Retirement*

Most of the discussion has been about restriction. The comparison is, if anything, simpler in the case of expansion, but since most of the points made apply in reverse order the analysis need not be elaborated in great detail.

In this case governments will choose, on the average, that policy instrument which generates the most favourable response, on the part of the public, which gives the most obvious "relief." In tax reduction, as with tax increase, the predicted incidence is straightforward. Individuals who find their current tax obligations reduced experience a real, and nonillusory, increase in real income. The incidence of debt retirement (monetization), on the other hand, is not nearly so clear. The government will, in this case, be purchasing bonds from the public with new currency, with cheques drawn on its own account in the central bank, cheques that will, of course, add directly to commercial bank reserves. Those individuals who sell bonds to the authorities receive an increment to current purchasing power, but they give up, in exchange, a claim against future interest income. Their wealth is not markedly changed in the process.

The genuine beneficiaries here are those who would otherwise have had to pay taxes to meet these interest payments in future periods. With less debt outstanding their future tax liabilities are reduced. A debt retirement or monetization process removes, once and for all, a real burden from their shoulders. Since, however, this "relief" is not so clearly understood, and, in any case, is deferred, the reaction will not be equivalent to that to be expected from current tax reductions.

As in the anti-inflation case, there will, of course, be all sorts of secondary effects. But, again, these should not be allowed to obscure the basic facts of the matter. These are that the primary incidence of antirecession *monetary* policy rests with those who pay taxes later, while the primary incidence of antirecession *fiscal* policy rests with those who pay taxes now (or receive the benefits of expanding public services if this variant is allowed).

x i. *Implications*

The observed asymmetry between the choice of monetary and fiscal instruments of policy over the cycle has been "explained" through the use of a simple model and the classical principles of public finance.

But we explain only to improve, so we must ask the important question: How can the behaviour of governments be modified?

Continuation of the asymmetry over long periods is clearly undesirable on many grounds. Interest rates will be pushed ever upward, and budget deficits will seldom, if ever, be matched by budget surpluses. This result should be condemned on ethical grounds, since it tends to place the costs of stabilization policy squarely on the shoulders of future taxpayers while concentrating the benefits in the here and now. Apart from the ethics of the matter, this pattern of policy runs directly counter to that which might be suggested if rapid economic growth should come to be accepted as an explicit aim of policy. Even if it serves no other purpose, the analysis here should suggest some of the political roadblocks that must be surmounted before a policy combination aimed explicitly at promoting growth could be introduced. As Professor Paul Samuelson and others have urged for the United States, such a policy would require that the asymmetry discussed here be replaced by that of "easy money and tight budgets."

Admitting the undesirability of the demonstrated practice does not suggest an alternative. One such might be the placing of fiscal policy back in its pre-Keynesian box, as circumscribed by the rule of the annually balanced budget, with the sole responsibility for stabilization falling on monetary policy. This alternative may seem superficially attractive to some who long for the revival of effective political controls of fiscal pressures. But myths once exploded are not easily reconstituted.

In any case, sole or primary reliance on monetary policy to achieve stabilization objectives involves an over-dependence on one market or set of markets to generate changes in a whole economic structure. This concentration inhibits the effectiveness of policy on the one hand, while subjecting those who operate in that market or set of markets to an "unfair" share of the stabilization task.

A second alternative, and one that was implied in the memoranda submitted by several economists to the Radcliffe Committee, would be the placing of sole or primary reliance on fiscal policy as the instrument of stabilization. This never-never land of "functional finance" ignores political facts altogether and assumes the presence of an all-wise, benevolent economic czar or commissar who moves tax rates and spending programmes up and down in complete indifference to the reactions of ordinary citizens. If we accept the fact that democratic process is worth preserving, the introduction of this model into practice will surely generate secular inflation, due to the bias previously discussed. And even the present asymmetry in policy seems preferable to continual inflation, despite its undesirable features.

The growth in importance of the automatic fiscal stabilizers offers some measure of improvement. In so far as these can become effective, the bias in fiscal policy is reduced. As has long been recognized, however, automatic stabilizers can, at best, help to correct cyclical swings, not to prevent them.

Improvement in governmental decision-making can only come, in the long run, as a result of the establishment of a new set of rules for behaviour, "rules" that will be rigid enough to influence the behaviour of politicians even in the face of constituency pressures. The analysis here suggests the importance of such possible rules. Symmetry should be preserved, over the cycle, in the employment of *each* of the policy instruments. That is to say, the budget should be balanced over the cycle, and open-market sales by the central bank should be balanced by open-market purchases, again over the cycle. If the trends in the economy justify a growth in the money supply, either or both of these rules may, of course, be slightly modified. Only by a rather rigid adherence to both these rules, however, can the natural political tendencies discussed in this paper be prevented from producing the distortions noted.

These rules are sophisticated ones, and democratic decision-making is not. But perfection should not be expected, and, above all, we should be tolerant of the politicians and critical of the economists. Only after the latter have succeeded in reformulating and securing acceptance among themselves of a new set of "principles for sound finance" can the politicians be called to task.

6

Fiscal Policy and Fiscal Preference

James M. Buchanan[1]

If the government budget is deliberately unbalanced for the ac-
complishment of macroeconomic objectives, how should the deficit
or surplus be created? Despite their recognition of the problem, the
standard public-finance textbooks do not examine the criteria for
this choice in specific detail. For the most part, primary emphasis is
placed on discussing the mechanics of the alternatives. Some leading
fiscal economists have recently urged that budget unbalancing should
be implemented through shifting tax rates. The early Keynesians
argued strongly for a concentration on shifting rates of government
spending.

The Keynesian and post-Keynesian argument for deficit creation
via the expenditure side of the budget was based on the allegedly
greater leverage effects of this policy. As compared with tax-rate
changes, comparable shifts in expenditure will exert a somewhat
larger multiplier effect on total spending in the economy. This result
stems basically from the simple arithmetic of the income multiplier.
Its importance for actual policy choice is reduced by the recognition
that the differential leverage can always be offset by quantitatively
larger tax-side adjustments. Early discussion stressed the disadvantages of expenditure adjustments due to time lags between policy
action, implementation, and project completion. More modern dis-

Reprinted by permission of the publisher from *Papers on Non-Market
Decision Making II* [now *Public Choice*], 1967.

1. This paper was developed as an outgrowth of the analysis contained in Chapter 8 of my book, *Public Finance in Democratic Process*
(Chapel Hill, 1967). In that chapter I tried to examine the effects of
modern fiscal policy on individual behavior in political process. In this
paper, the analysis is, in one sense, reversed. The emphasis is on the
possible effects that the recognition of individual fiscal preferences may
exert on fiscal policy norms.

cussion has included the differential institutional rigidities on the two sides in the American political structure.

Those who have argued for primary reliance on tax-rate changes suggest the desirability of making basic expenditure decisions independently of the macroeconomic state of the economy. Spending programs that are independently evaluated to be efficient should be initiated regardless of the position of critical macroeconomic variables, and programs that are not efficient should not be instituted merely because there exists some temporary deficiency in aggregate demand to be made up via fiscal-monetary policy. The weaknesses in this general argument have been noted by careful theorists, but, to my knowledge, the precise analysis has not been developed, either within an essentially organic or an individualistic-democratic reference system.[2] This analysis is limited to the second of these.

1. *The Assumptions*

I shall examine the question in a model of individual behavior in fiscal choice. This model has, to my knowledge, never been applied to the tax-expenditure fiscal policy alternatives, despite its apparent relevance and applicability. Some preliminary simplifying assumptions can be made at the outset.

It is assumed that overall macroeconomic policy dictates the maintenance of aggregate demand at some specific absolute level or growth in aggregate demand at some steady rate through time. Furthermore, this objective is to be accomplished exclusively through the introduction and withdrawal of funds through budget deficits and surpluses. Deficits, when and if these are created, are financed wholly by currency issue. Surpluses, when and if these are created, are disposed of by the destruction of currency. There are no non-fiscal means whereby the supply of money in the economy can be modified. Only one public good is provided, and this good is fi-

2. The most extensive discussion is provided by R. A. Musgrave. See, his *The Theory of Public Finance* (New York, 1959), pp. 517–20. Musgrave argues that primary reliance should be on tax adjustments, not on spending adjustments, in carrying out a positive fiscal policy. In qualifying this argument, however, Musgrave appears to recognize, even if imprecisely, the basic points that are developed in this paper. He is correct when he suggests, in opposition to other scholars, that if national income is effectively maintained as a result of the policy, the issue is not one of income elasticity for public goods. He fails to recognize that the issue does then become one of price elasticity.

nanced by a tax institution that imposes an invariant tax-price on each taxpayer. Note that this assumption is not so restrictive as it might initially appear to be; many modern institutions, for example, a proportional income tax or a progressive tax with constant share progression over varying budgets, will qualify. The purpose of this assumption is to allow us to examine individual "purchases" of public goods in a model that is, in some respects, analogous to the ordinary market purchases of private and divisible goods.

I shall assume that the policy in question is fully successful in achieving the objectives desired. Aggregate demand in the economy is maintained at the target level or grows at the target rate as a result of the policy combination that is adopted, regardless of the choice of instruments.

Attention will be concentrated on the fiscal choice behavior of a single reference individual. Despite this concentration, it is necessary that the analysis retain some relevance for group outcomes. To cross this bridge, it is possible to assume that the individual whose decisions we examine is the "median preference" person in the whole community or political group. This becomes helpful when we add the further assumption that collective-community decisions are made as a result of simple majority voting. The quantity of public good to be collectively supplied is determined by the application of simple majority voting rules. In this case, when the preferences of individuals are single-peaked, as they tend to be with an economic choice of the sort treated here, the reference individual's preferences become controlling for the whole community.[3]

11.   *The Analysis*

Initially, the budget is balanced and national income is being maintained or growing at its desired rate. The situation confronting the individual is shown in Figure 1. The curve D represents his demand or marginal evaluation curve for the public good. (In deriving this curve, income effects are neglected.) The tax-price which the individual confronts is shown by OP. This is the "cost per unit" at which the public good is available to him. He will tend to "vote for" the quantity, OX, at this tax-price, OP, provided only that he is allowed to vote incrementally and that he is not forced to make all-or-none choices. Through our assumption of the controlling influence of the

3. For the development of the notion of single-peaked preferences, see Duncan Black, *The Theory of Committees and Elections* (Cambridge, 1958).

median-preference person in majority-voting models, the individual is in equilibrium with respect to his preferred "purchases" of the public good. He does not desire either a larger budget, with more units of the public good, or a smaller budget, with fewer units. Total tax collections from this individual are shown by the rectangle, OXEP, and total public outlay, again measured in units partitioned among all individuals, is also represented by the rectangle, OXEP.

This pattern of reaction will be generated so long as the individual finds his estimated *marginal tax-price* below his *marginal evaluation* of the public good. Note particularly in this connection that the marginal tax-price need have little, in any, connection with the individual's *marginal tax rate*. The latter relates incremental tax payments to some tax base, presumably income, whereas the former relates incremental tax payments to the quantity of public goods supplied, that is, to the size of the budgetary outlay. Even if a tax reduction should fail to reduce the marginal tax rate on income, the individual might still treat this reduction as a reduction in the marginal tax-price, the rate at which he is enabled to "purchase" units of the public good through collective processes.

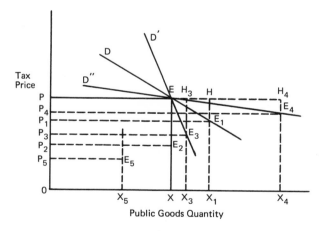

Figure 1. Public Goods Quantity

Conceptually, it is possible that the individual might treat any tax-rate reduction as an inframarginal rather than as a marginal shift downward in tax-price. The model does not seem realistic, however, when the complexities of converting tax obligations into tax-prices are recognized. At best, the individual can make some sort of crude estimate for the terms-of-trade with the fisc at the initial and at the post-reduction positions. His reaction behavior will probably be based on some gross estimates subject to wide ranges of error. It seems highly unlikely that he would try to take into account possible variations in tax-price over various quantities of public good, even should the tax-rate changes impose this result in reality. And, as noted, general tax-rate reductions will not normally generate this as a specific result, especially for the median or representative person in the community.

We now postulate a change in habits with respect to the holding of the monetary unit. As a result of a wave of net hoarding, or a threatened and predicted wave, aggregate demand in the economy will fall in the absence of offsetting fiscal policy action. This prediction, which we assume is certain, sets in motion the fiscal policy program previously outlined. A deficit will be created, and in sufficient volume to restore national income to its target level regardless of the instrument to be employed. But how is this deficit to be created? Which way of creation is the more desirable in this model of individual fiscal choice? It is relatively easy to show that if the fiscal preferences of the individual are to remain satisfied, the method of introducing this deficit depends critically on the tax-price elasticity of demand for the public good.

Regardless of the way in which it is introduced, the creation of a budget deficit must reduce the tax-price at which the public good is made available to the individual. If the government simply expands outlay and collects the same tax yields, the tax-price at which the individual "purchases" units of public good is lowered. If, on the other hand, the government reduces its tax yield, while leaving public outlay unchanged, the same quantity of public good is supplied at a smaller total tax outlay; the tax-price is lowered as before. The question is which of these two methods, or which combination of the two "should" be adopted, if the fiscal preferences of the individual are to be taken into account?

Let us first suppose that the expenditure-expansion method is adopted. Tax revenues are unchanged; the government continues to collect taxes at the same rates as before the predicted decline in aggregate demand. Public outlay on the collective good is expanded by an amount sufficient to maintain demand at its target level. From the construction of Figure 1, it can be seen that this method will be fully consistent with the continued satisfaction of individual fiscal preference only if the demand for the public good is characterized by unitary elasticity over the relevant range. The construction is so drawn that the rectangle $OX_1E_1P_1$ is equal in area to the rectangle $OXEP$. Hence, the revenue collected from the individual is the same in the two situations. Tax-price falls to P_1, and the quantity of the public good increases to X_1. The deficit is P_1E_1HP, which we have assumed is precisely sufficient to secure target levels of aggregate demand.

Let us now examine the opposite extreme in policy action. Spending is maintained at constant rates, while tax collections are reduced sufficiently to offset the threatened decline in aggregate demand. In terms of Figure 1, the same quantity, OX, of the public good is supplied, but the tax-price faced by the individual is lowered to P_2, the budget deficit now being P_2E_2EP. It is evident that this policy will violate individual fiscal preferences unless the tax-price elasticity of demand for the public good is zero. The individual is prevented, by this policy, from "purchasing" more units of the good despite the fact that the tax-price has been reduced.

A third alternative involves the creation of the deficit through *both* decreasing tax collections and increasing public outlay. For this method to be consistent with individual fiscal preferences, the tax-price elasticity of demand must be *less than unitary*. This is illustrated by the demand curve D', drawn so as to pass through the initial equilibrium point E. The rectangle $OX_3E_3P_3$, is smaller than the rectangle $OXEP$. Tax payments made to the government by the reference individual have fallen. The deficit is now $P_3E_3H_3P$; the quantity of public good is now OX_3.

A fourth case is that which involves increasing public outlay and also increasing tax collections, but by less than outlay increases. To be fully consistent with individual preferences here, the tax-price elasticity of demand must be *greater than unity* over the relevant range. This is shown by the demand curve D', also drawn to pass through E. The rectangle $OX_4E_4P_4$ is larger than $OXEP$; tax payments made by the individual exceed those made in the initial equilibrium. The deficit here is $P_4E_4H_4P$; public outlay has expanded by the amount XX_4H_4E, and the quantity of the public good has increased to OX_4.

For analytical completeness, the fifth possible combination should be mentioned, that in which the deficit is created by reducing public outlay and by reducing tax collections by a relatively larger amount. It seems clear that this set of policy actions could not be made consistent with any reasonable assumption about individual demands for public goods. In Figure 1, this combination can be depicted by a shifting to a public-goods quantity, say OX_5, a total outlay of OX_5H_5P, and a tax collection of $OX_5E_5P_5$. Here the individual "purchases" fewer units of the public good despite the lowered tax-price.

The conclusions of this analysis stem solely from the relative price effects that the deficit creation produces under the different policy mixes. Since it is postulated that, in carrying out the overall fiscal policy measure, aggregate demand attains desired target levels, the representative individual's income in the postpolicy equilibrium will be identical to that in the initial equilibrium. No income effects arise to confound the analysis. The conditions of individual fiscal choice are modified. Fiscal policy, which can only be operated by the insertion of a wedge between the costs of the public good to government and the payments made for this good by individual taxpayers, necessarily reduces the tax-price that the individual tax-payer-beneficiary confronts. From this point it follows that, if individual preferences are to be met, the method of creating the deficit depends on the elasticity of demand for the public good over the relevant range. It may be objected here that the individual demand for public goods may not remain unchanged before and after the presumed wave of net hoarding which sets off the fiscal action in the first instance. This objection would be critical only if some direction of shift in the demand for public goods could be shown to accompany the shifts in demand for private goods that make the policy action necessary. If no such relationship can be traced, meaningful analysis can proceed on the assumption that there need be no necessary accompanying shift in individual behavior in demanding public goods.

III. *The Implications*

The analysis does not suggest that fiscal policy action either "should" or, in the real world "would," tend to satisfy the fiscal preferences of citizens. It is interesting, however, to examine some of the implications of failure to meet such preferences, implications that lend themselves to conceptual if not to empirical refutation. Suppose that a deficit is created by reducing tax collections while keeping spending rates unchanged, roughly comparable to the 1964 pattern in the United States. What should have been observed as a result? At the new tax-price for the public good, at E_2 on Figure 1, the individual finds himself off his demand curve. He will, at this tax-price, seek to "purchase" additional units. He cannot, of course, do this independently. He will tend to behave in the political process in such a way that pressures toward expanded public spending will be generated. When given the opportunity, the individual will now "vote for" expansions in the budgetary outlay. Under conditions such as these, there will surely be a tendency for democratic process to

overexpand the required fiscal policy action, to exceed the macroeconomic objectives laid down in the program. This situation embodies the paradox that tax-yield reduction, unless the conditions
of demand are quite abnormal, becomes the very device for generating the loudest clamour for expanded public spending. Again
the post-1964 experience surely bears out the simple predictions.
Federal budgetary outlay increased rapidly, and there seems to be
general agreement that, by late 1965, the total effect was overly
expansive.

The situation would be reversed, of course, if the policy action
should be based in the assumption that say D″ were the appropriate
demand curve, whereas either D or D′ should be more descriptive.
Here, after the policy action, the individual might find himself at
E_4, again off his demand curve. In this case, he would bring pressure for a cutback in budgetary outlay. Aggregate spending would
tend to be reduced, and the macroeconomic objective may be under-
mined by democratic process.

The analysis suggests that, in any instance where individual
fiscal preferences are not satisfied, within reasonable limits, some
pressures toward budgetary changes will be likely to arise. These
will be generated, not as a result of the fiscal policy action per se,
but as a result of the modified fiscal choice position that the change
in budgetary policy produces. At the least, the analysis suggests
that some attention be given to the conditions of individual demand
for public goods when the choice is made among alternative means
of creating deficits and surpluses.

The analysis seems fully reversible when applied to the creation of budgetary surpluses. This exercise will not be carried out
in this paper. It is, of course, widely recognized that surpluses are
unlikely to arise from deliberate policy action in a democratic political setting.

IV. *Alternative Means of Injecting Money*

It should be emphasized that the results obtained in this paper depend critically on the assumption that new money can only be injected into the economy through budget deficits and withdrawn
through budget surpluses. This restriction insures that the tax-price
of public goods will change, and the desired quantity of public goods
will be changed in consequence, under ordinary conditions of demand. It is possible to develop alternative models that allow new
money to be injected by nonfiscal policy means. One such method
might be the simple random distribution of new bills among the

citizenry, wholly unrelated to their purchases of either private goods or public goods. In this instance, ignoring distributional elements, the new equilibrium should not be different from the old in terms of the desired mix between private goods and public goods. It may be argued that only in some such way as this could genuine "neutrality" in macroeconomic policy be guaranteed. Yet another model allows money to be injected via the private-goods budget. Money could be issued to individuals directly in proportion to their purchases of private goods. In this case, the prices of private goods will fall, while the tax-price for public goods will remain unchanged. This is the converse of the fiscal model examined in this paper, and similar conclusions could be developed. The point to be noted, however, is that this would not be a simple tax-reduction model, as seems to be implied in some of the literature. Tax reduction, in and of itself, reduces the relative prices of public goods, not private goods, and the policy model outlined in this paper becomes relevant. To inject money so that individuals sense a relative reduction in private-goods prices, a wedge must, somehow, be inserted between the prices paid by buyers and the prices received by sellers.[4]

It is not the purpose of the analysis here to suggest which method of injecting new money is best. The purpose is that of showing only that, if orthodox fiscal policy tools are employed, certain specific implications for the manner of creating deficits and surpluses emerge if "political acceptance" of policy action by the citizenry is acknowledged to be a desirable objective.

4. To an extent, this is accomplished by a reduction in certain *indirect* taxes. Implementing fiscal policy by cutting the rates on indirect taxes will reduce the tax-price of public goods, but, insofar as the tax liability is related to the purchase of private goods, the action may also reduce the gross price to which the individual adjusts his private-goods quantities. This suggests that it may well be more "neutral," with respect to the private goods-public goods mix, to inject money through a reduction in indirect than in direct taxation.

7

A Variable-Tax Model of Intersectoral Allocation

Charles J. Goetz

The recent history of public finance has been highlighted by attempts to elaborate an acceptable theory of the intersectoral allocation of resources between the "public" and "private" sectors. Among the numerous efforts in this regard, the works of Samuelson and Musgrave are perhaps the most widely known.[1]

The object of this note is to make explicit some of the peculiar restrictions which underlie the application of preference maps to the theory of private-collective allocation. In order to present these unique intersectoral problems in the most general fashion, they will be explored at the basic level of the individual choice situation. Although the existing theories tend to be stated in aggregate terms, the welfare concepts employed therein almost invariably take individual preferences, or at least individual market reactions, into account.

I. *Methodological Background*

A. *Multi-Good Preference Maps*

The three-dimensional preference maps familiarly used by economists are based on the individual's ability to construct ordinal rankings of various goods. In a simple two-good-model no problems

Reprinted by permission of the Foundation Public Finance/Finances Publiques, The Hague, Netherlands, from *Public Finance* No. 1, 1964.

1. Cf. Paul A. Samuelson, "The Pure Theory of Public Expenditure," *Review of Economics and Statistics,* Vol. 35 (November 1954), pp. 387–89; "Diagrammatic Exposition of a Theory of Public Expenditure," *Review of Economics and Statistics,* Vol. 37 (November 1955), pp. 350–56. Also, Richard A. Musgrave, *The Theory of Public Finance* (New York, 1959), Chaps. 4, 5, and 6.

arise with regard to units of measurement, since any arbitrary physical units of the goods involved can be measured on the axes of the preference map. Analysts, however, have frequently sought to apply the preference map of classes or representative "baskets" of goods falling within some generic category. Theory textbooks, for example, employ indifference curves showing rates of substitution between "money" and "goods" or "present goods" and "future goods." There is no objection to such constructions if the implicit assumption of determinate physical composition of the units is observed. Where the composition of the conglomerate units is indeterminate, the individual is faced with the manifestly impossible task of ranking unspecified selections from the general class or classes of goods involved.

The required specification of conglomerate units can be established by defining their composition as some constant, i.e., one unit of "fruit" invariably consists of one apple and two peaches. Although such a "standardized" conglomerate unit would be technically sufficient to determine preferences, the result will not be economically meaningful unless the composition of this standardized unit corresponds to that which the consumer would actually choose when free to adjust in the market. In other words, preference maps are of little interest unless they express the rates of substitution between those baskets of goods which reflect the actual market alternatives faced by the individual.

More useful for economic analysis, therefore, is a unit definition based on the optimal basket as determined by the consumer's tastes and a given set of relative prices for the possible components, since this is the basket to which the maximizing consumer will always adjust. Although there is no presumption that the composition of this basket must remain constant as the individual's opportunity set varies, the components of the basket are determinate for any level of purchasing power and hence can form the basis for construction of a preference map.

Little reflection is required to assure oneself that this latter concept of the optimal conglomerate market basket is implicitly assumed in economic models involving general classes of goods. When made completely explicit, the consequences of this assumption render the allocation of resources between the private and collective sectors a considerably more complex process than has previously been depicted.

B. Traditional Approach to Intersectoral Models

The traditional models of intersectoral allocation are constructed in terms of transformation curves between private and collective goods.[2] This familiar approach will therefore be employed as an underlying step in the construction of the more general models to be presented here.

On one axis of our two-sector preference map we wish to depict units of expenditure in the private or market sector. As indicated above, we can deal with a multigood sector if the composition of the basket of goods is determinate, i.e., we specify the relative prices of all goods in the private sector.

On the other axis of the map we wish to represent units of expenditure in the collective sector. If a multigood public sector is to be considered, the "basket" composing the conglomerate unit cannot be defined in the same manner as for the private sector. Since there exists no direct means of individual quantity adjustment, we cannot assume that the individual's "optimal" basket of public goods is the one which will actually be involved in trading. The conglomerate unit can still be defined determinately by (*a*) assuming that the levels of all public goods but one are held in *ceteris paribus;* or (*b*) assuming that the pattern of variation in public expenditure is somehow predictable. Since the existence of a multi-good public sector does not affect the main point of this paper, the models employed below will assume a single public good in order to simplify the exposition. Also the individual's utility function for this single collective good is assumed to be independent of the level or pattern of his private expenditure. Relaxing this independence assumption would actually strengthen the point considered below but would necessitate greater complexity in the diagrammatic presentation.

Using A and B as the two component goods in the relevant "class" of private goods, we can determine the contents of potentially observable baskets of private goods by tracing out the possible tangencies of the individual's indifference curves with the family of price lines which express the ruling intraclass relative prices between A and B.[3] The coordinates of line OE in Figure I*a* indicate

2. The term "collective goods" is deliberately used throughout in an effort to make a clear distinction from Samuelson's polar case of "public goods" which are characterized by absolutely equal availability to all. The "collective goods" referred to herein are distinguished from "private goods" only by their manner of provision.

3. The composition of conglomerate units need not be limited to two goods. Hence, goods A and B might themselves represent conglomerate units of subclasses whose optimal baskets were previously determined. Geometrical limitations require only that the ultimate comparison be between two units whose composition, though determinate, may vary without limit. Rigorously, A and B should subsume not only all goods but also all possible inputs as "negative goods."

the composition of the conglomerate basket of private goods for alternative levels of expenditure, given that the ruling relative prices remain as depicted by market transformation curve ab. Changes in the relative prices of A and B must be reflected in the slope of ab and would, of course, result in an alteration of the expansion path OE.

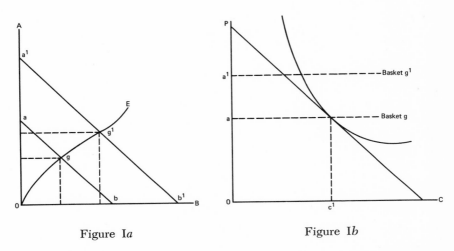

Figure I*a*   Figure I*b*

Measuring expenditure in terms of good A as a numeraire, the actual mix of private goods making up various levels of expenditure in the private sector can be identified in the intersectoral model depicted in Figure I*b;* the expenditure of Oa or Oa[1] in the private sector, for instance, will always be associated with the purchase of baskets g and g[1]. Our allocating consumer now can express the rate at which he would willingly forego private market opportunities in exchange for collective goods.

If we now confront an individual with the appropriate intersectoral transformation curve, i.e., the actual cost to him of exchange in the "collective market" between private goods P and the public good C, he will express a preference for that public-private goods mix which will equalize the relevant rates of transformation between expenditure in each sector. In terms of Figure I*b*, the individual would prefer to pay aP in taxes for Oc[1] units of collective goods while Oa is spent on basket of goods g in the private sector. This is a familiar conclusion, the only novelty of which lies in making explicit the fact that the preference map is valid only for the specified set of relative prices in the private sector. This restriction is of little importance in models where the cost of collective goods is financed in a manner such as to have either no effect or a predictable effect on the prices of goods purchased in the private sector. As demonstrated below, however, the effect of variable and unpredictable payment systems requires the abandonment of the traditional approach for models embodying the more complex matrix of choices actually available.

C. *Alternative-tax Models*

A peculiarity of the collective sector is that liability for the cost of collective goods need not be directly tied to the actual acquisition or consumption of public goods. Indeed, the price an individual pays for government services is commonly a function of his expenditure on or return from some private sector good. Moreover, there is an infinite number of combinations of tax bases and rates which will withdraw a specified amount of resources from the private sector. Hence, although the absolute opportunity cost of public goods is determined in the aggregate by the production function, the manner of withdrawing the required resources is a modifiable variable which is itself subject to collective choice.

Of all possible tax systems, only a completely "general" tax, such as the lump-sum poll tax, or a tax on pure economic rent, can eliminate the effect of a person's private market activity on the size of his tax liability.[4] Such taxes are of negligible practical importance. The rational individual will, therefore, ordinarily be faced with the necessity of modifying his purchases in order to minimize his tax burden. The varying effects of alternative tax systems on allocation within the private sector have been discussed at length in connection with the "excess burden" question, but the corollary consequences for private-collective *intersectoral* allocation have never been made clear.[5]

The changed set of private goods relative prices implied by any tax with an allocative effect necessarily alters the composition of the "optimal" basket of conglomerate private goods which would be bought at different expenditure levels. For example, in Figure I*a*,

4. Samuelson's classic articles, cited above, assume such lump sum taxes. Cf. "The Pure Theory," p. 388, and the implicit assumptions of the diagrams in the "Diagrammatic Exposition." This otherwise perfectly acceptable theoretical procedure would circumvent the practical problem we wish to raise here even if his other assumption of a single private good were relaxed.

5. An excellent summary and bibliography of excess burden literature is contained in David Walker, "The Direct-Indirect Tax Problem: Fifteen Years of Controversy," *Public Finance*, 10 (No. 2, 1955), 153–76.

the locus of expansion path E must adjust to the slope of a new market transformation curve between A and B, thus changing the identity of the baskets of goods represented by points on the private goods axis of Figure I*b*. Since the elements involved in the original ranking have been modified, the old preference map for private and collective goods is now clearly invalid. The individual's intersectoral preference map must be reformulated to reflect the artificially changed conditions of trade in private markets.

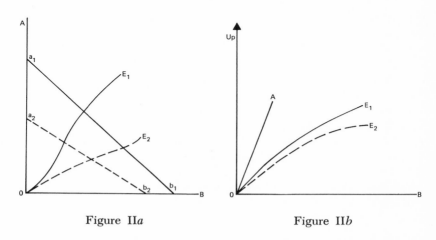

Figure II*a*   Figure II*b*

This effect of a tax-induced change of relative prices in the private sector is exemplified by the expansion paths E_1 and E_2 of Figure II*a*. Figure II*b* shows the individual's private sector preference surface as it would appear when turned on its side and shown in cross section along expansion paths E_1 and E_2. Two things are apparent: (1) the *absolute levels* of ordinal preference may differ at comparable points along the two paths; and (2) the *rates of change* to higher-ranked positions may likewise vary at comparable points on the two crosssections. The change in absolute levels of satisfaction is what has been discussed in the literature dealing with the so-called "excess burden" of tax systems. It is the change in slopes of the expansion paths, however, which necessitates the reformulation of the intersectoral preference map; in utility terms, such an alternation can be expected to increase or decrease the marginal utility of expenditure in the private sector relative to the marginal utility of expenditure in the collective sector. Interestingly enough, this fact raises the possibility of what superficially appears to contradict the economist's notion of the Law of Demand; although an economically "inefficient" tax system raises the total opportunity cost of government to an individual, it may actually increase the preferred purchase of collective goods if it simultaneously reduces the marginal satisfaction of private expenditure.

i i. *Taxes as Choice Variables*

A. *Tax Preference*

The role of variable tax systems in intersectoral allocation has been made explicit above, but the actual process of selection among tax institutions remains to be integrated into the individual's choice calculus. In order to do so, we must first dispense with the traditional assumption that the individual is choosing among equal-yield taxes with the objective of minimizing "excess burden." Realistically, the individual is interested in securing that tax system which will minimize the *total* utility loss from taxation, so that he will be concerned with the absolute size of his tax burden as well as the "efficiency" of the collection process. The individual, therefore, may gladly tolerate some degree of excess burden if he can thus secure the adoption of a tax system which reduces his individual share of the cost of collective goods. The dissimilarity of expenditure patterns favored by individuals of varying tastes and incomes provides ample scope for a citizen to strategically seek the raising of revenues through taxation of items which will account for a relatively low portion of his budget.

Relative preferences for alternative tax systems can easily be represented graphically by constructing a "tax map" embodying a matrix of taxes open to selection.[6] Holding constant the level of collective goods, and hence collective sector utility, an individual will be indifferent to any set of taxes which keeps him on the same private sector utility level. In Figure IIIa, for example, it will be immaterial to the taxpayer whether the tax system corresponds to t_1, t_2, t_3, or any of the innumerable other tax combinations which can be constructed tangent to the indicated indifference curve. This and every other set of constant-utility taxes can be represented in Figure IIIb by a series of indifference curves for private sector utility, utility *decreasing* for movements to the northeast. Not all tax systems are consistent with the postulated level of collective goods, however. We must therefore indicate by RR^1 the set of con-

6. The examples used below use percentage *ad valorem* rates as elements of the matrix, but the same figure can be adapted to other forms of variation.

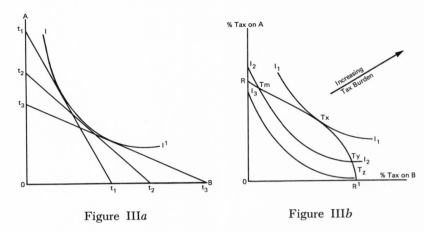

Figure IIIa   Figure IIIb

stant-revenue tax institutions which, when imposed on the entire economy, will yield a return equal to the cost of the required level of collective goods. Allocative effects of the alternative tax systems on the cost of public goods can be reflected in the RR^1 curve.[7]

We are now in a position to draw the conclusion that the taxpayer will prefer that the level of collective goods denoted by RR^1 be financed by tax combination Tz, on his lowest achievable indifference curve, rather than taxes Tm, Tx, Ty, or any of the other feasible choices which leave him with a lower level of private-sector utility. It happens that Tz yields a corner solution with no tax on A, implying that this particular sample individual has a relatively higher preference for A and lower for B than the economy as a whole. There is no guarantee, of course, that a majority decision can be mustered in support of tax Tz, in which case the individual will vote for the remaining alternatives in order of the level of their I curves, culminating with the least favorable choice, Tx.

Figure IIIb remains an incomplete picture of the individual's opportunity set, however, since it does not rule out the possibility that some movement from Tz to a more burdensome tax system beyond RR^1 may be more than compensated by the increase in utility from a higher level of collective goods provision. Accordingly,

7. Since at least some degree of specialization of resources exists, a change in the composition of private expenditure may entail a move along the production surface to an area of different real cost for the collective goods. For example, a tax which markedly stimulates the private purchase of automobiles could be expected to increase the resource cost of military trucks.

our last and most general model must remove the level of collective goods from *ceteris paribus* and show the simultaneous determination of tax system, tax burden, and collective goods provision.

B. A General Model of Intersectoral Allocation

Any point on the tax map will lie on some RR^1 constant-revenue curve representing a determinate amount of public goods. Since this is the case, the same principles underlying Figure III*b* can be used to construct a joint preference map which orders alternative states of the fiscal system according to the net gain (or loss) from the corresponding levels of collective goods provision and gross tax burden. The logic of such a construction is depicted in Figure IV*a* which, for illustrative purposes only, shows cardinal changes in utility measured from an initial state of no taxes and no collective goods. The utility effect of collective goods provision, U_c, can thus be measured against the utility effect on private expenditures, U_p. Such a comparison is depicted in Figure IV*a* for a cross section corresponding to some determinate set of taxes used to finance various levels of collective goods provision.[8] Converted into a net utility surface, or a simple ordinal preference surface, Figure IV*a* yields the individual's overall level of satisfaction as a function of the tax system. Such a preference map is exemplified by Figure IV*b*.

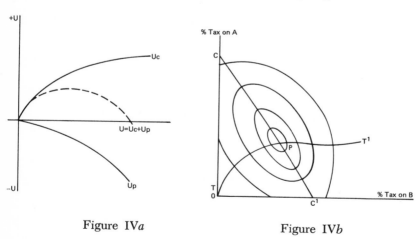

Figure IV*a*   Figure IV*b*

8. Figure IV*a* is similar to a diagram explained in a different connection by R. A. Musgrave, *op. cit.*, pp. 113–14. The individual analogy of his figure, however, would be only that "optimal" cross section determined by the locus of tangencies between R-curves and I-curves in Figure III*b*. This path may be irrelevant because unachievable.

This diagram, by depicting an integrated view of the individual choice situation, demonstrates that a general theory of intersectoral allocation requires simultaneous determination of the tax burden, its manner of imposition, and the level of collective goods. Concerned as they are with situations where at least one of these variables is determinate, the commonly encountered allocation models tend to give an incomplete, and perhaps misleading, picture of the basis of political preference.

The individual may, of course, be barred by the aggregate political decision from achieving his preferred utility peak at point P. We can, however, use Figure IVb to give us some idea of what pressures will influence aggregate political decisions.

Partition TT^1 can be drawn to indicate areas of disequilibrium in the bias of the tax system. Hence, TT^1 itself is the locus of the optimal (to the individual) tax system as determined by the tangencies of constant-revenue R-curves with the individual's lowest equal-burden I-curves as depicted in Figure IIIb. Points to the left of the partition TT^1 therefore indicate a desire for increased reliance on taxation of B, and vice versa. Similarly, partition CC^1 can be drawn to mark off the set OCC^1 of tax systems where the individual desires a movement to a higher R-curve with its correspondingly greater provision of collective goods. These partitions yield four quadrants where the "political pressure" exerted by the individual will be to move up his preference surface in the indicated directions:

Quadrant	Collective Goods	Preferred Decrease	Tax Emphasis Increase
I	Increase	A	B
II	Decrease	A	B
III	Decrease	B	A
IV	Increase	B	A

Only at point P is the person depicted in equilibrium both as to the level of his tax burden and its manner of distribution. At any other point, therefore, there exists some alteration of the fiscal system which could command his assent in the voting process. Only through a perusal of a multitude of such tax maps representing the preferences of other members of the electorate can the existence of coalitions determining the feasibility of a proposed move be ascertained.

C. Errors of Estimation

The models developed above can represent individual preferences only from an *ex ante* standpoint. The construction of E-curve expansion paths and, hence, the identification of the optimal private goods "baskets" presumes that the individual can predict after-tax income and commodity prices with accuracy. Errors in the prediction of after-tax market conditions may falsify—in either direction—the total and marginal burden of taxation in utility terms. The most obvious example of this is presented by an excise tax which improves the allocation of resources by cancelling out all or part of a preexisting market imperfection such as monopoly in a product or factor market.[9] Such instances of what may be called "negative excess burden" are a consequence of general equilibrium conditions for the economy as an aggregate and cannot reasonably be foreseen on the individual level. Indeed, it is questionable whether the trained economist can reliably recognize the induced price effects of a fiscal system even in retrospect. A problem therefore arises as to whether errors in this regard are recognizable or correctable.

The identification of alternative constant-revenue tax systems as expressed in the R-curves is also subject to error. The fiscal authorities may either over- or under-estimate: (1) the resource cost of a given level of collective goods provision or (2) the resource yield of supposedly alternative tax systems.

Regardless of the fact that an individual's preferences may not prove "correct" *ex post*, the theory presented above does provide a reasonably realistic description of the variables which affect collective allocation as it emerges in a political system with variable fiscal institutions.

III. *Conclusion*

The conclusions of this paper may be summarized as follows:

1. Intersectoral preference maps must be used with caution. Any tax with an allocative effect—a category to which all common taxes belong—can be expected to change the relative desirabilities of additional private and collective goods at the margin. Preference maps between public and private goods are, therefore, valid only when they specify the tax system used for financing.

2. The individual's intersectoral utility peak at P will probably not be politically achievable. In moving toward that point, however, both the level of collective goods disequilibrium and the bias of the tax system provide "tradeable" variables. In adjusting the bias of the

9. Cf. I. M. D. Little, "Direct *vs.* Indirect Taxes," *Economic Journal*, 41 (September 1951), 577–84; and Milton Friedman, *Essays in Positive Economics* (Chicago, 1953), pp. 110–13. Others have made essentially the same point.

tax system, the individual will accept "excess burden" in return for a strategically favorable variation in public sector size or in the allocation of collective costs.

3. The "correctness" of an individual's decisions will obviously be affected by his ability to predict after-tax market opportunities. Little prospect exists of avoiding or correcting errors in this regard. The performance of the fisc in identifying alternative fiscal systems should, however, be subject to at least a rough form of testing.

For welfare economists interested in formulating an interpersonal "social welfare function," the above may supplement the existing notions of individual adjustment to collective activity. For specialists in public finance or political economy who are concerned with the more modest goal of studying what tends to emerge within a particular political framework, the above provides at least a crude formal statement of the individual decision-making process which underlies tax preferences in the context of collective choice.

8

Excess Burden and the Voluntary
Theory of Public Finance

David B. Johnson and Mark V. Pauly[1]

The voluntary theory of public finance, originally suggested by
Wicksell and Lindahl, and recently clarified and extended by Samuelson, Buchanan, and others, postulates the voter-taxpayer as the
basic decision-making unit.[2] The voter is considered to be demanding, with his vote, marginal quantities of public goods whose price
to him is represented by the marginal tax he pays. This view of a
tax as the price paid for public goods was perhaps fostered by
Samuelson's seminal analysis, which uses what amounts to a two-
good (one public, one private) model. In such a model, taxes *are*
similar to prices. Amounts of the private good given up in order to
pay for each unit of the public good represent the "price" of that
good to the voter-taxpayer. These taxes are, in effect, lump-sum or
"head" levies that the individual levies upon himself or has levied on

Reprinted by permission of the authors and publisher from *Economica*, August 1969.

1. Helpful comments were provided by James Buchanan, Charles
Goetz, and Colin Wright.

2. Knut Wicksell, "A New Principle of Just Taxation" and Erik
Lindahl, "Just Taxation—A Positive Solution," Reprinted in Richard A.
Musgrave and Alan T. Peacock, eds., *Classics in the Theory of Public
Finance* (New York, 1958); Paul A. Samuelson, "The Pure Theory of
Public Goods," *Review of Economics and Statistics*, November 1954, and
"Diagrammatic Exposition of a Theory of Public Expenditure," *Review of
Economics and Statistics*, November 1955 Also, see for example, J. M.
Buchanan, *Demand and Supply of Public Goods* (Chicago, 1968), *Public
Finance in Democratic Process* (Chapel Hill, 1967); *The Calculus of
Consent* (with G. Tullock) (Ann Arbor, 1962); and W. J. Baumol, *Wel-
fare Economics and the Theory of the State*, 2d. ed. (Cambridge, Mass.,
1965).

him because of his desire for another unit of the public good.[3] In a similar sense, the price of a unit of a private good is like a lump-sum tax that the individual incurs because of his desire for a unit of that good.

A price paid for a private good, or a lump-sum tax used to finance a public good is "efficient" in the sense that neither causes an alteration in the individual's behavior other than the surrender of the required amount of income. In the real world, however, taxes are not usually of a lump-sum, "price-like" nature. Instead, government expenditures are financed by non-lump-sum devices embodying varying degrees of inefficiency. These tax devices are "institutionalized" because of the practical problems involved in altering the tax structure for each change in government expenditure and because government units at higher levels place constitutional constraints on the use of particular tax devices by governments at lower levels.

The traditional "excess burden" analysis is the usual method of discussing inefficient tax devices.[4] Such analysis has not, however, been integrated with the voluntary theory of public finance, in which the individual is assumed not only to react to taxes but also to determine public expenditure through the use of his vote. This paper will discuss the voter's decision calculus when public expenditures are constitutionally or institutionally constrained to be financed by inefficient tax devices. We will attempt to show how and why considerations of excess burden and inefficiency enter the voter's choice calculus, and how these considerations affect both the quantity of public goods he will choose and the number of tax devices he will use to finance those goods.

3. There does not exist a term in common usage which describes the type of tax envisioned by the Samuelson-Wicksell analysis. It is a tax which is related to the individual's marginal evaluation of each unit of the public good, i.e., for each unit of the public good, the individual pays a "lump-sum" or "head" tax, the amount of which cannot be altered by the individual's behavior. This tax may, however, vary among individuals or over quantities of the public good. The crucial point, as noted above, is that this tax is efficient. Throughout this paper we will call such an "ideal" tax a lump-sum tax. It should be recognized that this tax is not simply a fixed levy applied equally to all individuals. Rather it is a levy which varies directly with the individual's marginal evaluation of the public good.

4. See Arnold Harberger, "The Measurement of Waste," *American Economic Review, Papers and Proceedings,* May, 1964, pp. 58–76; "Taxation, Resource Allocation, and Welfare," *The Role of Direct and Indirect Taxes in the Federal Revenue System* (Princeton, 1964), pp. 25–70.

Section I will summarize the ordinary analysis of voter decision-making as originally suggested by Wicksell. Section II will indicate how the inefficiency of non-lump-sum taxes affects the individual voter-taxpayer's decision calculus. Individual welfare cost will then be incorporated into general optimality analysis in Section III. The last section contains our summary and conclusions.

The simple model with which we begin is based on the following assumptions:

1. A per-unit excise tax is imposed on a particular private good X_t.

2. The proceeds of this tax are earmarked for a specific public good X_p.

3. Decisions on the quantity of public goods to be provided are made by majority vote, with each individual possessing one vote.

4. All individuals have identical demands for the taxed good and the public good.

In addition, in order to use the welfare cost or excess burden approach, we further assume:

5. Before the imposition of the tax there were no other distortions (other inefficient taxes, monopoly, etc.) in the economy.

6. Costs of production are constant.

7. The public good X_p enters all utility functions in a strongly separable fashion, so that the public good is neither a strong substitute for or complement to the taxed good.

8. The marginal utility of money income is approximately constant with respect to changes in relative prices.

Although the analysis contained in this paper is directed only at a partial excise tax, it can apply as well to other types of nonoptimal taxes.

I. *Analysis of the Voter's Decision Calculus*

In the model we have described, or in any model in which the quantity of public goods is chosen by a voting process, the individual's decision whether to vote for or against the purchase of an additional unit of a public good will be the result of an economic choice reflecting individual preferences and costs. The usual description of the voter's choice calculus has been of the following form: The voter taxpayer will compare the marginal utility he gets from a unit of the public good with the utility he loses from having to give up private goods as a tax. He will vote for an expansion in quantity when the marginal utility of the public good exceeds the utility loss from the additional tax he must pay. He will vote against an increase when the marginal utility of the public good falls short of that of the tax.

Wicksell gave an early statement of these propositions:

> Now it is correct that efficiency requires approximate equality between this marginal utility [of the public good] and the price (or tax) paid therefore. Otherwise the individual would desire a restriction or further expansion of the public service and of the related expenditure.[5]

Similar analysis can be found in Lindahl,[6] and, more recently, in the work of James Buchanan:

> When the individual makes a decision, under any [voting] rule, he must try to compare the advantages that he will secure from the availability of the collective good and the costs that he will undergo from the increase in general tax.[7]

These generalizations are based on standard price theory. In the orthodox theory of consumer choice, a utility-maximizing individual is assumed to equate the ratio of the marginal utilities of two goods to the ratio of their prices. For a good X_j with a price p_j and a good X_r with a price p_r equal to unity, this condition becomes:

$$(1) \qquad \frac{\partial U^i/\partial X_j}{\partial U^i/\partial X_r} = \frac{p_j}{p_r} = p_j.$$

Wicksell's statement implies that an individual will cease trying to adjust his purchases of the public good X_p for which he pays a marginal tax-price per unit of T_p^i when:

$$(2) \qquad \frac{\partial U^i/\partial X_p}{\partial U^i/\partial X_r} = \frac{T_p^i}{p_r} = T_p^i.$$

This method of stating voter-behavior conditions treats the tax the individual pays for each unit of the public good in a manner similar to the treatment of the price of a private good. We wish to suggest, however, that when inefficient taxes are used to finance the public good, these generalizations from price theory are not appropriate. Any inefficient, nongeneral tax device not only affects the distribution of the tax burden and the net income of the individual

5. Wicksell, *loc. cit.*, p. 82.
6. Lindahl, *loc. cit.*, p. 216.
7. Buchanan and Tullock, *Calculus of Consent* (Ann Arbor, 1962), p. 168. See also Buchanan, *Public Finance in Democratic Process* (New York, 1966), pp. 13–14.

but it also changes the fundamental nature of the "price" the individual pays for the public good.

11. *Excess Burden in the Individual's Choice Calculus*

Consider an individual faced with a unit tax of $ t_0 per unit of some good X_t. Compared to a lump-sum tax which raised the same revenue, the welfare cost can be measured by:

$$(3) \qquad W^a = \int_0^{t_0} t \frac{dX_t^a}{dt} \, dt.$$

Welfare cost W is roughly measured by the triangular area under a demand curve above the pretax price, or the "welfare triangle." If the demand curve is linear, the welfare cost can be obtained from the expression:

$$(4) \qquad W^a = 1/2t(X_0^a - X_1^a) = 1/2t\Delta X_t^a,$$

where X_0^a is the amount of X_t individual a would have purchased in the absence of the tax and X_1^a is the amount he purchases when the tax is imposed. Since $\Delta X_t^a = t \, dX_t^a/dt$, (4) can be altered to:

$$(5) \qquad W^a = 1/2t^2 \frac{dX_t^a}{dt}.$$

Let us suppose that the individual is faced, in the world-of-equals model, with a constant marginal tax-price per unit of the public good equal to T_p^a dollars. That is

$$(6) \qquad T_p^a = \frac{dC^a}{dX_p} \text{ where } C^a = tX_t^a,$$

the total amount of tax collected from the individual.

If units of the public good were financed by an additional lump-sum tax for each additional unit of the public good, the tax-price of the public good to the individual would be simply T_p^a. If the public good must be financed by an excise, in order to purchase a unit of the public good the individual will have to pay an additional amount T_p^a and will also experience a different value of welfare costs. If the individual votes for the purchase of an additional unit of the public good, he not only votes to increase the tax rate enough to raise taxes from him in the amount of T_p^a (so that the tax rate t is some function of X_p), but he also votes to change the welfare cost he bears because of that tax.

The total cost to individual "a" of a unit of the public good equals $dC^a/dX_p + dW^a/dX_p$. It has been assumed that dC^a/dX_p

equals T_p^a. A value for dW^a/dt can be obtained by taking the derivative of (3) or (5), to obtain

$$(7) \qquad \frac{dW^a}{dt} = t\,\frac{dX_t^a}{dt}.$$

Considering X_t^a to be a function of the tax rate, and the tax rate in turn to be a function of the amount of X_p to be purchased, so that X_t^a becomes a function of X_p, we can then write

$$(8) \qquad \frac{dW^a}{dX_p} = t\,\frac{dX_t^a}{dt}\cdot\frac{dt}{dX_p} = t\,\frac{dX_t^a}{dX_p}.$$

The voter will therefore vote for that quantity of the public good under a single excise tax for which

$$(9) \qquad \frac{\frac{\partial U^a}{\partial X_p}}{\frac{\partial U^a}{\partial X_r}} = T_p^a + t\,\frac{dX_t^a}{dX_p}.$$

Since, in our model, the individual pays a constant share of a constant-cost public good, the marginal tax-price he faces is not altered as he extends his purchases of the public good through his vote. But the price distortion in the private market imposed upon the individual is altered as he votes for increases in the public good.

If the marginal utility of income is constant, marginal inefficiency will always be positive. Hence, the general conclusion from equation (9) is that the voter will vote for a smaller quantity of the public good under an inefficient tax than under an efficient one. Moreover, the greater the magnitude of marginal inefficiency, the greater will be this divergence in the quantity demanded.[8] It can be shown that marginal inefficiency will increase as the tax is increased if the demand curve for the taxed good is linear: This is so because (a) as the tax rate increases by equal increments, marginal inefficiency increases and (b) larger and larger increases in the tax rate are needed to finance additional units of a constant-cost public good as more units of the good are purchased.[9]

8. If the marginal utility of income declines considerably because of the price change, it is possible for *marginal* inefficiency to become negative, so that the individual will vote for *more* X_p under an inefficient tax. We are indebted to Professor Charles Goetz for clarifying this point. See C. Goetz, *Traditional Welfare Norms for Specific Taxes* (mimeo).

9. A mathematical proof of this proposition is in an appendix available from the authors.

In sum, this analysis suggests that even if either of two tax devices has the same distribution of tax payments over individuals, different quantities of the public good are likely to be selected under each of them. If the distribution of marginal inefficiencies associated with each tax device are different (e.g., because of differing elasticities of demand for the taxed good), the quantities of public good chosen will not be the same.

If X_p enters utility functions in a separable fashion, extension of this argument to a case in which there is more than one excise tax in existence is simple. Suppose taxes have been placed on goods 1 to n, but the public good must be financed by an increase in the tax on good X_i. Welfare cost in such a case can be defined as:[10]

$$(10) \qquad W^a = \sum_{i=1}^{n} \int_0^t \sum_{j \leq i} t_j \frac{\partial X_j^a}{\partial t_i} dt_i$$

or, in a "welfare triangle" form,

$$(11) \qquad W^a = 1/2 \sum_{i=1}^{n} t_j \Delta X_j^a .$$

Taking the derivative of (10) or (11), we obtain

$$(12) \qquad \frac{\partial W^a}{\partial t_i} = \sum_j t_j \frac{\partial X_j^a}{\partial t_i} .$$

If only one tax is in existence, this formula reduces to (7). If more than one tax is in existence, an increase in a given tax will, if the taxed goods are substitutes ($\partial X_j^a / \partial t_i > 0, \neq j$), generally produce a smaller increase in welfare cost than if there were no other taxes in existence. For this reason the larger the number of available tax devices, the larger quantity of public good one would expect to see provided.

III. *Welfare Optimality Conditions*

This association of excess burden or inefficiency with the use of a nongeneral tax device further suggests that the welfare optimality conditions must also be altered. The form of the marginal welfare condition for optimality in the supply of a public good X_p is, as given by Samuleson,

$$(13) \qquad \sum_a \frac{\partial U^a / \partial X_p}{\partial U^a / \partial X_r} = \frac{f_p}{f_r} .$$

10. See Harberger, "The Measurement of Waste," p. 61.

If X_r is a numeraire good with a price equal to marginal cost of unity, this becomes:

(13a)
$$\sum_a \frac{\partial U^a / \partial X_p}{\partial U^a / \partial X_r} = \sum_a T_p^a .$$

Hence, that quantity of public good at which condition (13a) is satisfied for every voter will be optimal. As indicated above, these formulations implicitly assume that taxes paid for public goods are similar to prices paid for private goods. Indeed, in a two-good model an excise on the only available private good is equivalent to a lump-sum or general tax. When taxes which generate inefficiency are employed, the form of the marginal condition must be altered. Equation (13a) must be changed to:

(14)
$$\sum_a \frac{\dfrac{\partial U^a}{\partial X_r}}{\dfrac{\partial U^a}{\partial X_r}} = \sum_a \left(T_p^a + t \frac{dX_t^a}{dt} \cdot \frac{dt}{dX_p} \right) .$$

Here both marginal taxes and marginal welfare cost are summed over all individuals in the community.

This formulation indicates that the Samuelson condition (13) or (13a) cannot be used to locate an "optimal" quantity under an inefficient tax, even if a distributional decision can be made or a social welfare function specified. If the optimum is constrained by the use of an inefficient tax, and if the marginal utility of income is unaffected, or affected only slightly by changes in relative prices, the optimum quantity of the public good will be less than that indicated by (13) so long as marginal inefficiency remains positive. The greater the marginal inefficiency, the greater must be the departure from an unconstrained optimum.

This conclusion also has important implications for the relative size of the public sector when inefficient tax devices are used to finance public goods. It has often been suggested that there is likely to arise a "social imbalance" in society's allocation of resources to private and public goods.[11] Our analysis suggests that such an "imbalance," may, to a degree, be made necessary by the inefficient manner in which individuals pay for public goods. Indeed, a movement from an "imbalance" to a "balance" which satisfies (13) could, if inefficient taxes were used, actually decrease everyone's utility. This analysis suggests, therefore, that meaningful discussions of such imbalance must consider not only the differential allocation of re-

11. John K. Galbraith, *The Affluent Society* (Boston, 1958), Chap. XVIII.

sources but also the differential efficiency of practical methods for collecting funds to pay for the public goods.

iv. *Conclusion*

Even in this highly simplified model in which individuals are equal and do not engage in strategic bargaining, it can be shown that an excess burden will always occur. Each individual will recognize that if all others maintained their purchases of the taxed good, it would be to his advantage to distort his consumption pattern and to reduce his purchases of the taxed good, thus attempting to shift a part of the cost to other individuals. If all others distort their behavior, on the other hand, the individual will not wish to maintain his purchases because he will suffer a disproportionate share of the tax burden. In game-theoretic terminology, the strategy of "maintain purchases of the taxed good" is dominated by the strategy of "reduce purchases." This situation is, in fact, another example of the ubiquitous prisoners' dilemma.

This analysis suggests that excess burden will be present in an individualist-democratic model, as well as in the more orthodox "dirigiste" context in which it was developed, so long as the public good is to be financed by non-lump-sum taxes. Excess burden is an essential characteristic of such taxes, regardless of the basic decision model employed, and regardless of the institutional framework.

This paper has been a first attempt at integrating the voluntary theory of public finance with the orthodox analysis of excess burden or inefficiency cost which arises when nonoptimal tax devices are used to finance public goods. Since the "price" the individual pays for a public good is not collected in the same way that the price of a private good is collected, but is, rather, what might be called an "inefficient price," the ordinary representation of individual voter rationality conditions, as given by Wicksell, and of welfare optimality conditions, as given by Samuelson, are incorrect when a nonoptimal tax is employed. An excise tax will induce individuals to shift their purchases away from the taxed commodity, causing a distortion in their consumption mix which represents a real cost of those individuals. This additional cost will lead the individual to vote for a smaller quantity of public goods under an inefficient tax than under an efficient one.

9

The Economics of Earmarked Taxes

James M. Buchanan[1]

Economists do not agree on the effects of earmarking. For example, Julius Margolis and Walter Heller suggest that the earmarking or segregating of fiscal accounts tends to reduce the willingness of taxpayers to approve expenditures on specific public services.[2] By contrast, Earl Rolph and George Break, along with Jesse Burkhead, discuss earmarking as one device for generating taxpayer support for expansion in particular services.[3] The staff of the Tax Founda-

Reprinted by permission of the publisher from *Journal of Political Economy*, October 1963. Copyright 1963 by the University of Chicago.

1. The background research on this paper was done in connection with a more comprehensive project on fiscal institutions that is supported by the National Committee on Government Finance, organized through the Brookings Institution. I am indebted to my colleagues, James M. Ferguson and W. Craig Stubblebine, whose persistent skepticism forced me to remove several errors from earlier drafts of this paper.

2. Margolis, in his stimulating paper, provides empirical support for this hypothesis in the case of expenditures for education (see Julius Margolis, "Metropolitan Finance Problems: Territories, Functions, and Growth," in *Public Finances: Needs, Sources, and Utilization* [New York, 1961] esp. pp. 261–66).

Heller criticizes the institution of the attached mill-levy because it serves to restrict unduly the willingness of taxpayers to support mosquito control programs and the like (see Walter Heller, "CED's Stabilizing Budget Policy after Ten Years," *American Economic Review*, XLVII [September 1957], 650, esp. n. 39).

3. In both cases here, the argument is applied to the financing of special functions in underdeveloped countries (see Earl Rolph and George Break, *Public Finance* [New York, 1961], p. 62, and Jesse Burkhead, *Government Budgeting* [New York, 1956], p. 469).

tion in a more comprehensive study have expressed views in accord with the latter position.[4]

This paper develops a theory of earmarking that explains the divergent predictions and also suggests certain hypotheses, the implications of which should be testable through the observation of political processes. In order to construct this theory, it is necessary to introduce models of the political-decision process that are not consistent with those that have been implicitly assumed in the orthodox normative evaluation of earmarking. The near-universal condemnation of the institution by experts in budgetary theory and practice is familiar and need not be summarized here.[5] This position cannot be supported on the basis of the efficiency considerations that may be derived from the models emphasized in this paper.

"Earmarking" is defined as the practice of designating or dedicating specific revenues to the financing of specific public services. It is discussed under such headings as "special funds," "segregated accounts," "segregated budgets," "dedicated revenues." Normally, earmarking as a term is used with reference to the dedication of a single tax source to a single public service within a multitax, multiservice fiscal unit, but the identical effects are produced by the creation of special-purpose fiscal units, such as school districts, fire districts, and sanitation districts, each of which is granted independent, but restricted, taxing powers. Quantitatively, earmarking is important in the overall United States fiscal system. At the local government level, the special-purpose units remain predominant in the financing of important services, education being the notable example.[6] At the state level, one study suggested that one half of all state

---

4. Tax Foundation, *Earmarked State Taxes* (New York, 1955).

5. For statements of the argument in standard works see M. Slade Kendrick, *Public Finance* (Boston, 1951), p. 331; W. J. Schultz and C. Lowell Harriss, *American Public Finance* (7th ed.; New York, 1959), p. 107; Philip E. Taylor, *The Economics of Public Finance* (rev. ed.; New York, 1963), p. 28; Harold M. Groves, *Financing Government* (New York, 1958), p. 500.

"Classical" statements of the standard position are to be found in C. F. Bastable, *Public Finance* (2d ed.; London, 1895), p. 689; Paul Leroy-Beaulieu, *Traité de la science des finances, II* (2d ed.; Paris, 1906), 30 ff.; Gaston Jeze, *Cours de science des finances, Théorie générale du budget* (6th ed.; Paris, 1922), pp. 82–103.

6. Independent school districts account for almost four-fifths of total school enrollment in the United States (see Margolis, *op. cit.*, p. 263).

collections in 1954 were earmarked.[7] At the federal level, the modern growth of the trust-fund accounts, such as that for highways, suggests that, proportionately, earmarked or segregated revenues are assuming increasing significance.

I.

The standard normative "theory" of earmarking adopts the reference system of budget-maker, the budgetary authority, who is, by presumption, divorced from the citizenry in the political community. An alternative working hypothesis of political order is the individualistic one in which the reference system becomes that of the individual citizen. In this model, the only meaningful decision-making units are individual persons, and the state or the collectivity exists only as a means through which individuals combine to accomplish collective or jointly desired objectives. The state is not an independent choosing agent, and "collective choice" results from separate individual decisions as these are processed by constitutional rules. The analytical device of the social welfare function, which guides the judgments of an independent budgetary authority, has no place in this model. The earmarking of revenues must be re-examined in the context of individual participation in the formation of collective decisions. When this approach is taken, it becomes apparent that the restrictions that such practices as earmarking may impose on the independence of a budgetary authority need not produce "inefficiency" in the fiscal process. Some such segregation of revenues may provide one means of insuring more rational individual choice; under some conditions, earmarking may be a "desirable" rather than an "undesirable" feature of a fiscal structure.

Institutionally, earmarking provides a means of compartmentalizing fiscal decisions. The individual citizen, as voter-taxpayer-beneficiary, is enabled to participate, *separately*, either directly or through his legislative representative, in the several public expenditure decisions that may arise. He may, through this device, "vote" independently on the funds to be devoted to schools, to sanitation, and so on, given the specified revenue sources. Only in this manner can he make "private" choices on the basis of some reasonably accurate comparison of the costs and the benefits of the specific public services, one at the time.[8] By contrast, general-fund budgeting, or

7. Tax Foundation, *op. cit.*
8. The necessity of relating decisions on public expenditures explicitly to decisions on taxes through the political process, and of assign-

nonearmarking, allows the citizen to "vote" only on the aggregate outlay for the predetermined "bundles" of public services, as this choice is presented to him by the budgetary authorities.[9]

The appropriate market analogue to general-fund financing (nonearmarking) is a specific tie-in sale, as opposed to independent quantity adjustment in each market, the analogue to earmarking. Independent adjustment is characteristic of privately organized markets for goods and services. The individual is not normally required to purchase goods and services in "bundles" of complex heterogeneous units. Insofar as some tie-ins are observed to persist in competitive markets, these reflect the advantages of superior efficiency to the purchaser. In the absence of genuine cost-reducing aspects of marketing separate goods in "bundles," any restrictions that are placed on the ability to adjust quantities independently must move the purchaser to some less preferred position on his utility surface. For example, any requirement that one stick of butter be purchased with each loaf of bread would surely produce "inefficiency" in choice, and could be implemented only through the exercise of monopoly power.[10]

II.

The model of individual fiscal choice that is required must remain extremely simplified. It is necessary to abstract rules from the

ing a definite revenue category to each single expenditure was stressed by Wicksell in his classic statement of the individualistic theory of public finance (see Knut Wicksell, "A New Principle of Just Taxation," in *Classics in the Theory of Public Finance,* ed. R. A. Musgrave and A. T. Peacock [London, 1958], pp. 72–118, but esp. p. 94. The original Wicksell work is *Finanztheorietische Untersuchungen* [Jena, 1896]).

9. Control over the budgetary allocation, at one stage removed, does exist through the voter's ultimate power to remove public officials through electoral processes. And, even for the budgetary allocation as presented, legislative power to modify the allocation of funds among the separate public service outlays is normally exercised. However, these powers to change the uses to which general-fund revenues may be put do not modify the basic "tie-in" features of the model until and unless the tax structure is simultaneously considered in the same decision processes.

10. For recent statements of the theory of tie-in sales see M. L. Burstein, "The Economics of Tie-in Sales," *Review of Economics and Statistics,* XLII (February 1960), 68–73, and his "A Theory of Full-Line Forcing," *Northwestern University Law Review,* LV (1960), 62–95 (see also Ward S. Bowman, Jr., "Tying Arrangements and the Leverage Problem," *Yale Law Journal,* LXVII [March 1957], 19–36).

complexities of alternative political decision rules and at the same time to retain for the model some relevance for collective results. To accomplish this, the "median" voter-taxpayer-beneficiary is introduced. "Median" here characterizes the individual's preference structure as typical of that describing his fellows' in the group. With single-peaked preferences the "median" individual becomes decisive under simple majority voting rules.[11] Hence, the behavior of the single "median" individual mirrors that of the effective decision-making group in the community. Through this device, collective results can be discussed in terms of the behavior of the single individual. The conception is similar to, although somewhat broader than, the community-of-equals assumption that has been employed frequently in fiscal analysis.

I shall assume that the goods or services provided publicly utilize a sufficiently small share of total community resources to allow income effects to be neglected in the behavior of the individual. Collective goods are assumed to be produced at constant marginal costs, and, finally, the costs of reaching collective decisions are neglected. Initially, I shall assume that the collective goods, whether supplied singly or jointly, are to be financed through the imposition of a particular form of lump-sum tax. This tax is designed so that the "terms-of-trade" between the individual and the fisc cannot be affected by the behavior of the former. The "tax price per unit" of the collective good made available to him is invariant over quantity, although the total tax bill is, of course, dependent on the quantity chosen by the community. This relatively pure model allows us to discuss the behavior of the individual free from any elements of strategic bargaining with his fellows that might be present were the terms of trade subject to influence by his own actions.

The choice calculus of the individual can now be analyzed in familiar terms. He is confronted by a fixed "supply price"; the supply curve, to him, for the collective good, singly or in a bundle, is horizontal at some predetermined "tax price." This tax price, to the individual, is some share of the total supply price or cost price of the good to the whole community. The quantity of collective goods made available to one person is assumed equally available to everyone else in the group. The distribution of taxes among the separate individuals is assumed to have been determined outside the model. In a world-of-equals model, an individual share might be taken simply as a pro rata part of total unit cost. In this more general setting, any

11. See Duncan Black, *The Theory of Committees and Elections* (Cambridge, 1958).

distribution of taxes is possible so long as this distribution is independent of the particular choice analyzed.

Consider first a single collective good. We can think of an individual marginal evaluation schedule or curve, which in this instance is equivalent to a demand curve, for this good in the same manner that we think of such a schedule or curve for a privately marketed good or service. Individual or private "equilibrium" is reached at a point where the demand price equals the individual supply price or tax price. In this collective good case, there is no opportunity for the individual, acting alone, to adjust quantity purchased to price. Hence, the attainment of his "equilibrium" position is possible, even for the "median" consumer, only through "voting for" or "voting against" extensions or contractions in public goods supply. The construction enables us to depict the voting choices of the individual with respect to the collective good in a manner analogous to the standard treatment of market choice, so long as we assume that marginal adjustments in public expenditure programs are possible. If marginal adjustments are not possible, and the voter is presented with a final choice of voting for or against specific expenditure proposals, elements of all-or-none offers enter his calculus, and the treatment requires modification.

The analysis is straightforward when we consider a single collective good or service. Since, however, we want to introduce the tie-in "sale" that general-fund financing implies, a two-good model becomes the simplest one that is helpful. For descriptive flavor, think of a community that supplies both police protection and fire protection services collectively. We seek to determine the possible differences between financing these two services separately, through a system of earmarking where each service is supported by revenues from a tax of the sort indicated above, and financing them jointly, with revenues from a general-fund budget derived from only one tax. In either case, the total amount of public expenditure is assumed to be determined by the rationally motivated choice of the voter-taxpayer. Will general-fund financing result in a larger or a smaller provision of one or both public services than that produced under an earmarked revenue scheme? Will total public outlay, on both services, increase, decrease, or remain the same as an institutional change from one revenue system to the other is made?

The answers to these and other questions must depend upon the particular form that a general-fund budgetary tie-in takes. It would be possible to define this tie-in with respect to physical units of service, such as, for example, the requirement that the same number of policemen and firemen be supplied. It will, however, be descriptively more realistic and analytically more convenient if we define the tie-in with respect to a budgetary allocation between the two services. In other words, general-fund financing takes the form of a specific proportion of the total budget devoted to each of the two services. There will always exist one budgetary allocation that will insure identity of solution as between the two institutions. That is, there is always one budgetary ratio that will cause the median individual to "vote for" the same relative quantities of the two services and the same public outlay with or without earmarking. This unique solution, which I shall label "full equilibrium," provides a starting point for a more careful analysis.

It is convenient to illustrate the analysis geometrically. In Figure 1 quantity units are measured along the horizontal axis, but these units are defined in a special way. Under the tie-in arrangement, a unity of quantity is defined as that physical combination of the two services available for one dollar, one hundred cents. Thus, the number of dollars expended is directly proportional to the distance along the horizontal axis. Now assume that the "full equilibrium" budgetary mix prevails, and that this is defined by the forty-sixty ratio. Forty cents out of each budgetary dollar is devoted to providing fire protection and sixty cents to providing police protection; each service is supplied at constant cost. We may now derive demand curves for fire protection services, D_f, and police protection services, D_p, respectively. These demand curves must be defined with respect to the dimensions indicated by the budgetary ratio. A unit of fire protection is defined as that quantity available to the individual for an outlay of forty cents, and a unit of police services is defined as that quantity available for an outlay of sixty cents. For expositional simplicity, I shall use linear demand functions. The vertical summation of the two demand curves, $D_f + D_p$, represents the demand for the bundle of services, available for one dollar per unit, when the forty-sixty ratio prevails. By definition of "full equilibrium," this composite demand curve cuts the tax-price curve, drawn at the one-dollar level, along the same vertical line measuring the independently chosen equilibrium quantities of fire protection and police protection respectively. The elements of circularity that are present in this whole construction are not damaging since the purpose is illustrative only.

Given the conditions of demand shown in Figure 1, there is no differential effect as between earmarking and general-fund financing of the two services at the forty-sixty budgetary ratio. The individual will choose, will vote for, the same quantity of services and the same overall public outlay under either one of the two institutional forms.

If separately presented, he will vote for an amount OX, of fire services, defined in forty-cent units, which can, of course, readily be translated into any other physical dimension. Similarly, he will choose an amount, OX, of police services defined in sixty-cent units. Or, if forced to take these two services in bundles, defined by the forty-sixty ratio, he will choose an amount, OX. In either case, he will vote for a total budget outlay that is directly proportional to the horizontal distance, OX.

Differential effects arise only when some budgetary ratio other than that required for "full equilibrium" is introduced. Assume now that the budgetary ratio is exogenously determined, and that a proposal is made to shift from a system of segregated financing to general-fund financing under, say, a fifty-fifty ratio, with underlying demand conditions for the two services remaining as depicted in Figure 1. It is necessary to translate the demand curves, D_f and D_p, into the modified dimensions, with physical units now being defined as the quantities available at fifty cents. The new demand curves, drawn in the fifty-cents dimensions, are shown as D'_f and D'_p. The effects of general-fund financing at this nonequilibrium ratio, which has been shifted in favor of fire-protection services, can be clearly indicated. As might be expected, more fire protection is demanded and less police protection than under earmarking. In the new dimensions, OX'_f represents the "full equilibrium" or earmarking quantity of fire protection services, and OX'_p the corresponding quantity of police services. In other words, OX, in the old dimension, is equivalent to OX'_f in the new; both represent the same physical quantity of fire protection services. General-fund financing under the new fifty-fifty budgetary ratio will produce a "tie-in equilibrium" at a quantity measured by OX'_{f+p}, which is determined by the intersection of the newly drawn composite demand curve, $D'_f + D'_p$, with the composite supply curve.[12]

Any shift in the budgetary ratio away from that required for "full equilibrium" will insure that general-fund financing introduces some distortion in the choice pattern of the individual. Forcing him to purchase the two services in a bundle, rather than separately, will move the individual to some less preferred position on his utility surface, given our framework assumption that decision-making costs are zero. Since, under independent quantity adjustment, he could always, should he desire, select quantities of fire and police services

12. The geometrical constructions in both Figure 1 and Figure 2 are drawn on the basis of a specific numerical model that will be supplied upon request.

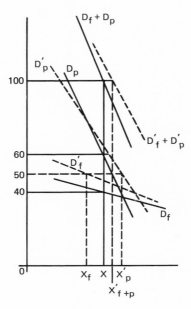

Figure 1

indicated by the second solution, the fact that he does not do so in the first solution suggests that such a combination must be less preferred than the initial combination chosen. The distortion produced by the nonequilibrium budgetary ratio will take the form of an expansion in one of the two services beyond the "full equilibrium" quantity and a contraction of the other to some less than "full equilibrium" quantity. Relatively, the service expanded will be that one that is differentially favored by the ratio. The analysis remains incomplete, however, until and unless further questions are answered. Will overall public outlay tend to increase or decrease and under what conditions? What are the characteristics of those services most likely to be substantially increased as a result of favorable-ratio general-fund financing?

   Total public outlay need not remain the same under earmarking and nonearmarking when a nonequilibrium budgetary ratio prevails, and the direction of change will depend on the configuration of the demand functions. Examination of the model produces the following conclusions: If the ratio turns in favor of the service characterized by the more elastic demand at the full equilibrium quantity (as in the example), total public outlay will be expanded as earmarking is replaced by general-fund financing. Conversely, if the ratio shifts in favor of the service characterized by the less elastic demand at the full equilibrium quantity, total public outlay will be reduced as a result of a similar shift in institutions. These results hold, however, only for limited shifts in the ratio away from the full equilibrium one. As the construction of Figure 1 suggests, the relative elasticities of demand may change as the "tie-in equilibrium" quantity changes. When and if relative elasticities change, the direction of change in total expenditure is reversed. Utilizing the linear demand curves of Figure 1, this point may be illustrated readily. As the ratio shifts initially in favor of fire protection, characterized by the more elastic demand at the initial quantity, total outlay will be increased by the tie-in scheme. Beyond some critical value, however, the elasticity of demand for fire protection, at the tie-in quantity, becomes less than that for police services, and total public outlay diminishes as the budgetary ratio continues to shift in favor of fire protection.[13]

Several of the relevant relationships are illustrated in Figure 2. On the horizontal axis is measured the percentage of fire protection service in a tie-in budgetary mix, from zero to one hundred. On the vertical axis is measured total outlay, on both and on each service, as determined by the demand pattern of the individual and the assumed cost conditions for the two services. Specifically, Figure 2 is derived from the same configuration as Figure 1, which embodies linear demand functions, although a similar set of relationships could be readily derived from any postulated initial conditions of demand. The full equilibrium ratio, defined previously as the forty-sixty one, must involve a total public outlay equal to the sum of the spending on the two services when "purchased" separately. If a ratio with zero fire protection services is introduced, total spending will be on police services alone; conversely, if a 100 percent ratio is present, all spending will be for fire protection. Thus, income effects being neglected, the vertical distance, E, at full equilibrium, must equal the sum of the distance, OP, and O'F. As the ratio shifts in favor of

13. Note that these conclusions can be stated in terms of relative elasticities only in the model that allows the quantity dimensions to shift as the budgetary ratio changes. This shifting of quantity dimension insures that, for both services, the quantity taken is the same. This, along with the additional requirement that the absolute changes in price for the two services must be precisely offsetting, allows shifts along two separate demand functions to be evaluated in terms of relative elasticity coefficients. Without these constraints, shifts along two separate demand functions could not be compared with respect to changes in total outlay solely in terms of relative elasticities. The latter would remain important, but some relative price factor would have to be added.

fire protection services, total outlay expands, as shown by the rising portion of the top curve to the right of E. Total outlay reaches a maximum at M, and then falls sharply to F as the ratio becomes more and more favorable to fire protection. As the ratio shifts in favor of police protection services, total outlay falls, as is indicated by the top curve to the left of E. It continues to fall to P where no part of the budget is devoted to providing fire protection.

The additional curves in Figure 2 break down this total outlay as between the two services and into actual and imputed components. Actual outlay is, of course, computed by taking the indicated percentage of total outlay as shown by the ratio on the horizontal scale. "Imputed outlay" on a service is defined as that part of total outlay on a bundle that is attributed to the service by the individual at each particular tie-in equilibrium. Imputed outlay on a service equals actual only at the full equilibrium budgetary ratio. For all other ratios, imputed outlay differs from actual, and the difference reflects the degree of "exploitation," negative or positive, that non-equilibrium ratios can generate. Imputed outlay falls below actual outlay on the service that is favored in the budgetary mix; it exceeds actual outlay on the remaining service. This is shown in Figure 2. To the right of 40 percent, imputed outlay on fire protection services, I_f, falls below actual outlay, A_f. To the left of 40 percent, the opposite relationship holds. And, of course, the relationship for police services are the inverse of those for fire services.

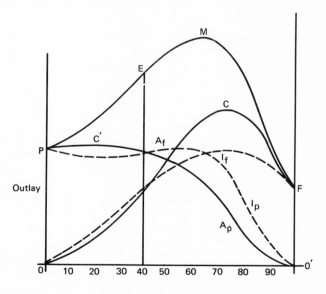

Figure 2. Percentage of general-fund outlay devoted to fire protection

Maximum total outlay is reached at M. As the ratio shifts beyond this point, total expenditures fall although the share of this total devoted to fire protection continues to increase. At some point, C, to the right of M, these two factors become mutually offsetting, and some maximum outlay on fire protection services alone is reached. Increasing the share in the budget beyond this "critical ratio" will result in fewer resources devoted to fire protection, always on the assumption that the voter-taxpayer retains the basic power of determining the level of total spending.

As the ratio shifts in favor of police services, in our model, total outlay falls continuously. Because of the increasing share, however, the quantity of police services supplied increases to some critical ratio, C', where actual outlay reaches a maximum.[14]

III.

The analysis, to this point, has been based on the choice calculus of the single median individual. Even before generalizing this analysis, we are able to draw some interesting implications for political group behavior. In any community specific individuals and groups will find particular interest in the performance of one or the other public services provided. Using the two-service model we can examine the predicted behavior of groups organized in support of either fire protection or police protection services. If both services should be initially financed through independently designated taxes, that is, if earmarking prevails, then groups in support of either service would have some incentive to attempt to secure a general-fund budgetary scheme favorable to its own service. Conversely, either group would try to retain earmarking if it predicts an unfavorable budgetary allotment under general-fund arrangements.

The characteristics of demand, however, make for considerable differences in the expected gains to be secured under favorable general-fund ratios. Relatively, the group that is organized in support of

14. The rising portion of the I_p curve at the left in Figure 2 requires some explanation. As the budgetary mix shifts in favor of police services, imputed expenditures on both services fall, as indicated. As a smaller share of the budget is allotted to fire protection, however, the degree of exploitation that consumers of police services can attain reaches some maximum. Beyond this point, the "relative-price reduction" that the tie-in involves is progressively diminished.

The derivation of this construction is clarified in the numerical example upon which both Figures 1 and 2 are based. It should be emphasized, however, that the general results do not depend upon the particulars of the example or on the shapes of the curves derived therefrom.

the service characterized by the more elastic demand stands to gain more by favorable tie-ins. In this way sizable amounts of "taxpayers' surplus" can be captured from the relatively less elastic demand service that is tied into the budgetary bundle.[15] Not only will the favored service be allotted a larger share of each budget dollar, but also total spending on both services increases. By comparison, the pressure group organized to support the relatively inelastic-demand service will not be able to secure so much advantage even from comparably favorable shifts in the budgetary ratio. A higher share of the budgetary dollar will be advantageous, but the degree of exploitation from "taxpayers' surplus" on the other service is severely limited. This group, therefore, stands to gain less and possibly to lose more from a general change in institutions leading away from segregated revenue sources. It will be much more likely to opt for the continuation, or the introduction, of segregated budget accounts.

Note that *both* pressure groups could never be observed to approve a shift from segregated to general-fund financing or vice versa if the budgetary ratio is known in advance, and known to be a non-equilibrium one. If the model has predictive value at all, observation should reveal that some groups support one financing arrangement and some the other. There is an appropriate market analogue. Rational monopolists producing two separate goods could never be observed to join in a mutually agreed tie-in sale without the pooling of revenues. Any particular tie-in, other than the full equilibrium one, must benefit one and harm the other.

As mentioned, Margolis refers to data that suggest somewhat larger expenditure on education under general-fund than under segregated financing schemes. If the analytical model presented here is valid, these facts suggest that education is favored in general-fund budgetary ratios. It seems probable, also, that total municipal spend-

15. This is, in general, consistent with the conclusions of Burstein with respect to the tie-in sales of the monopolist. As he suggests, the monopolist, selling a product that is necessarily price elastic, will seek to tie in the sales of an inelastic-demand product. The monopolist can, of course, control the relevant ratio (see Burstein, "The Economics of Tie-in Sales," *op. cit.*).

The analysis of earmarking, as developed here, is simpler than the comparable analysis of monopolistic tie-in sales. In the earmarking model, the unit cost of supplying services, either jointly or separately, is always equal to the "tax price" charged to "purchasers." In other words, the government does not seek to make profits. With the monopolist, the difference between unit cost and price is a central variable that the fiscal model need not include.

ing is larger in those cases where education is included in the general-fund budget. This supplementary hypothesis, if confirmed by observation, would imply that, over the relevant ranges, educational services are characterized by a relatively higher demand elasticity than companion services in the budget. There is independent evidence to support this implication. Public services, like education, that provide differentially higher benefits to particular subgroups in the community (in this case families with children) will tend to be relatively more demand elastic than services that are more "general" in benefit incidence (say, police protection). By requiring taxpayers who do not secure direct benefits from publicly provided educational services to purchase general community services, such as police, only through a tie-in arrangement with education, some "taxpayers' surplus" is captured, as Margolis has suggested. The bachelor who might vote against additional school district taxes (and expenditures) may vote for additional taxes to finance a bundle of services that includes education. The analysis does not imply, however, even if further research should confirm fully the hypotheses involved, that school superintendents and P.T.A. groups take no chances in pushing for the abolition of segregated financial sources. Such plans would, of course, backfire unless favorable budgetary ratios are secured.[16]

The behavior of subgroups in the political community that are not organized to support specific expenditures may also be noted briefly. Taxpayer groups, those whose primary objective is that of reducing the level of tax rates independently of any consideration for public spending levels, will tend to favor earmarking schemes if they expect that general-fund budgeting implies shifts in favor of the more elastic-demand services. For the same reason, these groups would desire general-fund financing in the converse case. Since, however, the gain to be expected in the latter institutional arrangement is likely to be slight, taxpayer groups normally might be predicted to support earmarking.

By comparison and contrast, the "bureaucracy," whose objective is primarily that of expanding the size and importance of the public sector, independently of costs, will directly oppose the taxpayer groups. If voter-taxpayer response is presumed, ultimately, to determine the total public expenditure level while the bureaucracy

16. As W. C. Stubblebine has pointed out, the analysis here seems appropriate to the behavior of certain charitable organizations. The model "explains" why the Boy Scouts seek to be included in general-fund Community Chest revenue-raising drives, while the Red Cross and the Cancer Society prefer independent (earmarked) financing.

chooses the budgetary mix, the model that seems to be implicit in much of the orthodox discussion emerges. Here the budget-makers should try to select a mix that approximates the full equilibrium ratio. If, however, these officials include consideration of bureaucracy objectives in their decisions, they will be biased toward shifting general-fund allocations in favor of the relatively elastic-demand services, and, in this way, toward insuring some overall expansion in public spending.

I V.

The first step toward generalizing the model involves the extension to more than two public services. Basically, the same propositions hold. The departures from independently determined or "optimal" levels of provision for particular services become larger as more services are included in the budgetary bundle. Partial segregation of fiscal accounts, with each including several services that are commonly financed, can be shown to be more "efficient," from the reference system of the voter-taxpayer-beneficiary, than overall integration into a comprehensive budgetary system, given the restrictions imposed on the model. Similar conclusions apply to the effects of segregated budget accounts created by special-purpose governmental units. Incorporation of decision-making costs into the model could, of course, modify these initial conclusions.

In the model discussed the separate services were assumed to be wholly independent. Extension of the analysis to cover those cases where services are either close substitutes or close complements will not affect the results. Services were also assumed supplied at constant cost, but this simplification does not affect the conclusions.

A major step toward generalizing the analysis is that which relaxes the specific tax assumptions. The individual, whose decision processes are examined, is confronted with a fixed "tax per unit." Only a form of lump-sum tax satisfies this requirement. Under most real-world taxing institutions, the tax price per unit at which collective goods are made available to the individual will depend, at least to some degree, on his own behavior. This element is not, however, important under the major tax institutions such as the personal income tax, the general sales tax, or the real property tax. With such structures, the individual may, by changing his private behavior, modify the tax base (and thus the tax price per unit of collective goods he utilizes), but he need not have any incentive to conceal his "true" preferences for public goods. His own tax liability, per unit, is to such a small extent modified by his own choice for public goods that he will not normally include this factor in his decision for or against public spending proposals. His behavior in participating in collective choice can remain broadly analogous to his behavior as a purchaser of goods and services in the market place.

In the formal model, it was assumed that the distribution of taxes among separate persons is in some way determined independently of the particular fiscal choices analyzed. The tax price per unit that the individual confronts does not depend on the outcome of the choice. This, in itself, seems "realistic." Local communities, for example, make decisions on expansions and contractions in public-spending programs in the expectation that costs will be placed on the ratepayers, and the distribution of these costs does not normally depend on the pattern of public services chosen. Similarly, assemblies at higher governmental levels vote on appropriations measures independently of the given tax structure. Conversely, tax reform does not imply change in budgetary allocation. The model employed can, therefore, apply equally to the calculus of the low-income citizen who, presumably, is required by the tax structure to pay a differentially low tax price for units of collective good and to the high-income citizen who is required to pay a differentially high tax price for the same good.

Complications produced by distributional elements must be faced when the results of the individual-behavior model are applied to fiscal experience. In the normal order of events, collective goods and services are "priced" to individuals in a discriminatory fashion. This fact makes it necessary that we interpret the conclusions concerning the relative elasticities of demand for public services quite carefully. In ordinary market analysis, when the demand for a good is classified as relatively elastic over a relevant price range, this conveys specific meaning since, presumably, all buyers confront the prevailing price. If, however, separate consumers buy at different prices, as they do in the case of collective goods, the elasticity of total demand depends on the pattern of discrimination that happens to be present. It becomes impossible to classify public services, even at known relative cost levels, into elastic and inelastic demand categories independently of the tax structure.

A further reference to Margolis' interesting evidence on educational spending illustrates this point. As suggested above, the data indicate that education secures favorable ratios in general-fund budgeting arrangements. If, in addition, municipal spending on all goods is higher when general-fund financing is adopted, the demand for educational services, *at the prevailing tax structure*, is relatively

more elastic than that for companion services. But a shift or change
in the tax structure can modify this relative demand elasticity, since
any change in the distribution of costs among individuals amounts
to a shifting of relative prices, as these are confronted by the separate individuals in the group. Margolis suggests that a shift to
general-fund financing for education may be needed in many localities in order to generate political support for expanded expenditures.
This expansion, however, would be secured at the expense of some
additional distortion in individual fiscal choice, along with a necessary contraction in accompanying services. A more fruitful, and
more "efficient," means of securing the same objective may lie in
some modification of the structure of taxes imposed by special-
purpose governments, some change in the pattern of discriminatory
rates.

v.

The theory of earmarking presented in this paper may be criticized
on many grounds. Any formal model based on individual behavior in
collective choice processes must remain remote from real-world political experience. Even when compared with models of market
behavior, a high degree of abstraction remains in this approach to
political decisions. Testable implications of the theory are difficult
to derive, and testing itself presents serious problems. Defense of the
approach comes down, quite simply, to the faith that "some theory
is better than nothing."

The analysis developed is intended only as a first step toward
understanding this important fiscal institution. A more complete and
more complex treatment may lead to normative conclusions that
would be somewhat more in conformity with ruling opinion. The
most important element omitted has been that of decision-making
costs, in its various institutional manifestations. If this is given due
weight, the basic individualistic model may indicate that the segregation of revenues remains "inefficient" relative to consolidated
revenue schemes. The point to be stressed here is only that, if this
conclusion should be forthcoming, the added features must be
demonstrated to outweigh the distortions upon which the model of
individual fiscal choice focuses attention.

10

Optimality in Local Debt Limitation

Richard E. Wagner

In response to epidemics of debt default during the mid-nineteenth century, most American states imposed limitations upon the ability of both themselves and their local governments to issue general obligation, full faith and credit debt. In the aftermath of the Panic of 1837 and the ensuing depression of 1839–42, during which up to 53 per cent of state debt was in default, states began restricting their ability to issue debt. Presently, only six states allow debt to be issued by a simple majority vote of the state legislature. Twenty states, by contrast, require constitutional amendment before debt may be issued, and the remaining states occupy an intermediate position on this spectrum of restrictiveness toward borrowing. The experience of the states was repeated by local governments during the depression of 1873–78, when up to 20 per cent of local debt was in default.[1] In response the parent states began imposing limitations upon the ability of their local governments to issue general obligation debt, with the limitations being instituted primarily through constitutional rules that limited indebtedness to some percentage of assessed property values. Since the conclusion of World War II, only 30 cases of local debt default have occurred. Only four defaults involved ordinary city governments; only two defaults exceeded $100 million, both of which were toll roads. Although restrictions upon the ability of legislative majorities to undertake debt financing are a ubiquitous feature of state and local fiscal organization, scholarly support for

Reprinted by permission of the author and publisher from *National Tax Journal*, vol. XXIII, no. 3 (September 1970).

1. Actual losses seem to average about ten per cent of the amount in default [11, p. 12].

124   Theory of Public Choice

debt limitation now seems minuscule, as debt limitation has been assailed strenuously on both empirical and conceptual grounds.[2]

The empirical rejection of debt limitation is based upon the observation that, regardless of their possible conceptual merits, the limitations have been fully circumvented. Besides issuing full faith and credit debt, governments also issue nonguaranteed debt, primarily revenue bonds to finance specific projects such as bridges and stadiums, which is not included within the debt limits. Although full faith and credit is not pledged, which makes it necessary for the bonds to carry a risk premium of from one-half to one per cent for shifting the locus of risk from taxpayers to bondholders, governments nevertheless seem to regard it as their duty to prevent default. Mitchell's evidence [11, pp. 35–44] suggests that while debt limits have reduced general obligation debt, they have encouraged the use of nonguaranteed debt to an offsetting extent. Debt limits, then, seem to have had no restrictive impact upon debt creation, as one form of debt has been fully substituted for another.

Other techniques are also available for circumventing debt limits.[3] Since debt limits are held to apply to *each* governmental unit, the creation of special purpose districts enables debt limits to be avoided. If a city should create a special school district, for instance, the city's debt limit would double, as the limit would apply separately to the city and to the school district. Long-term leasing arrangements are also used to circumvent debt limits. A city may contract for the construction of some facility by agreeing to lease it at some specified price for some specified period of time, with the city assuming ownership at the end of the lease. Although the effect of this leasing arrangement is indistinguishable from debt financing, the future contracted rental payments are not considered debt at law, so the debt limits are avoided.

Debt limits are also rejected on conceptual grounds, where it is argued that, even should they prove effective in limiting debt creation, there is no need for them. As borrowing becomes undertaken less prudently, interest rates rise in response to the additional risk. Lenders are willing to continue lending so long as they are compensated for the rising risk, and borrowers are willing to continue borrowing so long as they believe the marginal gains exceed the marginal costs. So long as a debt transaction is agreeable to both

2. For some recent works hostile toward debt limitation, see Bowmar [3], Heins [8], [9], and Mitchell [11]. For a survey of local debt restrictions, with a recommendation that they be abolished, see the report of the Advisory Commission on Intergovernmental Relations [1].

3. See Bowmar [3] for a thorough description of these techniques.

borrower and lender, it must be presumed efficient as it is simply evidence of the exploitation of mutual gains from trade. When the citizenry feels that additional debt is no longer worth the price asked by lenders, they will cease borrowing. And, moreover, individuals cannot avoid their share of local debt obligations through migration, as capitalization will effectively prevent avoidance. Thus the equilibrium level of debt produced by competitive forces will be optimal.[4]

In this paper we shall re-examine the conceptual basis for local debt limitation. The standard rejection of debt limitation is based upon a common methodological confusion about the appropriate specification of parameters and variables in economic analysis; it is illegitimate to base conclusions about the operation of a *system* of local government upon a model of the behavior of a *single* local government when that model holds constant the behavior of all other localities.[5] As a means of introducing the basic analytical framework, we shall first summarize briefly a simple model of an individual's choice of personal debt. In the next two sections we shall examine in turn the debt choice of a single local government, which is the frame of reference within which debt limits have been rejected, and the debt choice of a system of local government. We shall conclude with some implications of the analysis for local debt limitation.

I. *Individual Choice and Personal Debt Policy*

Since we are interested in governmental debt choice, not in personal debt choice, we do not attempt in this section to contribute to the theory of an individual's choice between current and deferred means of payment. Rather we only describe a simple model that will be utilized in the subsequent analysis. Although it is common to distinguish between consumption loans and investment loans, we shall focus upon the consumption demand for credit. Common distinctions, of course, are often evasive. A consumer durable is an asset that produces a flow of services over its lifetime, yet household bor-

4. Bowmar concludes, for instance: "Let the local citizenry, their governing officials, and the market mechanism itself carry the burden of decision in any given case . . . With choice left in the hands of those who will benefit or suffer as the result of their intelligently exercised rights, one may safely let the future take care of itself" [3, p. 900].

5. For a careful discussion of the relevant issues, in a different context, complete with illustrations, see Buchanan [4].

rowing to purchase a consumer durable is considered a consumption loan.

There are many circumstances under which one might want to acquire a consumption loan to make it possible to consume now and to pay later, but they all have in common a desire to achieve some smoothing of the inter-temporal distribution of utility from consumption. Individuals typically experience an income stream that rises during the earlier years of life, peaks during the middle years, and declines during the later years. If the opportunity existed, they would probably choose to reduce consumption in the middle years to finance additional consumption in both the earlier and the later years. There is no difficulty in saving during the middle years to increase consumption in the later years, but there is little opportunity to borrow to increase consumption in the earlier years because of the inability of individuals to mortgage their future earnings.[6] Even should individuals expect constant annual incomes throughout their lifetimes, however, they will probably experience variability about this mean income. If so, individuals would probably desire to reduce their consumption in their above-average years to finance additional consumption in their below-average years. Moreover, even should actual annual incomes be equal throughout one's lifetime, there would still be inter-temporal variability in the rate of consumption due to the irregular purchase of consumer durables. If consumer durables are fully paid for at the time of purchase, the bundle of services consumed is smaller in the years of purchase than in the other years. By borrowing in this instance, the consumer is able to spread his payments over several time periods, which produces a smoother time path of consumption.

The limiting case of desired inter-temporal smoothing entails equal rates of consumption in each time period. Equal rates of consumption are preferred whenever the marginal utility of income diminishes within any period, while at the same time the income utility schedule is identical over all time periods. There is an inherent uncertainty associated with the future, of course, so people rationally exhibit positive time preference, and the income utility schedule declines as the future recedes from the present.

As a general principle of rational inter-temporal choice, a consumer should allocate his income between any two years such that $f'_i(C)/f'_j(C) = (1 + r)^{j-i}$, where $U = f(C)$ is the total utility function of consumption in year i and r is the rate of interest between

6. See Thurow [12].

years i and j. Positive time preference is usually defined by the condition that $f'_j(C) = \lambda f'_i(C)$, where $0 < \lambda < 1$. Following Thurow [12], however, it seems preferable to introduce time preference explicitly by rewriting the condition for inter-temporal allocation as $f'_i(C)/f'_j(C) = (1 + r_1 - r_2)^{j-i}$, where r_1 is the rate of interest and r_2 is the rate of time preference. With the explicit introduction of r_2, we now assume that the income utility schedule is invariant over time. Depending upon the consumer's preferences for consumption in alternative years, r_2, and his ability to transfer consumption from one year to another, r_1, he will choose some amount of reallocation of consumption.

The primary policy implication of the formal analysis of personal debt choice is that individuals should be allowed to enter into whatever borrowing arrangements they can make; personal debt limitation can be rationalized only on paternalistic grounds. So long as the consumer is willing to borrow at the quoted rate of interest, borrowing enables him to achieve a more satisfactory inter-temporal distribution of consumption. And the lender will lend so long as he expects the transaction to be profitable. The effects of the lending transaction are primarily confined to the borrower and the lender, and ordinary considerations of mutual gains from trade suggest the absence of external constraints upon the terms of the contract.[7]

11. *Debt Choice in a Single Locality*

With collective borrowing, as with personal borrowing, the durability of certain components of consumption creates an incentive to substitute loan finance for tax finance. As with a privately purchased house, automobile, or refrigerator, the damming of a river to create an artificial lake for recreational uses or the construction of a new civic center creates a durable asset that supplies a stream of consumption services over a succession of time periods. If such expenditures are financed wholly through taxation, significant inter-temporal variability will be introduced into individual consumption patterns. By spreading the cost over a series of years as the debt is amortized, public borrowing permits a smoothing of consumption over time. Each individual citizen will have some most preferred combination of loan finance and tax finance which will depend upon

7. On the contrary, Thurow [12] argues that consumers should be able to borrow more than they are currently able, for the inability to mortgage future earnings reduces borrowing below optimal amounts.

the prevailing tax institutions, interest rates, length of the loan, and time preference. When collective decisions are made by majority vote, the collective borrowing choice will be effectively exercised by the individual whose preferences are median for the group [2], [5, pp. 144–59]. Majority rule equilibrium results when the median preference voter finds himself in his utility maximizing equilibrium, with offsetting numbers of voters desiring greater and lesser borrowing.[8] The median voter will choose an amount of borrowing that allocates his personal consumption between any two years such that $f'_i(C)/f'_j(C) = (1 + r_1 - r_2)^{j-i}$. The median voter will not choose a greater amount of local debt because the utility he would gain from his additional present consumption would be less than the utility he would lose from his additional sacrifice of future consumption.

It would seem, however, that the standard model of personal debt choice does not describe adequately the local debt choice exercised by the median voter. Since individuals possess freedom of migration among the component local governments within the nation, it would seem that the marginal cost of loan finance to the median voter would be lowered by a positive probability of out-migration. When faced with the choice of local debt, the median preference voter will rationally choose to allocate his consumption between any two years such that $f_i(C)/f_j(C) = \lambda(1 + r_1 + r_2)^{j-i}$, where λ is the probability of remaining a resident of the community over the $j-i$ year period.[9] If $\lambda = 1$, the standard conditions are satisfied and optimality will result. If λ falls below unity, however, the median preference voter will choose an excessive amount of debt for the locality. If, as an extreme illustration, the median voter attaches a probability of zero that he will remain in that same local government in year two, he will prefer to finance all public expenditures

8. Buchanan and Tullock [16, pp. 147–69] have shown that majority rule equilibrium may not be fully efficient. Budgetary inefficiency may result, for instance, if majority coalitions are able to secure benefits for themselves that are financed by taxes levied upon the entire population. If both taxes and benefits are uniform over the population, by contrast, majority equilibrium will probably be efficient. The same conclusions are true if debt finance replaces tax finance. Since we are interested not in alternative voting rules but only in the special characteristics of local government debt policy, however, we shall ignore issues of appropriate voting rules in this paper, which can be accomplished formally through an assumption of uniformity in both taxation and public expenditure.

9. This is the simplest way of introducing λ. It could also have been introduced as some more complex functional relationship without substantial difference in implication.

in year one by debt issue, regardless of the rate of interest. Debt finance would increase his real income by enabling him to consume the publicly supplied services without reducing his private consumption. If the median voter's probability of out-migration is less than unity, his demand for debt finance will fall, though he would still vote for excessive debt as a means of increasing his real income. Yet total internal migration must sum to zero, so local debt choices which are based on positive rates of migration would seem to generate an excessive amount of local debt.[10]

When a locality chooses debt finance, it obligates its members to make future tax payments to amortize the debt. The present value of these future tax payments to any individual member of the community is $T = \sum_{i=1}^{n} t_i (1 + r)^{-i}$, where n is the length of the amortization period, r is the rate of interest on the loan, i is the year of the loan, and t_i is the individual's tax share for debt amortization in year i. The total present value of the community's future tax payments from the debt issue is the sum of the individual present values. But in a system of local government, the present value of each individual's future tax payments is reduced by his probability of out-migration. If we let λ_i denote the probability that the individual will reside in the community in year i, the present discounted value of the individual's future tax payments associated with local debt finance is $T_L = \sum_{i=1}^{n} \lambda_i t_i (1 + r)^{-i}$. Only if $\lambda_i = 1$ over the entire amortization period will no migration discount be applied to the present value of the future tax payments. Otherwise, the median voter will support debt finance on the basis of an expected private cost that is less than social cost, and an excessive amount of local debt will be chosen.

In our model of a single locality in a system of local government, however, individuals will be unable to escape the consequences of their debt choices through out-migration. Capitalization will take place, which will place the full consequences of the debt choice upon those who make it. If an excessive amount of local debt is chosen, the entire debt-expenditure-tax package is less efficient than alter-

10. Along these lines, U. K. Hicks [10, p. 179] has argued that "With the mobility of modern life . . . there is a real danger that local communities may vote for loan finance to such an extent that when the present generation of taxpayers moves away they leave an encumbered estate behind them . . . The propensity to over-borrowing which appears to exist in the U.S.A. relies on the comfortable belief that the cost of the capital works can be wholly thrown on to future taxpayers."

native uses of those resources, and capitalized property values in the locality should fall sufficiently to offset the inefficiency.[11] Suppose, for instance, that some individual leaves the locality at the end of period j. His share of the present value of unpaid future taxes is $\sum_{i=j+1}^{n} t_i \, (1+r)^{-i}$. The capitalized value of his property in the locality will fall by that amount; at the time of out-migration the market forces him to realize his share of the loss from the choice of excessive debt. We need not, of course, restrict ourselves to the assumption that the locality relies wholly on property taxes. If the locality uses income taxes, for instance, an in-migrant would enter the locality only upon receiving a premium on his expected future earnings that would compensate him for acquiring a share of the consequences of the excessive debt. Regardless of the particular tax institutions used within the locality, capitalization will tend to prevent individuals from escaping through migration the consequences of the debt choices of their local governments.[12]

III. *Debt Choice in a System of Localities*

In our previous model of the debt choice of a single locality, we saw that capitalization operates to prevent inefficiency in local debt choices. Since a single locality in a system of local government contains a minuscule share of the nation's stock of productive resources, its own actions will have only an imperceptible impact upon the rate of return on capital. Thus the single locality must take the interest rate as given; its own debt policies will not affect the rate of return on capital. Since capital is highly mobile, its rate of return must be approximately equal throughout the nation. An inefficient debt choice within a single locality will thus reduce the capital values of

11. See, for instance, Daly [7] and Heins [9] on the capitalization of the consequences of local debt choice.

12. It has been asserted frequently that individuals are subject to a public debt illusion, under which they fail to account fully for the future tax obligations that debt finance entails. Although an inefficient local loan will reduce local capital values, the loss is not realized until some future time period when the property is sold. With imperfect foresight individuals act as if current flows are indicative of capital values. Since their income streams are not reduced during the present period to reflect fully the reduction in capital values, they underestimate the tax cost of loan finance. Thus they choose too much debt in the present, and are sorry about it in the future when they must realize their losses. The issues of debt illusion, though interesting, are not directly relevant for our analysis, so they shall be disregarded.

those residents living in the locality at the time of the choice. Residents of the locality will be unable to escape the consequences of their inefficient debt choices through out-migration.

When we examine the debt choices of a single locality, we hold constant the debt choices of all other localities. This procedure is illegitimate, however, if we want to examine the operation of the entire *system* of local government. When all localities make similar debt choices, there are no untaxed localities to which capital can flow. If all localities choose excessive debt, the net rate of return on capital must fall. With this reduction in the rate of interest, the excessive use of debt finance by localities will not produce capitalization. When only some localities choose excessive debt, some capitalization will result. But still the incomplete capitalization makes it possible to escape through out-migration some of the consequences of choosing an excessive amount of local debt.

Without full capitalization, then, if the median voter of any locality faces a significant probability of out-migration, the choice of an excessive amount of debt finance relative to tax finance becomes likely, as it increases the present value of the expected stream of future consumption. Yet as the median voter out-migrates, he becomes an in-migrant to another community, which also has chosen excessive debt for similar reasons. When we examine the entire system of local government, we see that the income effects of local debt choices vanish; the gain in real income that accrues to the median voter in his initial locality is canceled by the loss in real income he suffers when he takes up residence in his new locality. Yet there remains the price effect, which induces median preference voters to support excessive debt. The residents of all localities are caught in a large-number analogue to the prisoners' dilemma. It is individually rational for any locality to choose excessive debt. Since the actions of the other localities must rationally be taken as given—as they are beyond the control of any single locality—the choice of an excessive amount of local debt is a way of increasing the real income of the median voter. Yet other localities act similarly. Thus the increase in income produced by the creation of excessive debt in the locality of origin is offset by the additional taxes that must be paid to amortize the excessive debt in the community of destination. Although income effects cancel on the average, price effects remain, and it is the migration-induced reduction in the price of debt finance that produces the excessive use of debt finance by localities.[13]

13. For a demonstration, in a different context, that in-migration and out-migration do not produce offsetting effects, even though their magnitudes may be equal, see Weisbrod [13].

These points may be illustrated with reference to Figure 1, which indicates the debt choice of the median voter of a single locality. The axes indicate consumption in years two and one. If the median voter has a zero probability of out-migration, his budget constraint has a slope of $-(1 + r_1 - r_2)$, which is illustrated by the solid line ab. Under these conditions the median voter chooses to consume c_1, c_2 over the two year period. When, however, the indi-

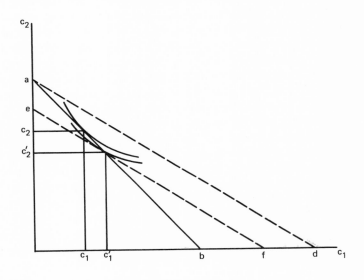

Figure 1

vidual senses a positive probability of out-migration, the price of consumption in year one is reduced relative to its price in year two. The slope of the budget constraint becomes $-(1 + r_1 - r_2)\lambda$, which is illustrated by the dashed line ad. If only a single locality issues debt, of course, capitalization restores the initial budget line ab. But in a system of local government with all localities issuing debt, capitalization will not take place. But the absence of capitalization implies that an out-migrant, though he might escape some of the burden of the debt choices within his original community, becomes liable for some of the burden of the debt choices of his new community. On the average for the entire system of local government, the income effect must cancel. Yet the price effect remains, which produces the budget constraint ef. The reduction in the price of debt finance that is produced by migration induces an alternative distribution of consumption, c'_1, c'_2, where total borrowing has increased.

Since the median voter also leaves behind his benefits when he migrates, the existence of a positive probability of out-migration also produces discounting of the present value of the future benefits from debt finance. If the time path of the future stream of benefits matches exactly the time path of the future stream of taxes, excessive debt finance will not result. With such exact matching of taxes and benefits through time, regardless of what point in time the median voter expects to migrate, he will always expect his taxes paid to equal his benefits received; a project that yields equal annual benefits for ten years, for instance, must be financed over a ten year period at a constant rate of amortization. Yet the cost discounting that is induced by migration makes it rational for individuals *not* to choose debt amortization in this manner, but, instead, to support mismatching of tax and benefit streams. If a median voter expects to reside in a community for ten years, for instance, he would rationally prefer a 20-year amortization period to a ten-year period. Although a median voter might support debt finance under a 20-year amortization period if he expects to live in the community only ten years, he might reject the debt issue if he had to live in the community the entire 20 years, or, similarly, if the amortization period were only ten years. The survival value of perfect matching of taxes and benefits through time seems weak, so excessive debt finance seems likely to result unless external constraints are placed upon local borrowing decisions.

I v. *Conclusions and Implications*

The case for imposing statutory limitations upon the debt creating freedom of local government rests, therefore, on the virtual certainty that such units will, in the absence of limits, issue amounts of debt in excess of socially optimum levels. The cost of local debt choices is discounted by the probability that the median voter will migrate to another locality. Since internal migration must sum to zero, however, this migration-induced reduction in the price of debt finance does not reflect the social cost of local debt choices. Rather, the cost of debt finance faced by a single locality will be less than the social cost of debt finance, so local governments will tend to rely excessively upon debt finance relative to tax finance.

Although it is probably correct that debt limits have been circumvented sufficiently to make them ineffective, this empirical observation does not refute the conceptual rationale for debt limitation, nor does it deny that debt limitation can be made more effective. We noted earlier that the primary means of circumventing debt limits are through the creation of special districts, the use of non-guaranteed revenue bonds, and the development of special lease-purchase arrangements. Each of these loopholes can be tightened. Lease-purchasing arrangements can be handled by considering the capitalized value of long-term rental contracts as debt. Nonguaranteed bonds can be counted within the debt limits, or, alternatively, local governments can be prohibited from acting to prevent default. Finally, incentives to the creation of special districts can be reduced by setting debt limits on some alternative basis, as, for example, by establishing maximum ratios of debt to per capita income within any county, which would make debt limits invariant to changes in governmental organization.[14]

Besides tightening loopholes in the administration of debt limits, the analysis contains other implications for debt policy. The shorter the period for which a loan is made, the greater the likelihood that the loan will be amortized before the median voter expects to migrate to another locality, and the less the tendency toward excessive borrowing. Since individuals are more likely to migrate among localities within a state than to migrate among states, localities would be subject to stronger tendencies toward overborrowing than states. This tendency seems to imply that, first, debt limitation should impinge more strongly upon local borrowing than upon state borrowing, and, second, debt issued by localities should contain a shorter period of amortization than debt issued by states.

The existence of a conceptual basis for local debt limitation does not imply by itself, of course, that actual debt limits are optimal, or that they are less inefficient than unfettered local borrowing. Collective choices themselves will sometimes generate external costs, and the external costs of state-imposed debt limits might exceed the external costs of unfettered local borrowing. So long as democratic processes of fiscal choice produce results as if state limits on local debt are chosen by majority vote among the constituent localities, the debt limit chosen by the state will be the limit preferred by the locality with the median preference toward debt limitation. And state limits on local debt will tend to be Pareto efficient if they tend to be equal to the mean of the limits preferred by the localities. If the limit preferred by the median preference locality is greater than the mean preference within the state, the state limit on local debt

14. Not only do debt limits, as currently administered, encourage governmental fragmentation as a device for avoiding the limits, but also they discourage what might otherwise be profitable consolidation because the consolidation would violate the limits. See Bowmar [3, pp. 892–93].

will be excessively permissive. If, by contrast, the limit preferred by the median preference locality is less than the mean preference within the state, the state limit on local debt will be excessively restrictive. Before debt limitation can be rejected in favor of unfettered local borrowing, however, not only must the median preference toward debt finance be less than the mean preference, which, other things equal, requires that the rate of out-migration in the median locality be less than the mean rate of out-migration, but also it must be shown that the inefficiency cost of local debt limitation is larger than the inefficiency cost of unfettered local borrowing.

References

1. Advisory Commission on Intergovernmental Relations, *State Constitutional and Statutory Restrictions on Local Government Debt*, Washington, 1961.
2. D. Black, *The Theory of Committees and Elections*, Cambridge, 1958.
3. R. H. Bowmar, "The Anachronism Called Debt Limitation," *Iowa Law Review*, 52 (1967), 863–900.
4. J. M. Buchanan, "Ceteris Paribus: Some Notes on Methodology," *Southern Economic Journal*, 24 (January 1958), 259–70.
5. ————, *Public Finance in Democratic Process*, Chapel Hill, 1967.
6. ———— and G. Tullock, *The Calculus of Consent*, Ann Arbor, 1962.
7. G. C. Daly, "The Burden of the Debt and Future Generations in Local Finance," *Southern Economic Journal*, 36 (July 1969), 44–51.
8. A. J. Heins, *Constitutional Restrictions Against State Debt*, Madison, 1963.
9. ————, "Elements of a Theory of Local Borrowing," *Proceedings of the National Tax Association*, 60 (1967), 75–86.
10. U. K. Hicks, "Autonomous Revenue for Local Government," *Western Economic Journal*, 6 (June 1968), 177–94.
11. W. E. Mitchell, *The Effectiveness of Debt Limits on State and Local Government Borrowing*, New York, 1967.
12. L. C. Thurow, "The Optimum Lifetime Distribution of Consumption Expenditures," *American Economic Review*, 59 (June 1969), 324–30.
13. B. A. Weisbrod, *External Benefits of Public Education*, Princeton, 1964.

11

Conscription, Voluntary Service, and Democratic Fiscal Choice

Richard E. Wagner

A consensus among economists seems to exist about the effects of military conscription upon the distribution of income and the allocation of resources.[1] Distributionally, conscription, as contrasted with voluntary military service, transfers income from conscriptees to nonconscriptees. Conscription places a special tax-in-kind upon conscriptees that would not exist under voluntary military service. Allocationally, conscription generates technical inefficiencies in the allocation of resources, which produces a lower level of real national income than would result under voluntary military service. Allocational inefficiencies include (1) excessively labor-intensive modes of production within the military sector, (2) increased uncertainty in individual planning decisions, and (3) increased rates of turnover in military manpower. Such technical inefficiencies move the community to some point inside the boundary of its production frontier. Although nonconscriptees secure redistributive gains at the expense of conscriptees, the technical inefficiencies that result make the entire game negative sum.

Our aim in this paper is to re-examine military conscription from an alternative, supplementary frame of reference. The standard frame of reference is one of market-oriented, private choice; the size and the composition of the public budget is taken as given, and the effects of alternative fiscal institutions (conscription and voluntary service) upon the distribution of income and the allocation of resources are then explored. Once we recognize that economists need

1. For recent analyses see Altman and Fechter [1], Bailey and Cargill [2], Berney [3], Bradford [8], Davis and Palomba [13], Fisher [17], Hansen and Weisbrod [18], Miller [20], Oi [21], and Renshaw [24].

not take fiscal choices as given data, however, it becomes appropriate to use economic analysis in examining the impact of these alternative institutions upon the budgetary patterns that emerge through democratic processes of fiscal choice.[2] In this paper we contrast conscription and voluntary service with respect to (1) the choice of size of the military budget, (2) the choice of output mix within the public budget, and (3) the choice of the degree of militancy in military-foreign policy.

1. *Conscription and the Democratic Choice of Military Budgets*

Let us initially assume a two-good world of "guns" and "flowers," with "guns" a surrogate for all military services and "flowers" a surrogate for all civilian, nonmilitary services. A community of n individuals bound by simple majority rule must decide to supply themselves with some quantity of guns. To establish the setting, we shall assume that, from an initial situation in which no guns are supplied, a sudden increase in the demand for military activity has created disequilibrium in the allocation of resources. We shall first describe the budgetary equilibrium that results when both the capital and the labor inputs into the supply of guns are secured through voluntary exchange. We shall then introduce the conscription of labor inputs and compare the impact upon the size of the budget.

We assume that each voter i has some utility function $U_i = f_i(F,G)$, where F denotes the quantity of flowers available to the individual and G denotes the quanitity of guns available to the collectivity.[3] If able, each individual would maximize his utility subject

2. This reversal of emphasis is explored in Buchanan [10]. For a more general discussion see Black [4].

3. For simplicity we have assumed that individuals are concerned only about the size of the military budget. Actually, of course, the composition is also relevant. The optimal composition of our military budget would depend, among other things, upon the identification of our enemies. Intermediate-range ballistic missiles would assume more importance relative to intercontinental ballistic missiles, for instance, if Canada and Mexico replaced China and the Soviet Union as our major enemies. For a discussion of joint optimality in both the size and the composition of the budget, see Buchanan [9, pp. 56–65]. Since we want to focus our discussion upon the size of the military budget, we shall assume that the composition of the budget is optimal.

We should perhaps also note at this time that the marginal utility of guns may not be positive over all sizes of the budget. Some people, for instance, may believe that increases in the military budget will initiate a negative-sum arms race.

to the budget constraint, $P_F F + P_G G = I_i$, where I_i is the income of individual i, and P_F and P_G are the prices of flowers and guns respectively. The standard conditions for consumer optimality, of course, are $\partial f_i / \partial F = -\lambda P_F$ for flowers and $\partial f_i / \partial G = -\lambda P_G$ for guns.[4] Individual citizens, however, are seldom able to choose their most preferred combination of guns and flowers. In a two-party system each citizen is offered only two quantities of guns from which to choose, corresponding to the platforms of the two candidates. Only a fraction of the citizenry will find that the quantity of guns proposed by one of the political candidates is also their most preferred quantity; and even in this event the preferred candidate may be defeated in the election. The remainder of the citizenry must choose among two candidates, neither of whom proposes that budgetary pattern that any of them most prefers. Those citizens who face this situation will vote for the candidate whose platform yields them the lesser loss of utility.[5]

For any individual i, $T_i = T_i(G)$ relates his share of the total tax charge for guns to the quantity of guns supplied, which in the two-good case is also his evaluation of the flowers sacrificed to procure the guns. Likewise, $E_i = E_i(G)$ relates his total evaluation of the guns supplied to the quantity of guns supplied. So long as $E'_i(G) > T'_i(G)$, the individual will prefer to have more guns supplied, as his marginal evaluation of the guns exceeds his marginal evaluation of the flowers that he must sacrifice to get those guns. The individual's most preferred rate of guns supply, size of military budget, is that

4. Although we ordinarily think in terms of tax rates and tax payments instead of tax prices, a simple relationship exists among these three concepts. If revenues are raised through an income tax, budgetary equilibrium will find $P_G G = t_i I_i$, where t_i is the average rate of tax paid by individual i. Since the same quantity of guns is made available to all members of the collectivity, we have $P_{Gi} \propto t_i I_i$ for any individual, i. With proportional income taxation, tax-prices will rise as income increases. With progressive income taxation, tax-prices will rise more rapidly as income increases because the average rate of tax itself rises as income increases.

5. Let (F^*, G^*) denote the most preferred bundle of guns and flowers for some individual. Each candidate announces some position toward the supply of G, which residually determines a quantity of F available to each individual. Letting the subscript $j = 1,2$ denote the two candidates, the individual would choose that candidate for which $f_i(F^*, G^*) - f_i(F_j, G_j)$ is smaller, assuming cardinality of utility. For a discussion of voter choice among two candidates under these circumstances, see Davis and Hinich [14].

for which $E'_i(G) = T'_i(G)$,[6] assuming satisfaction of the second-order conditions.[7]

Let $T = (T'_1(G), T'_2(G), \ldots, T'_n(G))$ denote a row vector of marginal tax prices, where $T > 0$. Similarly, let $E = (E'_1(G), E'_2(G), \ldots, E'_n(G))$ denote a row vector of marginal expenditure evaluations, where $E > 0$. From these vectors, define a vector of net marginal preferences, P, such that $P = -T+E$. In voting on marginal increases in the quantity of guns, any individual i will favor more guns so long as $P_i > 0$, for he will value the additional guns more highly than the flowers he must sacrifice. A collective decision to expand the supply of guns will result so long as $P_i > 0$ for $k > (n + 1)/2$ individuals, where n is odd.[8] Equilibrium in the collective supply of arms will be attained when:

$P_i > 0$ for $(n - 1)/2$ individuals $i = 1, 2, \ldots, j - 1$
$P_i = 0$ for 1 individual $i = j$, and
$P_i < 0$ for $(n - 1)/2$ individuals $i = j + 1, j + 2, \ldots, n$.

The first group has above-median preferences, the last group has below-median preferences, and individual j is the median preference voter. In this median voter model, some quantity of guns, say G_0, will be supplied. Individual tax payments, r, will be $r = G_0 T'_i(G)$,[9] and total tax payments, R, will be $R = G_0 T_\mu$.[10]

We can now examine the effect of conscription upon the collective supply of guns. Conscription is a form of discriminatory taxation,

6. For analytical simplicity we develop our model with the use of marginal valuation functions rather than with the use of the standard framework of utility maximization. Although models based on marginal valuation functions are not suitable for locating equilibrium positions, they are appropriate for showing the characteristics of equilibrium positions. For a discussion of marginal tax prices and marginal expenditure evaluations as they relate to public goods supply, including a discussion of their usefulness and their limitation, see Buchanan [9, pp. 39–43].

7. We would normally expect $E''_i(G) < 0$, and $T''_i(G) > 0$, which satisfies these conditions. For the most part, however, we shall assume $T''_i = 0$, as this assumption of constant marginal tax-price per unit both simplifies and lends precision to some of the analysis without restricting it unduly.

8. With n even, the required condition is $P_i > 0$ for $k > (n/2) + 1$ individuals.

9. This is a consequence of our assumption that $T_i(G) = 0$. To handle nonconstant marginal tax pricing, the general case would be $r = \int T_i'(G) \, dG$.

10. μ is a column vector of unities which is necessary to reduce R to a single number.

though obviously not a form considered unconstitutional.[11] When
the tax-in-kind imposed upon conscriptees is added to the prevailing set of monetary taxes, we find that conscriptees pay higher tax
prices for guns than nonconscriptees of equal income. The imposition of conscription by itself is merely a transfer of income from conscriptees to nonconscriptees. Let λ denote a column vector of multi-
pliers, $\lambda = (\lambda_1, \lambda_2, \ldots, \lambda_n)$, such that $G_0 T_\mu = G_0 T_\lambda$. Conscription
then alters the structure of tax prices such that $\lambda_i > 1$ for conscriptees
and $1 > \lambda_i > 0$ for nonconscriptees. Per unit tax prices become
$T'_i(G)\lambda_i$, and individual tax payments become $G_0 T'_i(G)\lambda_i$. Through
the operation of democratic processes of fiscal choice, however, this
change in the structure of tax prices will produce a change in the
quantity of guns chosen by the collectivity. We shall examine how
the change in fiscal institution produces a change in budgetary policy
both when conscriptees are excluded from the voting population
and when conscriptees are included in the voting population.[12]

When conscriptees, or those in the pool from which conscriptees
are chosen, are excluded from the voting population, their P_i's will
not influence collective choice, except to the extent that there are
voters who are personally interested in particular members of the
pool more strongly than they are interested in themselves. Since
$T'_i(G)\lambda_i < T'_i(G)$ for nonconscriptees, $P_i > 0$ must continue to hold
under conscription for those $(n-1)/2$ individuals for whom it
held under voluntary service. Similarly, the median preference individual, j, must now find $P_i > 0$. And for the $(n-1)/2$ individuals
for whom $P_i < 0$ held under voluntary service, some will now find
$P_i > 0$, under reasonable assumptions about the variability of P about
the median preference individual, j, and about the structure of con-
scription-induced changes in T.[13] G_0 is no longer an equilibrium

11. For a discussion of constitutional restrictions against discriminatory taxation, see Tuerck [26].

12. There is some question as to whether "voters" should refer to
individuals or to families, and as to whether "conscriptees" should refer
ex post to those conscripted or *ex ante* to those in the pool from which
conscriptees will be chosen. The amount of the tax-in-kind paid by conscriptees will be smaller if the family and the *ex ante* interpretations are
used. Since we are interested primarily in comparing the differential impact of changing from conscription to voluntary service, however, for the
most part it seems more important to maintain consistency in usage between the models than to select "the" framework that is most appropriate
in some absolute sense.

13. These two caveats about reasonable assumptions both pertain to
conceivable but improbable circumstances. First, significant discontinuity

level of guns supply once conscription replaces voluntary service. Expansion in the supply of guns will result because $P_i > 0$ for $k > (n + 1)/2$ members of the voting population, and it will continue until a new equilibrium is attained where, say, G_1 is supplied. This new equilibrium will satisfy the previously described condition for equilibrium under majority rule.

With conscriptees, or those in the pool from which conscriptees are selected, having voting rights, the analysis may be modified slightly, and we shall examine two polar cases. In the first case, we assume that all conscriptees are in the group for whom $P_i < 0$ under voluntary service. Even if we assume that this group is composed wholly of conscriptees (i.e., that $(n - 1)/2$ of the population is conscripted), the preceding analysis holds without exception, for $P_j > 0$ after conscription. If less than $(n - 1)/2$ of the voting population is conscripted, some individuals who formerly found $P_i < 0$ now find $P_i > 0$ due to the shift in tax prices, and an additional increase in the supply of guns will result.

Giving conscriptees voting rights, then, can affect the outcome only when at least some conscriptees are in the group for whom $P_i > 0$ under voluntary service. As with the first polar case, we can assume that all conscriptees are in this group.[14] For the conscriptees, the most likely event would seem to be that $P_i < 0$ after conscription.[15] For the supply of arms to expand in this case, the reverse

---

could exist in the distribution of P_i about P_j. For the set of below-median preference individuals, there may exist some gap by which T_i exceeds E_i. If so, it is possible that reductions in T_i could still leave $P_i < 0$ for all individuals in the set. It seems more reasonable, however, to assume continuous variability about P_j, especially in large number situations.

Second, in combination with discontinuity in P, the expansion in guns would not occur if the tax-price reductions were given in highly selective fashion. The simplest form would occur if the reductions were given only to those $(n - 1)/2$ individuals for whom $P_i > 0$ held under voluntary service. Above all, none of the tax-price reduction can be given to the median preference individual, j. Selective tax-price reductions can be given to the $(n - 1)/2$ individuals for whom $P_i < 0$ held under voluntary service, so long as this inequality condition is not violated. Since tax instruments ordinarily apply generally to the entire population, however, the blatant tax discrimination that would be required seems unlikely.

14. The most reasonable assumption is perhaps that of random variation in $E_i'(G)$, which would produce an expectation of equal distribution among both sets under voluntary service.

15. This is not necessarily true, however, as it requires that λ_i for conscriptees be sufficiently large. Before conscription, we assume $T_i'(G)$

movement in P_i must take place for a greater number of nonconscriptees, and the final outcome will depend upon the reordering of conscriptees and nonconscriptees that takes place.

If the collective supply of arms increases to G_1, the military budget increases by $(G_1 - G_0)T_\lambda$, when expressed in real terms—in terms of sacrificed flower values. For the minority coalition, conscriptees, $G_1T'_i(G)\lambda_i > G_0T'_i(G)$, for both $G_1 > G_0$ and $\lambda_i > 1$. For the majority coalition, nonconscriptees, by contrast, $G_1T'_i(G)\lambda_i$ may be $\gtreqless G_0T'_i(G)$, as $G_1 > G_0$ is opposed by $\lambda_i < 1$. If we assume some inelasticity in the demand for military services, total payments by nonconscriptees will be reduced, though by less than the increase to conscriptees.

When we extend our analysis to examine behavior in collective choice, we see that conscription will generate allocative inefficiencies, even if we assume that there are no technical allocative inefficiencies in the ordinary sense of the term.[16] It seems reasonable to suppose that military services are one of those activities for which preferences are distributed normally, or at least symmetrically about the mean. If so, budgetary choice under majority rule is likely to be an optimal institutional arrangement, provided that taxes are levied nondiscriminatorily among the citizenry [11, pp. 167–68]. Conscription, however, is a form of discriminatory taxation; conscriptees are charged higher tax prices for guns than equally situated nonconscriptees. Budgetary choice will be exercised by a majority coalition, which takes account of only the marginal cost to its members. When tax discrimination prevails due to conscription, however, the marginal cost to the members of the majority coalition, which in per capita terms is

$$\frac{\sum_{i=1}^{j} T'_i(G)\lambda_i}{j},$$

is less than the marginal cost to the members of the entire community, which in per capita terms is

$$\frac{\sum_{i=1}^{j} T'_i(G)\lambda_i}{n} + \frac{\sum_{i=j+1}^{n} T'_i(G)\lambda_i}{n}.$$

Since the budgetary choice will be based upon a marginal private cost to the members of the majority coalition that is less than the

---

$< E_i'(G)$ for conscriptees. After conscription, $T_i'(G)\lambda_i > E_i'(G)$ must hold before it can be asserted that $P_i < 0$ for conscriptees.

16. Such as those inefficiencies listed above.

marginal social cost to the members of the entire community, tax discrimination is subject to the standard Pigovian critique about the divergence between marginal private cost and marginal social cost [11, pp. 164–167; 12, pp. 10–13].

When conscription introduces technical inefficiencies into the allocation of resources, moreover, a new dimension must be added to our examination of democratic fiscal choice. Any technical inefficiency increases the quantity of flowers that must be sacrificed to get any given increase in the quantity of guns. Inefficiency in this case exists in both a utility and a production sense. The community no longer resides at some point beneath its production frontier. This additional, excessive quantity of flowers sacrificed under conscription is also part of the price of guns. The price of guns under conscription thus has two components: (1) the payments that people make directly (both monetary and in-kind) and (2) the indirect payments that become paid as they are transmitted through the general operation of the economy rather than through direct charges placed upon taxpayers, even though, of course, the payments must ultimately be extracted from identifiable individuals.

Choice, of course, is based upon one's perception of sacrifice, not upon some computation of "true" sacrifice.[17] Under ordinary circumstances an increase in the quantity of guns will require a reduction in the quantity of flowers. "Incidence" describes the distribution of this cost among the citizenry. Some such pattern of cost can be computed for any increase in the quantity of guns supplied. If individuals do not directly associate the increase in the quantity of guns with a reduction in their real income, however, they will sense the fiscal action as costless.[18] Incidence, as ordinarily defined, is irrelevant to an examination of behavior in fiscal choice. Under conscription fiscal choice is based upon a perceived tax-price (direct tax-price) that is less than the real (or correctly perceived) tax-price (direct tax-price plus technical allocative inefficiency). Since the lower, perceived tax-price of guns is the one relevant for explaining collective choice, the technical allocative inefficiencies associated with conscription, by generating an under-estimation of the price of guns, will produce an even greater increase in the quantity of guns supplied under conscription.[19]

17. For an interesting development of some of these issues, in a more general context, see Boulding [6].
18. For a seminal work on fiscal perception, see Puviani [23].
19. Our analysis has been developed within a framework of direct democracy. Following such examples as Downs [16], we could have introduced party competition and indirect democracy. This would have

11. *Conscription, Voluntary Service, and the Collective Choice of Budgetary Mix*

In addition to arms, various nonmilitary services are also supplied collectively, and an institutional shift from conscription to voluntary service will change both the size and the composition of the budget. To examine both types of budgetary change, we must introduce a third good into our model. We now let "flowers" denote a surrogate for all nonmilitary public services. "Guns" and "flowers" together then correspond to the "public goods" of the more familiar public goods-private goods frame of analysis. We let "bread" denote the private good. Besides voluntary military service, compulsory national service has received considerable support as a replacement for conscription. Since January 1, 1970, moreover, a lottery selection of conscriptees has been used in place of the former means of selection.[20] As we shall see, each of the institutional alternatives will affect differently both the size and the composition of the public budget.

Selection of conscriptees by lottery should not produce results significantly different from those produced by the former means of selecting conscriptees. Presumably, the same number of conscriptees will be chosen and they will pay the same rate of tax-in-kind. Lottery selection will change only the identities of those conscripted, which may, of course, produce second-order consequences. Second-order consequences aside, however, lottery selection only changes the rules for selecting conscriptees, so the status quo would be maintained between guns, flowers, and bread; lottery selection, by itself,

---

produced a two-stage model: an analysis of fiscal choice within legislative assemblies, and an analysis of voter choice among legislative candidates. In terms of the framework of this paper, however, the additional complexity would not produce any significant difference in results. Within each district the winning candidate would tend to have median preferences, and within the legislative assembly the median preference among the legislators would dominate. (Davis and Hinich [14] have shown that in a multi-issue setting, the mean preference will tend to survive in a system of two-party competition.)

There is currently, of course, considerably less agreement over the appropriate balance between "realistic" and "simplified" assumptions in the theory of collective choice than there is in the theory of private choice. Yet, Buchanan and Tullock [11, pp. 230–31] are probably correct in arguing that the analysis of collective choice has remained underdeveloped at least partly because an excessive concentration on political "reality" has impeded the development of fruitful models of collective choice.

20. See Tax [25], for a collection of papers discussing the major alternatives.

should produce no significant change in either the size or the composition of the public budget.

Compulsory national service, by contrast, would extend labor conscription to the provision of flowers. As a result, the price of public goods (guns and flowers) would fall relative to the price of the private good (bread). Operating through such democratic processes of fiscal choice as we have examined above, the real size of the budget would rise. Within the budget, moreover, the price of flowers would fall relative to the price of guns, so the budgetary mix would tend to shift towards a relatively greater supply of flowers.[21]

If conscription should be replaced by voluntary service, the implicit taxes levied upon conscriptees would be transformed into explicit taxes levied upon taxpayers. Such an institutional change would increase the budgetary outlays required to supply any given quantity of guns. With the increase in the tax-price of public goods, democratic processes of fiscal choice would tend to operate to reduce the real size of the budget and to increase the real quantity of bread supplied. Within the budget the price of guns would rise relative to the price of flowers, so the composition of the budget would change in the direction of a relatively greater supply of flowers.

Since lottery selection would not differ from the former form of conscription, only voluntary service and national service would affect the pattern of budgetary choice. The real size of the budget would fall under voluntary service and rise under national service. Within the budget both alternatives produce a decrease in the relative supply of guns. We cannot say a priori, however, what will happen to the real supply of flowers under voluntary service, where flowers occupy an increased share of a smaller budget. Nor can we say what will happen to the real supply of guns under national service, where guns occupy a reduced share of a larger budget.

III. *Conscription, Voluntary Service, and Democratic Warfare Choice*

Discussions of alternative institutional forms for procuring military manpower are usually qualified with an observation that while vol-

21. As with conscription in the supply of guns, moreover, compulsory national service in the supply of flowers is likely to generate technical inefficiency in the allocation of resources. Although such inefficiencies are part of the cost of flowers, this cost is not apparent to any individual, but exerts itself through the operation of the economy. This fiscal illusion will lead people to underestimate the cost of flowers, so an even greater expansion in the quantity of flowers supplied will result.

untary service would probably work well during peacetime, conscription would probably be required during periods of national emergency.[22] Such an observation appears deceptively reasonable, for it ignores the manner in which the institutions of collective choice themselves influence the existence of a state of national emergency. For an individual, a state of personal emergency can be defined in terms of the cost of failing to take some corrective action within some short period of time; the greater the cost or the shorter the time period within which action must be taken, the more critical the situation. A person confronts a more critical situation, for instance, if he is bitten by a fer-de-lance than if he is bitten in the same place by a copperhead.

An additional dimension is introduced, however, when we ask whether a collectivity is confronting a critical situation. The citizenry must reach some agreement that a situation is critical, and individuals may reasonably differ as to both their estimation of the objective consequences of failing to take remedial action and their willingness to gamble on different patterns of outcome. Thus, aside from social consensus, there is no unambiguous criteria for distinguishing critical from noncritical situations. A critical situation exists whenever a ruling coalition says, through its pattern of choice, that one exists. The institutional framework within which collective choices are made will itself partially determine whether some state of affairs will become considered critical. Under such circumstances we should expect to find that a situation revealed as critical under one set of institutions may not be revealed as critical under an alternative set of institutions.[23]

In our preceding analysis of the collective choice of the quantity of guns, we allowed continuous variability in the quantity of guns. Decisions about warfare, however, are largely binary. Either we must or we must not decide to undertake military action. Either we must continue or we must cease some military action to which we previously committed ourselves.[24] In examining collective choice

22. See, for example, Hansen and Weisbrod [18, p. 401].

23. Although "crisis" has no objective meaning, it is, of course, a prominent part of the rhetoric of political competition. The description of a situation as "critical" is commonly used in an attempt to gain support, and we seem to have currently arrived at a point where everything is "critical"—another illustration of the tendency toward price uniformity under competition.

24. If some room exists, of course, for variability in the size of the military force used to fight the war. Different force sizes alter the probabilities of military success, and considerable variability in force size is possible within the context of a positive choice to undertake some military

about war, therefore, we must examine the threshold between positive and negative decisions. A positive decision to fight a war, once made, will not be revoked by a marginal decrease in preferences for the activity, but will be revoked only if the decrease in preferences bridges some discrete threshold.[25] The relevance of models of continuous variation in this context lies in comparing the differential impacts of alternative institutions upon the probable bridging of the threshold. By observing the differential between alternative institutions in a context of continuous variation, our analysis can say something about the relative likelihoods that the threshold will be bridged.[26]

There are four sets of circumstances under which we may examine the implications of alternative institutions for the likelihood that the threshold will be bridged and a decision will be changed. On the one hand, we may distinguish between those situations in which a war is currently being fought and those in which it is not. On the other hand, we may distinguish between those cases in which the perception of threat is diminished and those cases in which the perception of threat is intensified. Thus a war may currently be in progress, with perceptions of threat (preference for the war) either diminishing or intensifying. Or we may currently be free from warfare, with perceptions of threat (preferences for some potential war) either diminishing or intensifying. Of the four cases, only two are of analytical interest, as only they introduce phenomena associated with bridging the threshold necessary to reverse previously chosen courses of action. These two cases are (1) a diminution of the perception of threat while a war is in progress and (2) an intensification of the perception of external threat while we are currently free from warfare. We shall examine only the first case, as the analysis is applicable symmetrically to the second case.

Let us assume, then, that some time in the past a decision to engage in warfare emerged through normal democratic processes. Since that decision was made, however, preferences for the military action have fallen among at least some of the citizenry, without offsetting increases in preferences among the remainder of the citizenry. We now want to compare the impact of conscription and voluntary

---

action. The scope of this type of variability seems limited, however, and a significant element of discreteness must exist in warfare choice.

25. For a comparison of threshold-sensitive models with hypersensitive models, see Devletoglou [15].

26. Although, because of the discreteness, the collective decision may remain unchanged, as stickiness in the face of small changes is characteristic of threshold-sensitivity.

service upon the likelihood that the threshold will be bridged which would revoke the decision to engage in military action.

In the simplest, most responsive model of democratic choice, the reduction in support for the war will potentially influence the choice of the collectivity only to the extent that the preferences of the median voter have changed.[27] It is possible, of course, that the reduction in preferences occurs wholly among individuals whose preferences do not lie in the median range. Those strongly hostile to the initial decision to engage in warfare, for instance, could become even more hostile. Or those strongly in favor of the initial decision could become somewhat less favorable. Under such circumstances, when conscription is practiced, the initial decision will be continued. Even if the fall in preferences lies within the median range, moreover, the necessary threshold may not have been bridged.

Under voluntary service, by contrast, so long as at least some of those with reduced preferences are those who supply military labor, the previous warfare decision may be rescinded even though there has been no change in preferences among the median ranges of the citizenry. When the situation seems less critical to those who supply military labor, the war can be continued only if tax-prices are increased sufficiently to finance the higher wage payments required to maintain the necessary quantity of labor.[28] If the preferences of those supplying military labor do not fall, of course, the tax-price increase will not take place. In this case conscription and voluntary service have the identical impact upon the democratic warfare decision. Whenever some of the reductions in preference lie among those providing military labor, however, democratic institutions of budgetary choice are more likely to produce a change in the warfare decision under voluntary service than under conscription. With increased tax payments required to maintain the supply of military labor, the price of the war would rise to the voters in the median range of preferences (as well as to the other voters), so long as the revenues were raised through general forms of taxation. Even though

27. In more complex, less responsive models, a change in the preferences of the median voter transmits itself less directly into changes in collective choice. In such circumstances, the simpler model only indicates general tendencies.

28. For a recognition of the possible effects of preference changes upon the tax-prices required under voluntary service, see Hildebrand [19]. "Men are more likely to volunteer at a given rate of pay when they are convinced that the nation's security is threatened than when they are doubtful that such is the case. . . ." [19, p. 641]. See also Boulding [7].

preferences for the war among voters in the median range have not changed, the price they must pay for the war will rise. The stronger this rise in tax-price, the greater the likelihood that voters in the median range of preference would like to see the warfare decision reversed, and the greater the likelihood that political competition will produce such a reversal. Although the increase in tax-price may not be sufficiently strong to bridge the decision threshold, the threshold seems more likely to be bridged, or seems likely to be bridged more rapidly, under voluntary service than under conscription.[29]

To summarize, then, conscription seems to increase the likelihood that a "national emergency" will happen.[30] When, for whatever reason, the members of a democratic society differ in their willingness to undertake warfare, a positive warfare decision seems more likely under conscription than under voluntary service. The cost to the members of the controlling coalition of choosing to have a "national emergency" is less under conscription than under voluntary service. A greater number of situations, then, are likely to be revealed *ex post* as critical under conscription than under voluntary service. "National emergency" cannot be defined independently of the institutions within which collective decisions are made; democratic processes may produce a declaration that a national emergency exists under one set of institutions but not under another.

IV. *Concluding Remarks*

Economists need not limit their analytical activities by taking the pattern of budgetary choices as a given datum. In this paper we have compared the impacts of conscription and voluntary service upon the probable pattern of collective choice, rather than upon the probable pattern of private choice. We have seen that institutional arrangements that permit conscription will produce both a larger, real-sized military budget and a less isolationist (or more

29. It might be expected that a conscript military would contain more members from middle-income families than a volunteer military (which would be more heavily weighted with members of lower-income families). If middle-income families have more political influence than lower-income families, an opposing tendency would exist. Middle-income conscriptees, however, are more likely to receive technical assignments than lower-income conscriptees (who would more likely be assigned to the infantry), which would soften the impact of this opposing consideration.

30. Similarly, a "national emergency" is more likely to continue to exist under conscription than under voluntary service.

interventionist, depending upon one's linguistic preferences) military-foreign policy. Collective decisions concerning military activity, moreover, seem likely to be more sensitive to changes in individual preferences under voluntary service than under conscription. At the same time, preferences themselves may change more rapidly under voluntary service than under conscription, as the greater variability in tax-prices associated with voluntary service seems likely to generate a more sensitive learning process by which preferences form and change.[31]

Simple economic principles also suggest that institutional change from conscription to voluntary service is more likely to result during a period of declining demand for guns (increasing demand for flowers) than during periods of either stable or rising demands. During periods of stable or rising demands for guns, the replacement of conscription by voluntary service requires that additional taxes be extracted from the citizenry. During periods of declining demands for guns, by contrast, the replacement of conscription by voluntary service requires only that potential tax reductions be foregone. Even should the objectively measured costs be the same in both instances, individuals will tend to subjectively evaluate the former situation as more costly than the latter.[32] Institutional change thus appears to be less costly when the cost is a tax reduction foregone than when its cost is an increase in current taxes.

At the same time, conscription is more likely to be re-introduced during periods of rising demand for guns (falling demand for flowers) than during periods of stable or declining demands. During periods of stable or declining demands for guns, the cost of continuing voluntary service is the potential tax reduction that could be achieved if conscription were instituted. During periods of rising demands for guns, by contrast, the cost of continuing voluntary service is the sacrifice of currently consumed private services that need not be sacrificed if conscription were instituted. In this case, the latter cost will tend to be subjectively evaluated as more burdensome than the former cost, so conscription is more likely to be re-

31. For some suggestive comments on the role of price as a teacher of preferences, see Boulding [5, p. 7].

32. For an interesting discussion of the sensory perception of cost when choices are made in a temporal sequence, see Buchanan [10, pp. 58–64]. Such considerations explain why public services are sensed to be more costly when they are initially undertaken than at a later point in time when their continuation is accepted. This is also the essential message of the "displacement effect" expounded by Peacock and Wiseman [22, pp. 24–28].

instituted during periods of rising demands for guns than during periods of stable or declining demands.

References

1. S. H. Altman and A. E. Fechter, "The Supply of Military Personnel in the Absence of a Draft," *Am. Econ. Rev.*, Proc., 57, May 1967, 19–31.
2. D. Bailey and T. F. Cargill, "The Military Draft and Future Income," *Western Econ. Jour.*, 7, December 1969, 365–70.
3. R. E. Berney, "The Incidence of the Draft," *Western Econ. Jour.*, 7, September 1969, 244–47.
4. D. Black, "The Unity of Political and Economic Science," *Econ. Jour.*, 60, September 1950, 506–14.
5. K. E. Boulding, "The Economics of Knowledge and the Knowledge of Economics," *Am. Econ. Rev.*, Proc., 56, May 1966, 1–13.
6. ————, *The Image*, Ann Arbor, 1956.
7. ————, "The Impact of the Draft on the Legitimacy of the National State,: in [25, pp. 191–96].
8. D. F. Bradford, "A Model of the Enlistment Decision under Uncertainty," *Quart. Jour. Econ.*, 82, November 1968, 621–38.
9. J. M. Buchanan, *The Demand and Supply of Public Goods*, Chicago, 1968.
10. ————, *Public Finance in Democratic Process*, Chapel Hill, 1967.
11. ———— and G. Tullock, *The Calculus of Consent*, Ann Arbor, 1962.
12. J. R. Davis and C. W. Meyer, "Budget Size in a Democracy," *So. Econ. Jour.*, 36, July 1969, 10–17.
13. J. R. Davis and N. A. Palomba, "On the Shifting of the Military Draft as a Progressive Tax-in-Kind," *Western Econ. Jour.*, 6, March 1968, 150–53.
14. O. A. Davis and M. J. Hinich, "On the Power and Importance of the Mean Preference in a Mathematical Model of Democratic Choice," *Public Choice*, 5, Fall 1968, 59–72.
15. N. E. Devletoglou, "Threshold and Rationality," *Kyklos*, 21, No. 4, 1968, 623–36.
16. A. Downs, *An Economic Theory of Democracy*, New York, 1957.
17. A. C. Fisher, "The Cost of the Draft and the Cost of Ending the Draft," *Am. Econ. Rev.*, 39, June 1969, 239–54.
18. W. L. Hansen and B. A. Weisbrod, "Economics of the Military Draft," *Quart. Jour. Econ.*, 81, August 1967, 395–421.
19. G. Hildebrand, "Discussion," *Am. Econ. Rev.*, Proc., 57, May 1967, 63–66.
20. J. C. Miller, III, ed., *Why the Draft?* Baltimore, 1968.
21. W. Y. Oi, "The Economic Cost of the Draft," *Am. Econ. Rev.*, Proc., 57, May 1967, 39–62.
22. A. T. Peacock and J. Wiseman, *The Growth of Public Expenditure in the United Kingdom*, Princeton, 1961.

23. A. Puviani, *Die Illusionen in der öffentlichen Finanzwirtschaft,* trans. M. Hartmann and F. Rexhausen, Berlin, 1960.
24. E. F. Renshaw, "The Economics of Conscription," *So. Econ. Jour.,* 27, October 1960, 111–17.
25. S. Tax, ed., *The Draft,* Chicago, 1967.
26. D. G. Tuerck, "Constitutional Asymmetry," *Papers on Non-Market Decision Making,* 2, Charlottesville, 1967, 27–44.

12

A Public Choice Approach to
Public Utility Pricing

James M. Buchanan[1]

In orthodox discussions of economic policy, economists tend to assume that they are providing advice to a benevolent despot who will, costlessly and willingly, implement those measures which analysis suggests to be efficient. This often unrecognized assumption about the political order may not exert relevant feedback effects on the policy analysis itself in many cases. In fact, some such assumption may be necessary to achieve an appropriate division of labor between economists and other social scientists. In certain important areas of policy, however, the model of political decision-making that is assumed may influence the analysis itself. If this is not understood, economists may be frustrated by their entrapment in a theory of policy that explains little about the behavior of the effective decision-makers. The replacement of the benevolent-despot model by the more plausible, even if still simplified, model that assumes individuals make their own collective decisions may be highly productive in particular applications.

This paper is one such application. The traditional and much-discussed problem of pricing and investment for decreasing-cost enterprises is examined in a model based on the assumption that individuals make collective as well as private decisions. As the analysis demonstrates, this change in the underlying decision-making model produces relatively sharp contrasts with orthodox analyses at specific points. In a fully closed behavioral model, the analysis shows

Reprinted by permission of the publisher from *Public Choice*, vol. VII (Fall 1968).

1. The Analysis contained in this paper was first presented in seminars at Purdue University and Northwestern University during the fall of 1967.

that when the necessary equality between marginal cost, marginal price, and marginal evaluation is satisfied, *average price must equal average cost*. The policy conflict between average-cost pricing and marginal-cost pricing for increasing-returns facilities does not exist. Somewhat less dramatically the analysis may be interpreted as a defense of the multipart tariff or club principle of pricing for decreasing-cost facilities.

I.

If the necessary marginal conditions for Pareto optimality are fully satisfied, the marginal cost of supplying-producing a unit of product must be equal to the buyer's marginal evaluation of a unit. If the consumer or purchaser is allowed to adjust independently to price offers, this equality is behaviorally generated when "marginal" price is made equal to marginal cost. It is essential to insert the modifying adjective "marginal" before "price." Marginal price need not equal average price, and in a general sense this equality *cannot* be realized when average costs fall throughout the relevant output range, the standard characteristic of the facility that embodies the controversial, and thereby interesting, pricing-investment problem.

This summarizes the argument of the paper, but it will be useful to illustrate the argument geometrically in the familiar textbook diagram that economists have accepted, taught, and reproduced. In Figure 1, average-cost pricing, interpreted in the traditional sense, would require a price of p_a, with an output of q_a. By apparent contrast, marginal-cost pricing, as a rule, would require a price of p_m, with an output of q_m. The alleged conflict reduces to one between the profitability criterion, every facility standing on its own bottom, and the general welfare criterion, resources optimally allocated to the facility in question, provided that the required total conditions are also met.

Initially, I suggest that we forget the paradigmatic model depicted in Figure 1. Consider a simpler example, a one-man Crusoe economy where the isolated individual is confronted with the possibility of producing one good at increasing returns. We assume that all of his other activities are in equilibrium adjustment and that no "profit" opportunities are available among these alternatives. Under these conditions, we ask: Will the isolated individual produce the decreasing-cost good, and, if he does so, how much will he produce?

The obvious response is that the individual will produce the good if the necessary total conditions are met and that, if produced, the output will be extended to the point where the necessary marginal conditions are satisfied. The isolated individual will behave optimally. It remains useful, nonetheless, to look at the simple geometry of the individual's behavior here. Figure 2 depicts the individual's tastes for the good in question in relation to some numeraire good, one that we assume to be fully divisible over quantity units and one that is itself produced at constant costs. The "public utility" good is measured along the abscissa; the numeraire or "private" good is measured along the ordinate. The transformation function is shown as TT', and the equilibrium position is shown at E. In this position, the individual is giving up an amount, TY, of the numeraire good in exchange for an amount, OX, of the decreasing-cost good. He attains a higher utility level by producing-consuming this good than by remaining at T. At equilibrium, he is paying a marginal price, defined by the slope of the transformation curve, equal to marginal cost, defined also by this slope. This is brought into equality with his own marginal evaluation of the good, defined by the slope of the appropriate indifference curve. It should be noted, however, that, at E, the individual is paying an average price that is higher than marginal price. Average price is measured by the ratio, TY/YE, in Figure 2.

Figure 3 incorporates a straightforward translation of the data depicted in Figure 2 into the more familiar Marshallian coordinate dimensions. The ordinate now measures price and cost per unit, defined in the numeraire. The marginal cost curve, MC, is derived by taking the absolute values for the slope of the transformation curve,

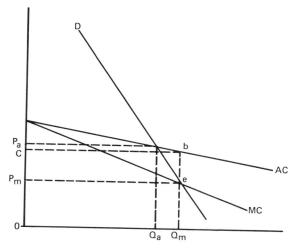

Figure 1

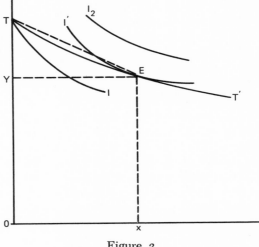

Figure 2

TT′, over all quantities. The average cost curve, AC, is derived by taking the appropriate ratio between total cost and output at all levels. This latter curve, that for average cost, can also be interpreted as representing the "price offer" curve that the isolated individual confronts. This traces, conceptually, the set of prices and associated quantities that the individual faces as he tries to make a decision. He can, for example, "purchase" x_o units at a p_o price per unit. The third basic curve in Figure 3, that for marginal evaluation, ME, is derived by taking the slopes of successive indifference curves as these cut the transformation curve, TT′, in Figure 2. Equilibrium is again shown at E, where marginal evaluation equals marginal cost. At this point, all of the necessary conditions for optimality are fully satisfied. Note especially that there is no conflict between average-cost and marginal-cost "pricing" here. The individual, at E, pays an average price, p_a, which is equal to average cost, and a marginal price, p_m, which is equal to marginal cost. In the average price sense, he is, of course, off his "demand curve." In such a model as this, however, the very notion of a "demand curve" drawn in the orthodox manner is highly questionable.[2]

As drawn in Figures 2 and 3, the total conditions are satisfied, along with the marginal conditions. The limiting case would be that

2. Economists' proclivity to think always in terms of positions on the demand curve, as normally derived, may have been one of the factors that has inhibited critical recognition of the simple points made in this argument.

in which the transformation possibilities exhaust the total valuation placed on the public-utility good by the individual. This is the perfectly-discriminating monopolist example of standard theory. Geometrically, in our one-person case, this would require that the TT′ curve in Figure 2 lie along but just below an indifference contour over some positive range. The individual would secure no net surplus over inframarginal ranges, and, in the limit, he would remain indifferent as between a resource commitment to this activity and a noncommitment.

Little more needs to be added to the formal structure of the argument, but the theory of public-utility pricing has been conducted along quite different lines. Some departure from the simplified model may, therefore, be necessary to convince the adherents to orthodoxy. For present purposes, we remain in a one-person model, but let us allow the individual to split himself into two quite separate and distinct capacities or roles. This may be done by supposing that he has, somewhere in a past life, heard about Hotelling, Lerner, and the marginal-cost pricing rule. Having done so, the individual decides, if he produces the good at all, he must offer it to himself, as a consumer, at a price that is equal to marginal cost and that this price must be uniform over the whole quantity range. That is, marginal price must be equal to average price.

He will recognize, however, that under these restrictions the "revenues" collected from his payments as a direct consumer will not cover the outlays that he must make as a producer. It becomes necessary, therefore, to analyze his behavior, not only as a consumer, but also as a taxpayer-purchaser of the facility. Initially, let us assume that he adopts a policy of complete passivity in this role. He decides that he will make consumer decisions on the basis of marginal-cost pricing rules but that he will simply make up any losses that might be incurred through residual "taxation." He sets prices at marginal cost. Hence, as a consumer he confronts a price-offer curve or schedule now shown by the MC curve of Figure 3. Faced with this, and limiting himself to his consumer's role, he reaches an equilibrium position, of sorts, where the appropriately derived marginal evaluation curve, ME′, cuts the new curve for marginal price, MC′. The actual marginal cost curve becomes, in this construction, the curve of average cost to the consumer. Equilibrium is attained at E′, with an output of the facility set at X′.

This output is clearly excessive. It is nonoptimal because, at the margin, the individual's evaluation falls below his anticipated outlay. Through the attempt to price at marginal cost, in a confused effort to follow the standard welfare norms, the individual has so modified

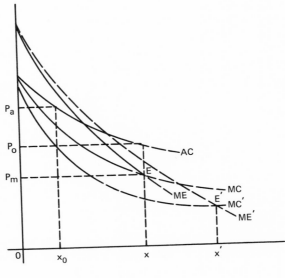

Figure 3

his conditions of choice that he is trapped into an excessive produc-
tion-consumption of the public-utility good.

11.

Serious objection may, however, be raised to the one-man model at
this point. The many-person model differs from the single-person
model precisely in those respects that generate the apparent contradiction in results. Individual consumers-purchasers, when acting in
the large-number setting, do not act as if their own purchases exert
an influence on price. They accept price as a parameter for their
own behavior. When this point is recognized, the conflict between
average-cost and marginal-cost pricing seems to be restored.

    This objection is partially justified, but the explanatory potential
of the one-man model may be retained provided that we introduce
the appropriately-restrictive assumptions about the individual's behavior. Let us continue to assume, now, that the individual bifurcates
himself into two capacities or roles, those of consumer-buyer-user on
the one hand and taxpayer-producer on the other. As before, let us
assume that price at all outputs is set equal to marginal cost. In a
significant departure from the model examined above, however, we
now assume that the individual, in his role as consumer-buyer, acts

as if price is parametric. By this assumption, we convert the behavior of the individual, as consumer-buyer, into a pattern that is directly analogous to the behavior of the consumer-buyer in a large-number market setting.

In this modified model, the consuming-buying behavior of the individual can be represented by an orthodox demand curve (which is not a marginal evaluation curve). Equilibrium will be established where this curve cuts the orthodox marginal cost curve. The construction of Figure 1 illustrates this standard analysis. Total revenues that are generated by this combination of pricing policy and individual response will not cover total outlays that are anticipated at any level of output. In the model discussed immediately above, we assumed that the individual in his second role as a taxpayer-producer of the facility reacts passively and finances any deficit that might emerge. It should be obvious that this assumption cannot be maintained in any remotely realistic model for behavior. By necessity, the choice behavior of the individual in his role as taxpayer-producer must be explicitly examined. Under what conditions will he choose to invest the required resources in the facility, given the postulated response behavior as a consumer-buyer?

We may begin by examining the individual's choice behavior as a taxpayer-producer in a reasonably straightforward cost-benefit calculus. What are the tax-costs, considered *ex ante*, that the facility or enterprise embodies over varying output ranges? What are the "public" benefits? Tax-costs may be identified without difficulty. These are simply the total outlays anticipated minus the total revenues that will be collected at the planned-pricing scheme. In the geometry of Figure 1, the total tax-cost at output q_m would be the rectangle p_m ebc. It becomes relatively simple to derive a curve for total tax-costs over all possible outputs, given the production function and the predicted direct buyer response pattern. From this we may derive schedules or curves for both average tax-costs and marginal tax-costs; these are depicted in Figure 4. The curve, MTC, represents marginal tax-cost. Note that, by construction, marginal tax-cost becomes zero at the output where the individual attains consumer-buyer equilibrium. Total tax-cost is minimized at this output, given the preference and production schedules. The individual's marginal evaluation of the facility over differing output ranges must also be derived before we can determine whether he will, as a taxpayer-producer, attain equilibrium at the *same* output. This requires that we measure the difference between the value that the individual places on successive units of consumption and the direct-user prices that he must pay under the marginal cost pricing

rule. Geometrically, the curve for taxpayer-producer marginal evaluation is measured by the difference between the appropriately
drawn curve for direct-user marginal evaluation and the supply
curve that the individual confronts (horizontal at price p_m).[3] This
subtraction process yields a curve which is the marginal evaluation
for the individual as taxpayer-purchaser of the facility as a "public"
enterprise. This is shown as ME_t in Figure 4. Note that, again by
construction, this curve also reaches the abscissa at the same output
which defines consumer-buyer equilibrium.

Marginal tax-price (cost) equals marginal taxpayer evaluation
of the facility which produces output x; marginal user price (set at
marginal cost) equals marginal user evaluation at this same output.
The necessary marginal conditions for Pareto optimality are met,
and there seems to be no conflict between the individual's behavior
as a direct consumer-user and his behavior as a taxpayer-purchaser.

Nothing has yet been said about the total conditions, however,
and the analysis remains incomplete until the investment decision
is examined. We have postulated that, as a consumer-buyer-user,
the individual acts as if his own rate of purchase of the good has no
influence on price. We have also assumed that price is set at the
uniquely determined level where marginal user demand equals anticipated marginal outlay (cost). But what about the companion
calculus of the individual in his role as taxpayer-producer-purchaser
of the facility? If we adopt the same convention for this aspect of his
behavior, the marginal tax-price will always be set at the unique level
where marginal taxpayer demand equals marginal tax-cost, which is
zero. But with a direct user price of p_m (Figure 1 or Figure 3), and
a tax-price of zero (Figure 4), total outlays cannot be covered. The
enterprise cannot possibly be viable on these assumptions.

The escape route from this genuine dilemma seems obvious. We
cannot adopt the same assumptions about individual behavior in the
two roles. As a direct consumer-buyer, we may continue to assume
strict price-taking reaction on the part of the individual. As a taxpayer-producer-purchaser, however, the individual must be allowed
the possibility of acting differently, that is, not as a "price taker." In
this latter capacity, the individual must be assumed to realize that,
because of the nature of the production function, any decision on

3. The two marginal evaluation curves must be kept distinct, one
for the individual as direct user-consumer and the other for the individual
as taxpayer-producer-purchaser. The marginal evaluation curve for the
individual as direct user is not drawn in Fig. 4. If income effects are
neglected, however, the orthodox demand curve of Fig. 1 becomes this
marginal evaluation curve.

his part to purchase-produce a larger output of the facility will reduce average costs on all inframarginal units. In other words, the "tax-price offer" curve confronting the individual as taxpayer-purchaser must be that shown by ATC in Figure 4. Faced with such an offer curve, the individual adjusts his "purchases" to the point where marginal tax-price equals marginal taxpayer evaluation. He reaches full behavioral equilibrium at x, where marginal tax-price is zero, but where average tax-price is xR. This average tax-price is, by construction, equal to $p_m p_a$ (Figure 3).

In this more complex model for individual behavior in the one-person setting, the simplistic conclusion reached at the outset is restored. Even though we have allowed the isolated individual to behave, in his role as a direct consumer, in precisely the manner of the single consumer among many buyers in a large-number market setting, his pattern of rational response as a taxpayer-purchaser of the decreasing-cost facility insures that both the required marginal and total conditions for optimality will be satisfied. This means, of course, that he will extend the output of the facility to the point where marginal cost equals marginal evaluation, but that he will pay an average price equal to average cost. There is no conflict between average-cost and marginal-cost criteria. If, by mistake, the individual should extend the output of the facility only to the point where direct user payments equal total anticipated outlays, the point shown by q_a in Figure 1, his marginal taxpayer evaluation of the facility would clearly exceed marginal taxpayer cost. The individual would stand willing, in his role as a taxpayer-purchaser, to contribute something toward the expansion of output beyond this limit.

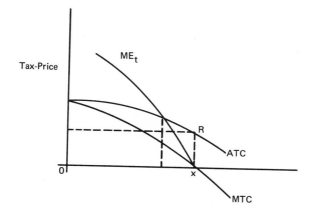

Figure 4

III.

To this point the one-man model for behavior has been consistently employed, even if the various assumptions about behavior may have appeared somewhat extreme. This model is helpful in forcing concentration on the *dual* capacity or role that the single individual must play when his behavior as a direct consumer is postulated to be inconsistent with the characteristics of the production function. This model may also be a helpful stage toward analysis of the more complex collective-decision process which all decreasing-cost facilities must introduce. Given the institutions of the market, when there are many buyers no single person considers the influence that his own rate of purchase exerts on price. He adjusts to prices parametrically; he behaves as a price-taker. If all consumers do this, however, they *must* behave differently when they take up their roles as voters-taxpayers considering the problem of public or collective investment in the facility. In this latter role, rational behavior dictates that they behave precisely as the individual in the isolated situation was shown to behave. Given the appropriate institutions for making collective decisions, they will tend to approve investment in the facility so long as the total conditions are met.

These results seem evident on their face, but some of the problems involved in aggregation are interesting in themselves. When we move beyond the one-person model, it becomes necessary to specify the characteristics of the collective organization and its rules for reaching decisions. Initially, we may assume that *all* persons in the collectivity are consumers-users of the good that is produced by the decreasing-cost facility or enterprise that we are examining. For absolute simplicity in analysis, we assume first that all persons are identical and that there are only two.

The marginal evaluation that each person places on the facility, as a "public facility," is measured by the difference between marginal consumer evaluation and user price, as noted in the one-person model. To distinguish the two evaluations here, we refer to *marginal taxpayer evaluation* and *marginal consumer evaluation*. The former is, in the limiting case where there are not interpersonal or intemporal consumption externalities, simply Marshallian consumer's surplus. To get at the total taxpayer evaluation for the facility, we need to add the separate individual curves *horizontally*, as we do with an ordinary derivation of a market demand curve. Note that, initially, we do not add curves vertically, as with a genuine public good. The curve for aggregate taxpayer evaluation intersects the marginal taxpayer cost curve at the output which is generated by direct user pricing at marginal cost. To this point the two-person model remains identical to the single-person model. As such, however, the construction tells us nothing, either in an explanatory or a representational sense, concerning the allocation or pricing of the facility, as a "public" enterprise. At the margin, aggregate marginal taxpayer evaluation equals zero, which is equal to marginal taxpayer cost; the necessary marginal conditions are met. As noted in the single-person models, however, some measure of taxpayer evaluation over inframarginal ranges of facility output must be made in order that some of the surplus be captured for the financing of public investment.

Individuals must "vote for" investment in the facility, with variations in capacity reflecting the alternatives of collective choice. As a "voter," the single person knows that the collectivity faces a *public* production possibility indicated by the curves for average and marginal tax costs, ATC and MTC in Figure 5. The question becomes one of comparing an individual share in this cost with an individual marginal evaluation. There may be, of course, a sub-infinity of possible sharing arrangements, all of which satisfy the necessary marginal requirements. Since we have assumed the two persons are identical, let us further assume prior agreement on equal sharing of collective costs. This allows us to draw curves for individual average and marginal tax-cost, ATC_i and MTC_i in Figure 5.

The difficulty arises in deriving curves or schedules for individualized marginal evaluation. As we have assumed throughout the analysis, the good is fully divisible among separate users. The aggregate curve for marginal taxpayer evaluation was derived by the *horizontal* not by *vertical* summation of the individual curves. But these latter, derived from individual evaluations of discrete units of output, cannot be used to represent evaluations for output capacities of the facility. What evaluation will an individual, as a potential taxpayer-voter-beneficiary, place on, say, a facility that has the capacity of supplying two units per period. Clearly, this evaluation will depend on his anticipations about the *sharing* of this output among users. With some appropriate sharing rule, the model can be converted into one that is fully analogous to a public-goods model. If the individual thinks that he will secure one-half of the output of the facility in each period, which he knows will be priced to him as a direct user at marginal cost, he will value the two-unit facility equally with *one unit* of user output. In the two-man setting, therefore, an individual's marginal taxpayer evaluation of a unit increase in the capacity of the facility, considered strictly as a collective enterprise that will follow marginal-cost pricing rules, will be one-half his evaluation of a one-unit increase in the quantity of the good that will be made available to him directly as a user, at marginal-cost prices. Geometrically, therefore, we can derive curves for the individual marginal "voter-taxpayer" (ME_t^i) by taking one-half the slopes of the marginal taxpayer evaluation curves drawn as in the one-man model. One such curve is shown as ME_t^i in Figure 5. By this device, we have effectively converted the fully divisible good into a purely public good for purposes of examining the collective decision process. Note that we can now generate the aggregate taxpayer evaluation curve, ΣME_t in Figure 5, either by adding the conventional output-unit evaluation curves (ME_t^i) horizontally or by adding the derived "facility" marginal evaluation curves (ME_t^i) vertically.

The geometry here is really more complex than the point requires. It is evident that there exists no scheme whereby the individual member of the collectivity, as taxpayer-voter, can react to a uniform tax-price and, at the same time, reach behavioral equilibrium that is consistent with his behavior as a direct user. As a taxpayer-voter, the individual must be confronted with either a tax-price offer that embodies a reduction in unit charges as a larger facility is selected or a tax-price offer that embodies an all-or-none choice in which both quantity and charges are fixed. In either case, as the geometry makes clear, the test for the satisfaction of the total conditions being met is the observed unanimity among all members of the group.

The model becomes considerably more complex, of course, when individual differences are introduced. For now, we assume that all members of the community remain direct users. Here, under the same construction, individual marginal taxpayer evaluation curves would differ, and agreement among all members of the collectivity could be reached only if separate persons should be confronted with differing price-offer conditions, either declining over facility size or all-or-none offers at the fixed-size facility. The problem here becomes one that is similar to, but somewhat more complex than that faced in any public-goods decision process. Voluntarily, individuals will not, of course, contribute to the cost-sharing for the nonuser financing of the facility, and collectively, there is no direct means of ascertaining individualized evaluations which are required to determine the efficient set of differential price-offers. With nondecreasing cost public goods, however, tax-prices may be uniform over quantity, but not necessarily so. In the case under consideration here, tax-prices must, by the nature of the problem posed, decline over facility size. The voting alternatives become, therefore, neces-

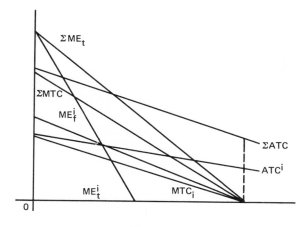

Figure 5

sarily somewhat more complex than those which represent the essentials of the public-goods problem generally speaking.[4]

Let us now introduce the further complication that some members of the collective group are not demanders-users of the decreasing-cost facility. At marginal-cost prices, these persons demand none of the good. It seems self-evident that, in any collective decision-process, and neglecting possible consumption externalities, this group will unanimously oppose any proposal that will embody their own support of tax charges to finance the facility. The argument strongly supports the financing of decreasing-cost facilities by the imposition of multipart tariffs levied directly on users, and on users only. The convenient fiction of the lump-sum tax that has been used by economists who ignore the collective decision process had best be discarded as fiction. This is perhaps best indicated by asking the simple question: Who would vote to impose a lump-sum tax on himself? Conceptually at least, there always exists some scheme for sharing the costs of the facility, over and above those financed by marginal-cost user prices, among direct users, so long as the facility is efficient in the overall sense. No such scheme could possibly exist

4. Samuelson apparently disagrees. In his comment on my interpretation of his own basic contribution to the theory of public goods, Samuelson appears to suggest that decreasing-cost phenomena are an inherent aspect of "publicness." See P. A. Samuelson, "Pitfalls in the Analysis of Public Goods," *Journal of Law and Economics*, X (October 1967), 199–204.

for sharing costs among nonusers in the absence of consumption externalities.

Practically, therefore, the analysis here lends support to the early arguments by Coase and others that multipart tariffs provide the best means of financing decreasing-cost facilities.[5] The objections raised by apparent purists to multipart pricing are clearly invalid in the general setting developed here. The analysis provided a general approach that also allows for the introduction of any degree of "publicness" or "indivisibility" to be introduced without difficulty. There is no necessity that the marginal taxpayer evaluation add up to the same as the Marshallian consumer surplus. Indeed this is the exception or the extreme rather than the rule.[6]

Finally, the methodological relevance of the analysis deserves stress. Problems of economic efficiency should always be examined within the framework of models that hold some potential applicability for the making of real-world decisions. The one-man models presented initially here are absurd simplifications, and the two-person models later introduced may seem little improvement. But in my view, even such models as these are considerably more meaningful than the Hotelling-like models which assume the presence of some benevolent despot whose shining will guides us all to bliss.

5. See R. H. Coase, "The Marginal Cost Controversy," *Economica*, 13 (August 1946), 169–82.

6. In this connection see, B. Weisbrod, "Collective Consumption Services of Individual Consumption Goods," *Quarterly Journal of Economics*, 78 (August 1964), 471–77; and Millard F. Long, "Collective-Consumption Services of Individual-Consumption Goods: Comment," *Quarterly Journal of Economics*, 81 (May 1967), 351–52.

IV

GROUPS AS PUBLIC CHOOSERS

13

Politics, Policy, and the Pigovian Margins

James M. Buchanan[1]

Since Sidgwick and Marshall, and notably since Pigou's *The Economics of Welfare*, economists have accepted the presence or absence of external effects in production and consumption as a primary criterion of market efficiency. When private decisions exert effects that are external to the decision-maker, "ideal" output is not obtained through the competitive organisation of economic activity even if the remaining conditions necessary for efficiency are satisfied. The market "fails" to the extent that there exist divergencies between marginal private products and marginal social products and/or between marginal private costs and marginal social costs. This basic Pigovian theorem has been theoretically refined and elaborated in numerous works, but its conceptual validity has rarely been challenged.[2] The purpose of this paper is to bring into question a fundamental implication of this aspect of theoretical welfare economics, namely, the implication that externalities are either reduced or eliminated by the shift of an activity from market to political organisation.

Reprinted by permission of the publisher from *Economica*, February 1962.

1. Although independently developed, this note draws upon and extends certain ideas that have been developed in a larger work undertaken in collaboration with Gordon Tullock. See, *The Calculus of Consent* (Ann Arbor, 1962). I should acknowledge Tullock's indirect as well as his direct influence on the general ideas presented in this paper.

2. The work of Ronald Coase should be mentioned as a notable exception. Coase's criticism of the Pigovian analysis concerns the implications of externality for resource allocation. For a preliminary statement of Coase's position see his "The Federal Communications Commission," *Journal of Law and Economics*, II (1959), especially pp. 26–27. A more complete statement appears in "The Problem of Social Cost," *Journal of Law and Economics*, III (1960).

I shall try to show that this implication will stand up to critical scrutiny only under certain highly restricted assumptions about human behaviour in modern political systems. When these restrictive assumptions are modified, the concept of divergence between marginal "social" product (cost) and marginal private product (cost) loses most of its usefulness.[3]

"Imperfection" and "failure" are descriptive nouns that tell something about the operation of the organism, the activity, or the organisation that is under discussion. These words, and others like them, are meaningful only if the alternative states of "perfection" and "success" are either specifically described or are assumed to be tacitly recognised by participants in the discussion. In the analysis of market organisation, the "perfectly-working" order has been quite carefully defined. The necessary conditions for Paretian optimality are now a part of the professional economist's stock-in-trade, and these conditions are known to be satisfied only when all of the relevant costs and benefits resulting from an action are incorporated into the calculus of the decision-maker that selects the action. By contrast with this state of perfection, almost all ordinary or real-world markets are "imperfect," in greater or lesser degree. Most private decisions exert external effects. So far, so good. If this were the end of it, however, there would be little point in all of the effort. Economists must imply or suggest that the imperfectly-working organisation is, in fact, "perfectible": that is, they must do so if they are to justify their own professional existence. The analysis of an existing social order must, almost by the nature of science itself, imply that some "improvement" in results can be produced by changes that can be imposed on the variables subject to social control.

3. It should be noted that I shall not be concerned with the conceptual ability of welfare economists to make specific policy prescriptions, a problem that has been central to much of the modern discussion. It is now widely acknowledged that welfare economics, as such, can provide few guides to positive policy-making in a specific sense. But the analysis continues to be employed for the purposes of demonstrating the existence of market failure. If, as J. de Graaff suggests, "*laissez-faire* welfare theory" was "largely concerned with demonstrating the optimal properties of free competition and the unfettered price system," it is surely equally accurate to suggest that modern welfare theory has been largely concerned with demonstrating that these conclusions are invalid: that is, that competitive markets do not satisfy the necessary conditions for optimality. Graaff's own work is, perhaps, the most elegant example. See his *Theoretical Welfare Economics*, Cambridge, 1957 (Citation from page 170).

Such improvements in the organisation of economic activity have, almost without exception, involved the placing of restrictions on the private behaviour of individuals through the implementation of some *political* action. The various proposals that have been advanced by economists are sufficiently familiar to make a listing at this point unnecessary. They run the gamut from the relatively straightforward tax-subsidy schemes of Marshall to the more sophisticated and highly intricate proposals for multipart pricing, counter-speculation, collective simulation of ideal market processes, and many other intriguing methods designed to promote and to insure the attainment of economic efficiency. Indeed, economists tend to be so enmeshed with efficiency notions that it seems extremely difficult for them to resist the ever-present temptation to propose yet more complex gimmicks and gadgets for producing greater "efficiency." In almost every case, and often quite unconsciously, the suggested improvement is assumed to be within the realm of the genuinely attainable. And, if some sceptic dare raise a question on this point, the economist is likely to respond to the effect that his task is not that of the politician, that he does not appropriately concern himself with the political feasibility or workability of his proposals. But if political obstacles to realisation are not, in fact, discussed, the implication is clear that the proposals which are advanced are attainable as a result of some conceivable politically imposed modifications in the institutional framework within which decisions are made. It seems fully appropriate to charge welfare economists, generally, with an implicit acceptance of this implication of their analyses. If this were not the case, it is difficult to see why, for example, William J. Baumol should have attempted to construct a theory of the state, of collective action, on the basis of the externality argument,[4] why K. W. Kapp should have entitled his work, *The Social Costs of Private Enterprise*,[5] and why Francis Bator should have called his recent summary analysis, "The Anatomy of Market Failure."[6]

I shall not be concerned here with the analysis of market imperfection or failure, as such. The primary criticism of theoretical welfare economics (and economists) that is advanced in this note is that its failure to include analyses of similar imperfections in realistic and

4. William J. Baumol, *Welfare Economics and the Theory of the State*, 1952.

5. K. W. Kapp, *The Social Costs of Private Enterprise*, 1950.

6. Francis Bator, "The Anatomy of Market Failure," *Quarterly Journal of Economics*, LXXII (1958), 351–79.

attainable alternative solutions causes the analysis itself to take on implications for institutional change that are, at best, highly misleading. To argue that an existing order is "imperfect" in comparison with an alternative order of affairs that turns out, upon careful inspection, to be unattainable may not be different from arguing that the existing order is "perfect."[7] The existence of demonstrated imperfection in terms of an unattainable state of affairs should imply nothing at all about the possibility of actual improvement to an existing state. To take this step considerably more is required than the preliminary analysis of "ideal output." This is not to suggest, of course, that the preliminary analysis is not essential and important.

In what follows I shall try to show that, with consistent assumptions about human behaviour in both market and political institutions, any attempt to replace or to modify an existing market situation, admitted to be characterised by serious externalities, will produce solutions that embody externalities which are different, but precisely analogous, to those previously existing. Indeed, the Pigovian analysis lends itself readily to the analysis of political imperfection.

I.

In order to analyse political processes in a manner that is even remotely similar to the methods of economic theory, great simplification and abstraction are required. To the political scientist, accustomed as he is to working with more "realistic" models of human behaviour, the simplified models with which the economist must analyse political institutions can only seem to be grossly inadequate caricatures of the operation of complex organisational structures. This rather sharp methodological gap between the two social sciences incorporated in "political economy" provides an important reason why the political scientist has not filled, and could hardly be expected to fill, the analytical void left open by the incompleteness of welfare economics.

I shall assume the existence of a community composed of separate individuals in which all collective decisions are reached by a voting rule of simple majority with universal suffrage. More complex, and realistic, models introducing representation, political parties, leadership, etc., could be employed but without significantly altering

7. Professor Frank Knight's statement that "to call a situation hopeless is equivalent to calling it ideal" may be reversed. To call a situation ideal is merely another means of calling it hopeless: that is, not perfectible.

the conclusions reached. Almost any political order described by the term, "democratic," in the modern Western usage of this term may, for present purposes, be simplified into this extreme model of "pure" democracy. Characteristics of the political structure may modify the majority equivalent in the simple model. That is to say, a model of two-thirds or three-fourths majority may be more appropriate to the analysis of some political structures under certain conditions than the simple majority model. This quantitative variation in the voting rule equivalent, however, does not affect the conclusions of this paper. Each particular rule, save that of unanimity, leads to conclusions that are identical to those reached in the simple majority model. The magnitude of the distortions produced is, of course, affected by the voting ru'e. The analysis here is concerned solely with indicating the direction of these effects, not with their magnitude. A distinction among the various "majority equivalents" is not, therefore, necessary.

In the first model, the orthodox assumptions of positive economics will be retained insofar as these concern individual motivation and action. Private individuals are assumed to be sufficiently informed and rational to conduct the required calculus and to reach decisions on the basis of a comparison of private costs and benefits at the relevant margins. No considerations of the "public" or the "social" interest are assumed to enter into this individual calculus within the relationship in question except insofar as this should coincide with individual interest. In determining his voting behaviour on each issue confronted by the group, the individual is assumed, quite simply, to act in that manner which he considers to advance his own interest. The model embodies, therefore, a rather straightforward extension of the behavioural assumptions of orthodox economic theory, as a predictive, explanatory theory, to political choice-making.

If no institutional restrictions are placed on this majority-rule model of the collective choice process, the characteristics of the "solution" should be intuitively clear. The minimum-size effective or dominating coalition of individuals, as determined by the voting rule, will be able to secure net gains at the expense of the other members of the political group. These gains secured through the political process will tend to be shared symmetrically (equally) among all members of the dominant coalition. In the simple majority-rule model, this involves, in the limit, 50-plus percent of the total membership in the dominating coalition and 50-minus percent of the total membership in the losing or minority coalition. That such a solution will, in fact, tend to emerge under the conditions of the model seems hardly subject to question. It is helpful, however, to note that such a solution, and only such, satisfies fully the Von Neumann-Morgenstern requirements for solutions to n-person games which, of course, all political "games" must be.[8]

It is useful to apply the familiar Pigovian calculus to this model of political behaviour. To the individual member of the effective majority, the political process provides a means through which he may secure private gain at the expense of other citizens. In determining the margins to which political activity shall be extended, the individual member of the dominant coalition will include in his calculus a share of the net benefits from public activity that will be larger than the offsetting individualised share or proportion of the net costs of the activity. In the calculus of the individuals effectively making the final collective decision, marginal private benefits will tend to exceed marginal social benefits and/or marginal private costs will tend to fall short of marginal social costs. The distortions produced are, therefore, precisely analogous, in opposing directions, to those present in the market solution characterised by the familiar Pigovian divergencies. In essence, the value of a political vote in this model lies in its potential power to impose external costs on other members of the group. Externalities must be present in any solution reached by the voting process under all less-than-unanimity rules. If the possible "perfectibility" of market organisation is to be determined under these conditions, it is clearly necessary to compare two separate imperfections, in each of which significant divergencies of the Pigovian sort may exist at the individualised margins of decision-making. Since there will be nothing in the collective choice process that will tend to produce the "ideal" solution, as determined by the welfare economist, the presence or absence of a Pigovian marginal divergency in the market solution, even of sufficient seriousness to warrant concern, provides in itself no implication for the desirability of institutional change.[9]

8. J. Von Neumann and O. Morgenstern, *Theory of Games and Economic Behavior*, 3d ed., Princeton, 1953, p. 264.

9. I am not suggesting that deliberate exploitation of minority by majority need be the only purpose of collective activity, even in this polar model. The point is rather that, independently of the motivation for collective activity, majority-rule institutions of decision-making create opportunities within which Pigovian-like externalities may arise. There will, of course, arise situations in which the self-interest of the individual dictates the collectivisation of an activity in order that the application of general rules to *all* members of the group can be effected. It is precisely in such cases that, conceptually, unanimity may replace majority rule as the decision device, and the propositions of modern welfare economics become

I I.

This conclusion holds so long as consistency in individual behaviour patterns over market and voting processes is retained, independently of the specific motivation that may be assumed to direct this behaviour. The oversimplified model of Part I may be criticised on the grounds that individuals do not act in the way postulated: that is, they do not follow their own interests when they participate in the formation of social decisions for the community. Several responses might be advanced to such criticism, but it is not the purpose of this note to defend the validity, methodologically or otherwise, of the self-interest assumption about behaviour. The relevant response to the charge of unrealism at this point is surely the frank admission that, of course, individuals do not always act as the model of Part I postulates. A model is a construction that isolates one element of behaviour and upon this the analyst may erect conceptually refutable hypotheses. The model of majority rule in the simple pure democracy is not different in this respect from the competitive model of economic theory. Both models isolate that part of human behaviour that does reflect the rational pursuit of private gain by individuals in particular institutional relationships and both models fail to the extent that individuals do not, in fact, behave in this fashion in the relationships under consideration.[10]

---

fully appropriate. But so long as majority rule prevails, the "political externalities" are present, whether these be purposeful or ancillary to collective action designed to accomplish other ends.

10. Care must be taken to distinguish between the self-interest assumption, as the basis for a "logic of choice" and the self-interest assumption as the basis of a predictive, explanatory theory of human action. In the first sense, all action of individuals must be based on self-interest, and it becomes meaningless to discuss alternative models of behaviour. The pure logic of individual choice is not without value, but it should be emphasized that the argument of this paper employs the second version of the self-interest assumption. If conceptually refutable hypotheses are to be developed, the behaviour of choice-making individuals must be externally observable in terms of measurable criteria of choice. In the market relationship, this degree of operational validity is often introduced by stating that the minimal requirement is that individuals, when confronted with choice, choose "more" rather than "less." But "more" or "less" take on full operational meaning only when they become measureable in something other than subjective utility of the choosers. The "measuring rod of money" must be allowed to enter before the generalised logic of choice can produce even so much as the first law of demand.

Any number of models of individual behaviour can be constructed. The only real limitation lies, ultimately, in the testing of the predictions made. It will not be necessary, however, to develop any large number of additional and complex models to illustrate the central point of this note. One additional extremely simple model will suffice for this purpose. In this second model I shall drop the assumption that individuals, in both their market and in their political behaviour, act in pursuit of their own narrowly defined self-interest. Instead, I now postulate that individuals act in the other extreme: I assume that each individual, in all aspects of his behaviour, tries to identify himself with the community of which he is a member and to act in accordance with his own view of the overall "public" or "social" interest. Each member of the group tries to act in the genuine interest of the whole group as this is determined for him through the application of some appropriately chosen Kantian-like rule of action.

The results are again almost intuitively clear. Since each member of the group acts on the basis of identifying his own interest with that of the larger group, no deliberate exploitation of minority by majority can take place through the political process regardless of the voting rule that is applied. Differences that may arise, and which must be resolved by voting, stem solely from differences in individual conceptions of what the group interest on particular issues is. The Pigovian-type marginal divergencies between private and social costs or benefits disappear from the individual calculus in this model of behaviour. It is in application to market, rather than to political, behaviour that this model seems somewhat unorthodox. Under the assumptions of the model, the individual in his market behaviour will also try to identify himself with the group as a whole and to act in accordance with what he considers to be the "public" interest. If his chimney pours out smoke that soils his neighbors' laundry, he will assess these costs as if they were his own in reaching a decision concerning the possible introduction of a smoke-abatement device. The familiar analysis of welfare economics simply does not apply. Each individual decision-maker does, in fact, attempt to balance off "social" benefits against "social" costs at the margin. While, as in the collective sector, differences may arise among members of the group concerning the proper definition of social benefits and social costs, these differences cannot be interpreted in the standard way. The Pigovian divergence between marginal private product and marginal social product disappears in both the market and the political organisation of activity in this universal benevolence model. The policy conclusions are, however, identical with those reached from the use of the extreme self-interest model. If chimneys smoke, or if the majority is observed to impose discriminatory taxes on the minority, these facts carry with them no implications for institutional changes. In this case, they must represent the decision-makers' estimates of genuine community interest. Neither "real" nor "apparent" externalities can, in themselves, provide grounds for suggesting organisational changes.

I I I.

From the analysis of these two extreme and contrasting models of human behaviour, the inference is clear that so long as individuals are assumed to be similarly motivated under market and under political institutions there can be no direct implications drawn about the organisational structure of an activity on the basis of a Pigovian-like analysis of observed externalities. The orthodox implication of Pigovian welfare economics follows only on the assumption that individuals respond to *different* motives when they participate in market and in political activity. The only behavioural model appropriate to the Pigovian analysis is that which has been called "the bifurcated man." Man must be assumed to shift his psychological and moral gears when he moves from the realm of organised market activity to that of organised political activity, and vice-versa. Only if there can be demonstrated to be something in the nature of market organisation, as such, that brings out the selfish motives in man, and something in the political organisation, as such, which, in turn, suppresses these motives and brings out the more "noble" ones, can there be assumed to exist any "bridge" between the orthodox externality analysis and practical policy, even apart from problems of specific policy prescription.

The characteristics of the organisational structure within which choices must be made may affect the nature of the value system upon which individual action is based. It seems probable that the individual in his voting behaviour, will tend to choose among alternatives on the basis of a somewhat broader and more inclusive value scale than that which will direct his behaviour in the making of market choices. One reason for this is that, in political behaviour, the individual is made fully conscious of the fact that he is choosing *for* the whole group, that his individual action will exert external effects on other members of the group, that he is acting "socially." In his market behaviour, on the other hand, the external effects of individual choice are sensed only indirectly by the chooser.[11] But this recog-

---

11. For a further discussion on these points see my "Individual Choice in Voting and the Market," *Journal of Political Economy,* LXII (1954), 334–43.

nition that the individual value scale may be, to some extent, modified by the institutional structure within which choice is exercised is quite different from accepting the idea that the motivation for individual action is wholly transformed as between two separate structures. While it may be acknowledged as "realistic" to assume that the model of individual choice based on self-interest motivation—the "economic" model—is somewhat more applicable to an analysis of markets than of voting processes, this is far removed from accepting the applicability of the universal benevolence model for the latter. At most, the influence of the different organisational structures, as such, on motivation would seem to be conceptually represented by a reasonably narrow distance on some motivational spectrum. If, at the elementary stages of analysis, a choice must be made between that conception of behaviour that assumes this possible institutionally generated difference to be absent or negligible (models that I have called consistent) and the conception that assumes wholly different behavioural patterns solely due to the institutional structure, the first alternative seems obviously to be preferred. Yet, as I have shown, it is the second, and clearly extreme, conception of human behaviour that is implicit in much of the discussion of Pigovian welfare economics.

This assumption of behavioural dichotomy, as opposed to behavioural consistency, is most openly expressed in the early literature on socialism, especially that of the Christian and Fabian varieties. The criticism of the market order of affairs was often made by referring to the pursuit of private gain, and the case for socialism was based on the replacement of this pursuit of private gain by that of public good. Although this rather naïve conception has perhaps lost some of its appeal since World War II, it continues to be implied in much of the popular discussion. While this is not in itself surprising, it does seem notable that the analytical structure based on this conception of human behaviour should have remained largely unchallenged in the scientific literature.[12]

IV.

Up to this point the discussion has been concerned with the most general case in which no limitations are placed on the activities that

12. The behavioural inconsistency here has been, of course, indirectly recognised by many writers. The only explicit reference, however, to the private-cost social-cost analysis, to my knowledge, is contained in the paper by William H. Meckling and Armen A. Alchian, "Incentives in the United States," *American Economic Review*, L (1960), 55–61, and, even here, the reference is only a passing one.

may be organised through the political process. Can the implications of the Pigovian welfare analytics be rescued by restricting the movement of the political-institutional variables? If collective action can take place only within prescribed limits, which can be assumed to be fixed by constitutional rules, a model may be constructed in which the policy implications of the Pigovian-type of analysis do not run into immediate conflict with reasonable assumptions concerning human motivation. To accomplish this result, however, the range of possible political action must be restricted to such an extent as to make the analysis practically worthless.

Let it be assumed that constitutional rules dictate that all human activity shall be organised privately and voluntarily except that which involves the provision of genuinely collective goods and services. These are defined as those goods and services which, when a unit is made available to one individual member of the group, an equal amount, one unit, is also made available to each other member of the group. These goods and services are completely indivisible. Let it be further assumed that the constitution states that the provision of such goods and services, if politically organised, shall be financed by taxes that are levied on the "marginal-benefit principle." That is to say, each individual shall be required to contribute a "tax-price" that is exactly proportional to his own marginal rate of substitution between the collective good and money (all other goods). This marginal tax will be different for different individuals in the group because, although the good is genuinely collective, the relative marginal utility of it will vary from individual to individual.

If the provision of such a good or service should be organised privately rather than collectively, and if individuals are assumed to be motivated by self-interest considerations, the market solution will be characterised by the presence of significant externalities. The individual, acting privately, will take into account only that share of total marginal benefit or product that he expects to enjoy. By comparison, he will take into account the full amount of the marginal costs which, by hypothesis, he must bear individually. In other words, he cannot exclude other members of the group from the enjoyment of the benefits provided by the good; but there is no way that he may include these other members of the group in the payment of the costs. This market organisation produces, therefore, the familiar result; the private calculus of individuals embodies the Pigovian divergence at the margins of decision. Compared to a Pareto-optimal situation, relatively too few resources will be devoted to the provision of the common good or service.

Under this situation, a shift in organisation from the private or market sector to the collective sector will, under the conditions specified, tend to eliminate the Pigovian divergence, even if the self-interest motivation of individual action is retained. If the individual, in making a political or voting choice concerning the possible marginal extension of the provision of the collective good or service, is required to include in his calculus a share of the total marginal cost of the extension that is proportional to his individualised share of the total marginal benefits provided by the extension, a "solution" will tend to be produced by political choice that will meet all of the necessary conditions for Pareto optimality. If the total marginal costs of extending the activity fall short of the total marginal benefits, individuals will not be in equilibrium and they will, accordingly, vote to extend the activity. At the "solution," all of the necessary conditions are satisfied, and total incremental benefits equal total marginal costs. No externalities exist.[13]

The reason for this result is not difficult to understand. By imposing the restriction that the individual voter must pay for the marginal unit of the collective good or service in proportion to the marginal benefit enjoyed, it is insured that the individual's private calculus becomes a miniature reflection of the aggregate or "social" calculus that would be made by an omniscient, benevolent despot acting in the interests of all persons in the community. The individual voter cannot, because of the restrictions on the model, impose external costs on others in the group through the political process. In his private voting decision he will recognise that additional units of the collective good will yield benefits to others than himself. But he will, under the self-interest assumption, not be influenced by these spillover benefits at all. There are, however, also spillover marginal costs that the provision of the additional units of the collective good will impose on his fellows, and the neglected external benefits will tend to offset these neglected external costs.

This highly restricted model has several interesting features. First of all, note that the sharp difference in result as between the market and the political solution emerges only if the self-interest assumption about human motivation is consistently adopted and applied. If, by contrast, the universal benevolence assumption is introduced, the market organisation and the political organisation will tend to produce similar results, as in the earlier analyses. Secondly, if the self-interest assumption is adopted, the political result

13. This solution is that which has been rigorously defined by Paul A. Samuelson. See his "The Pure Theory of Public Expenditure," *Review of Economics and Statistics*, XXXVI (1954), 386–89; "Diagrammatic Exposition of a Theory of Public Expenditure," *Review of Economics and Statistics*, XXXVII (1955), 350–56.

in the restricted model here will tend to be identical under *any* voting rule. Any rule will, under the constitutional restrictions imposed, tend to produce a solution that satisfies all of the necessary conditions for Pareto optimality. The single individual acting as a dictator, the simple majority, and the rule of unanimity: each of these will tend to produce the same results. These separate rules for making political decisions only become important because they reflect differences in the ability of some members of the group to impose costs on other members, an ability that is specifically eliminated by the constitutional restrictions postulated.

It is not, of course, surprising to find that the Pigovian analysis has relevant policy implications only for the provision of genuinely collective (perfectly indivisible) goods and services. Indeed, the statement that externalities exist in any private market solution is one means of stating that genuinely collective elements characterise the activity under consideration. This restricted model indicates clearly, however, that the good must be wholly collective if the implications of the Pigovian analysis are to apply. If an activity is only quasi-collective, that is to say, if it contains elements that are privately divisible as well as collective elements, the political solution must also involve externalities. The restricted model analysed here is perhaps even more useful in pointing up the extremely limited tax scheme that is required for the analysis to apply at all. Even for those goods and services that are wholly collective in nature, the provision of them through the political process will produce Pigovian-like externalities at the margin unless taxes are collected on the basis of marginal benefits. In the real world, very few, if any, goods and services are wholly collective. And even if these few could be isolated, they would not be financed by taxes levied on this principle of incremental benefits enjoyed. Such a principle is not only politically unimaginable in modern democracy, it is also conceptually impossible. Its application would require that the taxing authorities be able to determine, in advance, all individual preference functions. It must be concluded, therefore, that the restricted institutional model in which the implications of the standard externality analysis might apply is nothing but a conceptual toy. In the real world, political results must embody externalities as collective decision makers: individuals are able, by political means, to impose costs on other individuals.

v.

In Part III it was demonstrated that the generalised implications of the Pigovian analysis could be supported only on the adoption of a highly questionable conception of human motivation. In Part IV it was demonstrated that these implications would be drawn from a consistent motivational model only if this model should be so highly restricted as to make the analysis of little practical value. It is much easier, however, to explain the reasons for economists neglecting to examine these aspects of their analyses than it is to justify their neglect. As Knut Wicksell suggested many years ago, most economists are content with assuming the presence of a benevolent despot. Insofar as their analyses point toward policy at all, as they must, the improvements in efficiency advanced are assumed to be attainable within the realm of the politically possible. The almost universal neglect of the imperfections that might arise from the political attempts at applying the economists' efficiency criteria represents a serious deficiency in the work of welfare economists and economists generally. To shy away from considerations of the politically feasible has been deemed an admirable trait, but to refuse to examine the politically possible is incomplete scholarship.

14

Institutional Elements in the Financing of Education

William Craig Stubblebine[1]

Generating financial support for education has commanded and will continue to command concern on the part of parents and educators, business and government. Expert studies purport to show a discrepancy between realized and desired levels of support estimated at several billion dollars.[2] At the same time, a wide range of fiscal institutions—e.g., full tuition charges, tax financing, tax credits, systems of grants-in-aid from the public treasury, etc.—has been proposed as a means to eliminate, or at least to diminish, this discrepancy. The diversity of these recommendations suggests that their advocates differ in their evaluation of the relative effectiveness of these fiscal institutions in financing education.

One obvious need is an explicit comparison of these fiscal institutions in terms of the funds, both private and public, generated in support of education. This unique topic delineates the investigation presented here.

It should be emphasized at the outset that my concern is not with the optimal amount of education to be financed. While it seems

Reprinted by permission of the author and publisher from *Southern Economic Journal* (Supplement), vol. XXXII, no. 1, pt. 2 (July 1965).

1. The author acknowledges his general indebtedness to many published works. For purposes of the Conference for which the paper was prepared, only the most specific references are cited. I should like to acknowledge the helpful comments of James M. Buchanan and Bertram F. Levin. In part, the research was carried out with support from the University of Delaware General Faculty Research Fund.

2. *America's Needs and Resources, A New Survey* (New York, 1955), where the total expenditure for an adequate educational program in 1960 was estimated at $21.9 billion (at 1950 prices) and actual educational expenditures were expected to be $15.3 billion (at 1950 prices)—a discrepancy of $6.6 billion.

safe to say that education has strong characteristics of a public good, the absence of a fully developed theory of externalities precludes an attempt to define optimal levels—as does the inchoate nature of the data on the magnitude of externality relations and of the education-economic growth relation at the relevant margins of decision making. In addition, comparisons in terms of the quality of education, in terms of the distribution of funds among geographic regions or economic classes, and in terms of sociological implications are excluded both for reasons of manageability and data deficiencies. Similar considerations arise with any attempt to compare the fiscal equity of the institutions studied.

One can seek further justification for these exclusions by noting that their reconciliation turns on normative considerations. By contrast, the study reported here is essentially descriptive in concept. The concern is not with how people should respond to opportunities to support education, but how they may be expected to respond to the constraints of given fiscal institutions. In any event, even this relatively narrow topic is sufficiently complex to warrant separate treatment.

In no way is it the intention to deprecate the excluded areas. They *are* important. Any comprehensive discussion of education requires a blending of many goals, some of them conflicting. The generation of financial support is but one. The present topic deserves attention only to the extent that it can be of assistance in guiding debate on educational questions.

Before introducing the primary model, let me anticipate one frequent, and favorite, criticism of studies such as this. The models, at least initially, are unabashedly analytical. It is a familiar device of social scientists, and of economists in particular, to use models which depart significantly from the complex real world. The procedure is so familiar and so discussed that one might pass over it without mention. That the technique survives in spite of legions of critics suggests a great strength—not necessity as is frequently the justification—but strength. The defense of simple analytical models is this: abstract models may be more successful than more complicated[3] models in revealing the essential or predominant influences. This is, I believe, the case with the models presented here.

1. *The Model*

Let us begin by imagining a community (society) of homo sapiens organized as family units, but without any other social or political

---

3. As opposed to "sophisticated."

grouping. These family units operate (that is, make decisions) within a pre-existing constitution and legal system. Activity is normally private rather than collective. Within the constitutional constraints, whatever collective actions taken are resolved by simple majority. Voting is by community-wide referendum. The fiscal institution is constitutionally specified. Finally, each family unit is assumed to maximize its welfare (or utility), given its preferences and the community's constitutional-legal constraints.

Several assumptions of this model are noteworthy. Of primary concern is the "choice behavior" (act of choosing) within a given institution, not among institutions. Constitutionally specifying the fiscal institution removes the higher, and ultimately determinant, choice among institutions. Second, there is one and only one community, and one and only one level of government. Thus, complications introduced by multi-community societies and/or multi-level governments (e.g., national, state, and local) are eliminated. Finally, there are no "legislative representatives." The setting of pure democracy serves to eliminate the complex problem of predicting outcomes of the decision-making process in representative assemblies. The shorn model nevertheless goes far in laying bare the elemental choice behavior of the family unit. In a democratic free-market oriented society, the resolution of these choices *is* the community choice.

To lend substance to the model, let us refer to a Basic Arithmetic Model wherein the community is composed of n ($=20$) family units. m ($=15$) family units have one child, $n - m$ ($=5$) have no children. Of the m family units with children, m' (#'s 1-10) have "average" educational preferences for their children and m'' (#'s 11-15) have "high" educational preferences. Family units *within* each of the three groups have identical educational preferences, as depicted in Figure 1 ("average educational preferences"), Figure 2 ("high educational preferences"), and Figure 3 ("no-children educational preferences"). Family units without children consume education vicariously through education of children of other family units. Relative to other families, they have "low" educational preferences. For family units with children, preferences for education of other children in the community is summarized in preferences for their own children's education.[4]

4. Perhaps this particular methodological step requires justification. Under several of the fiscal institutions, there is a one-to-one correspondence between the educational resources devoted to one's own child and those devoted to all children. In other cases, no such correspondence holds, though one might argue that the correspondence is close.

All family units have annual money incomes of y $(=\$1,000)$; total community income is Y $(=\$20,000)$. All have (nonhuman) capital assets of k $(=\$1,000)$; total community (nonhuman) assets are K $(=\$20,000)$. All annual income is spent, hence there is no new saving or dissaving, and capital assets are constant through time. The community operates under an existing constitutional provision which requires collective spending of G $(=\$2,000)$ per annum on "public goods." Resources represented by G are raised through an appropriate proportional tax on annual income. The operating budget, exclusive of capital investment, is strictly balanced at all times. (Given G and Y, the appropriate tax is 10%; post-tax family income, y_t, is $900.) The per unit per pupil opportunity cost of education is c $(=\$10)$ per year, constant over all units. It is assumed that each family acts to maximize its own level of satisfaction.[5]

Having established the Basic Arithmetic Model, one is now in a position to compare the levels of education supported by the community (the dependent variable) under various selected fiscal institutions (the independent variable). All other data of the basic model are held constant. The results are tabulated in Table 1.

If not particularly surprising, the results are interesting. The largest educational support is generated within institutions which mix private and public financing (Models C-1, C-2, and D-1). The smallest support is generated by full parental financing (Models

---

Preference systems are assumed to have the usual characteristics favored in the economists' theory of maximizing behavior. Thus indifference curves relating money income and educational units are convex to the origin, whether this be money income and per child educational units for families with children or money income and total (community) education for families without children. These preference systems incorporate a host of variables among which the most significant are likely to be the child's future earning stream both absolutely and vis-a-vis other children (which is, at least partially, a consequence of the community's economic growth), his personal capacity to enjoy life, and the future health-welfare-stability of the community.

If a separate community educational variable is attributed to families with children, the "usual" preference characteristics are no longer certain. More education for my child—hence less for other children—surely improves his position vis-a-vis other children. At the same time, less education for other children may so diminish economic growth that my child is absolutely worse off. On the other hand, it might not. On balance, the sensible course seems to be to assume that the error introduced by treating the correspondence as if it were one-to-one is *de minimis*.

5. Or acts as if it were maximizing something which may be termed satisfaction.

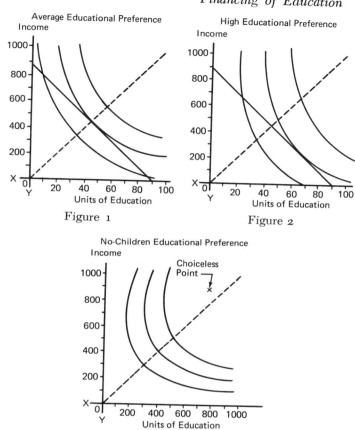

Figure 1

Figure 2

Figure 3

A-1, D-2). Full public financing generates "middling" support (Models B-1, B-2, B-3). In studying the institutions themselves it will be helpful to keep these results in mind.[6]

11. *Full Private Financing*

If one thinks of education under full private financing, one imagines a system of schools which the children of the community attend each day. Depending upon the size of the community and upon the most

6. A still simpler model—one with only average educational preferences—would produce identical results under both full public financing and mixed financing, as shown in Fig. 1 under the column headed "average." For this reason it would be less illustrative of critical character differences than the model used. The reasons will become apparent in the discussion which follows.

Table 1

Results of the Basic Arithmetic Model[1]

| | | Units consumed by families with | | |
| | | "aver- age" | "high" | the Com- mu- |
Model Number	Fiscal Institution	educational preference		nity
	A. Full Private Financing			
A-1	without philanthropic subsidies	45	67	785
A-2	with philanthropic subsidies	50	76	880
	B. Full Public Financing			
B-1	with capital asset taxation	63	63	945
B-2	with personal income taxation	63	63	945
B-3	with general sales taxation	63	63	945
	C. Mixed Private Financing and Public Financing from General Tax Revenues			
C-1	with per pupil grants to educational institutions	63	79	1025
C-2	with per pupil grant to parents	63	79	1025
	D. Mixed Private Financing and Public Financing through Tax Adjustments			
D-1	with tax credits	63	79	1025
D-2	with tax deductions	48	67	815

1. Given the preference systems shown in Figures 1, 2, and 3, anyone familiar with the use of indifference maps may derive these results with ease.

efficient resource combination, there may be only one school or several competing schools. The schools themselves are bundles of economic resources—building, materials, teachers, and managers.[7] The quantity of resources required for any given school is a function both of the number of educational units furnished each pupil and of the number of pupils in attendance. The funds necessary to command these resources are raised by tuition charges imposed upon pupils or the parents of these pupils. The magnitude of the tuition charged would be dependent upon the quantity of education fur-

7. While privately financed, the schools may be either privately or publicly owned and operated.

nished to the pupil. Given either an actual or an "as if" competitive environment, per unit per pupil tuition charges equal the resource costs.[8]

Without philanthropic assistance

Corresponding to the first of the fiscal institutions examined, a constitutional provision prohibits any real or money transfers between family units designed to aid or alter in any way the purchase of education by any family. This is a crucial characteristic for it eliminates any means whereby families without children may alter the choices of families with children—even when it would be to their advantage to do so.[9] Each family unit must bear the full cost of educating its children.

For purposes of this paper it can be taken as given that the individual family unit knows its preferences or utility function, its money income, prices of all available goods and services (including education), and the constitutional-legal constraints on choices. With this knowledge the family seeks that combination of its purchases which maximizes its utility, that is, maximizes

(1) $U^i = U^i(e^i, x_1^i, \ldots, x_r^i, g^i)$ $(i = 1, \ldots, 20)$

subject to

(2) $y^i = p_e^i e^i + \Sigma p_j x_j^i + t^i$[10] $(j = 1, \ldots, r)$.

For families with children, utility maximization corresponds to adjusting the quantity of education purchases so as to satisfy

(3) $u_e^m/u_r^m = p_e^m/p_r$[11] $(m = 1, \ldots, 15)$.

8. In a society largely conditioned to fixed school terms, whether the education produced be considered good or bad, additional units of education are best associated with increased quality. In fact, where competition is efficient, differences in educational expenditure per pupil can only represent differences in quality. (This applies with equal force to our competing public school systems of the United States.)

9. Other than persuasion which is not taken into account here.

10. For simplicity, utility functions exhibit no externality relations other than the one associated with educational choices.

11. The definition of each variable is as follows: Right superscript—the designated family unit;

U^i—the utility function of the (ith) family unit;

e^i—units of education consumed by the family (for families without children the educational variable becomes Σe^i);

Using the familiar indifference map, this corresponds to selecting that combination of post-tax–post-purchase money income and educational units at which the budget line is tangent to the highest attainable indifference curve.

In terms of the Basic Arithmetic Model, we find from Figure 1 that families with average educational preferences choose forty-five units of education. Those with high educational preferences choose sixty-seven units (Fig. 2).[12] Families without children do no selection and, hence, find themselves at a choiceless point the coordinates of which are post-tax income and total community education (Fig. 3). As a whole, the community consumes 785 units, or resources worth $7850.

With philanthropic assistance

Dropping the constitutional provision which prohibits private or philanthropic assistance to education alters the constraints within which families choose educational levels. The subsidization of purchases is one means by which families without children may influence the choices of child-rearing families. In order that some determinacy may be introduced into the Basic Arithmetic Model, let this subsidizing institution be constructed as follows: Families can assist the education of children by equally contributing to a fund which will return to parents a portion of their per unit pupil expenditures. The per unit level of the subsidy is identical for all pupils over all units.

The significant difference between this and the first institution is that the community solution now involves joint maximization of utilities. The level of education chosen by parents depends upon the amount of the subsidy; the size of the fund, hence the amount of the

---

x_j^i—units of the jth activity $(j = 1, \ldots, r)$ consumed by the family;

g^i—public goods provided for in the constitution available to the family;

y^i—annual money income of the family;

t^i—tax contribution of the family to constitutionally required collective spending of G;

p_e^i—per unit price of educational units to the family;

p_j—constant competitive price of the jth activity;

u_j^i—$\partial U^i/\partial x_j^i$.

12. This is one of the cases in which the education of one's own child is not in one-to-one correspondence with total community education. For its general implications, see footnote 4, *supra*. In particular, it means that the units chosen here are an approximation, but probably a good one.

subsidy, depends upon the level of education chosen by parents. Some agency acting for the community, in this case the fund, must reconcile the preferences of individual family units. The choice of any one family unit is no longer independent of the choices of other family units.

Given the preference functions and the specified subsidizing institution, a mathematical-geometrical solution is relatively easy to obtain. Each of the infinity of per unit subsidies will determine some unique quantity of education purchased by parents; their sum over all families constitutes the unique community total. Conceptually, a somewhat more realistic alternative is for the fund to announce various per unit subsidies. Parents could indicate to the fund the quantities of education they would choose. Any incentive that parents may have to dissemble in announcing their choices will be minimized by their uncertainty as to how these choices will affect the size of the fund established. If this is not sufficient, the fund may penalize those who do dissemble. In either case, the response information provides the nonchild family with a locus of attainable positions (i.e., a budget line) on which to base its level of contribution. And, in turn, this provides parents with a similar locus on which to base their educational purchases.

Solved geometrically in terms of the Basic Arithmetic Model, we find that the per unit subsidy level is approximately one dollar. This generates purchases of fifty units by families with average educational preferences and purchases of seventy-six units by families with high educational preferences. Thus, the community consumes 880 units with a resource value of $8,800.[13]

As between the two institutions of full private financing, philanthropy should lead to a higher level of educational support. Several comments on the model constructed here seem called for. As a technical matter, the fund would be likely to find that differential subsidies would repay larger dividends than would uniform per unit subsidies in altering parental choices. Specifically, the fund would tend to concentrate its resources on families with high educational preferences (especially if contributors are sensitive only to total education and not to distribution among families). While this too can be solved by introducing a variable for subsidy differentials among

13. Here again the results are approximate since the correspondence is not one-to-one between child and total community levels of education. An additional error might be introduced if parents also could contribute to the fund.

families, for present purposes it hardly seems worth the computational effort required. The result would not be likely to alter the ranking of the institutions in terms of the funds generated. A real world fund might well reach this same conclusion.

More significantly, it is apparent that a ban on philanthropic assistance disadvantages all members of the community. Gains-from-trade would exist; agreement for removal of the ban could be secured unanimously. By definition, creation of the fund is a type of collective action, albeit private.

Next, it was assumed that families without children contribute equally to the fund. Somewhat different results would be likely to occur if these families contributed serially on a family-to-family basis. Either of two situations may arise: the "free rider" problem which has been discussed extensively in the literature, and the "impotent giver" problem (considerably less discussed).[14]

In the first situation, the initial subsidizer will elicit some change in the community's level of education, as will all who follow him. At some point, any given subsidizer may conclude that his retirement from the process would now be advantageous to him. As far as he is concerned, withdrawal of his contribution alters the outcome but little. If this decision is reached by all more or less simultaneously, each will find his expectations disappointed as education diminishes to its no subsidy level. In turn, this initiates a new round of subsidization. The consequences of such an oscillation for education and for the community's welfare may well be deemed intolerable by the whole, or at least a major part, of the community.

The second situation is a sort of inverted free rider problem. Cooperatively, subsidizers might gain significant advantages for all. But acting individually, each may conclude that the educational changes elicited by his contribution is too slight to repay his sacrifice of private goods and services. Each feels too impotent to stimulate education. As a result, no subsidy is forthcoming.

The solution to these problems leads us back to the observation that the fund is a type of collective action. Unanimous agreement, at least among potential subsidizers, may be reached to establish some institution which assures the continued cooperation of all concerned. Collective action in the form of a private fund to which each contributes equally is one possibility. Some coercive tax institution is an even more potent possibility, particularly if the community has a sizeable population (e.g., a nation). Here may well be

14. One of the few discussions which comes to mind is that of W.S. Vickrey, "One Economist's View of Philanthropy," *Philanthropy and Public Policy*, F.G. Dickinson, ed. (New York, 1962), especially pp. 40–44.

found the basis for coercive, collective organization of education associated with government.

Some evidence may be adduced from the history of educational finance. However important to the quality of education, private financing without philanthropy has been quantitatively insignificant. From the beginning of recorded time, some subsidization has been forthcoming privately or publicly. While individual men of wealth have from time to time acted independently, private subsidization usually has involved cooperation, often with some element of coercion. As one example, established churches have succeeded at times past in imposing a general obligation on the faithful to support church schools. In the main, however, the trend has been toward deliberate public decisions to support education through coercive taxation. Today the bulk of education is financed publicly.

iii. *Full Public Financing*

Full public financing collectivizes the community's choice as to the level of education, distribution of educational resources among pupils, and source of command over educational resources. Choices concerning these variables are made publicly, not privately. Some public body, in the form of a constitution or an operating government, must make these choices for the community as a whole and for every individual member. To be sure, if the society is democratic in organization, family preferences may condition public decisions. But parents have no freedom to supplement or to reduce the education of their children independently of the public choice. This, the absence of independent action, is the salient feature in any definitive construction of full public financing.

With the passing of extensive public domains, full public financing is synonymous with taxation, that is with compulsory payments by individual economic units. To specify a particular public fiscal institution is to specify the source or tax base of payment and the rate or tax structure applied to the base. For present purposes, the constitution is assumed to specify either capital assets or annual money income or annual consumption as the source base and a proportional rate structure whatever the base. Similarly, the constitution provides that exactly the same number of educational units must be devoted to each child. With two of the choices constitutionally constrained, only the level of education is subject to community choice.

In keeping with previous assumptions, the collective decision on the level of education is rendered in a community-wide referendum. For simplicity, the referendum takes a very special form. In place of the usual yes or no, each voter indicates the level of education he prefers. Polling officials then order the indicated levels from highest to lowest. Each vote for a given quantity is also counted as a vote for any smaller quantity. That level which receives a simple majority is declared the community's collective choice. By construction it corresponds to the middle or *median* preference of the electorate. Note that, assuming competitive utilization of resources, the community's choice as to the level of education determines simultaneously the proportional tax rate, and vice versa.

Rational choice on the part of the family voting unit need be little more difficult than an analogous fully private choice. As a theoretical-mathematical matter, the rational voter-taxpayer-beneficiary will realize that the community resource requirement of any educational unit is the product of the per unit cost and the number of children in the community, that is, cm. The tax rate per unit of education per unit of base is simply cm/B. Per unit of education, the family with children pays $p_e^i = (cm/B)b^{i}$.[15] Combined with its preference function, money income, and the price of other goods and services, the family may proceed as before to select and to vote that level of education which maximizes its utility. The difference here is that family choice and community choice coincide only for median families. For all others, the community choice is either too high or too low.

By contrast with the full private-cost of $10, the per unit public price of education to families is $7.50 in the Basic Arithmetic Model.[16] At this public price, high preference families seek ninety-three units of education per child, average preference families sixty-three units. Families without children would prefer a community total of 900 units, or sixty units per child. With the 5-10-5 population distribution, the median, and in a sense controlling preference, is sixty-three units. Total community education is 945 units at a resource cost of $9,450.

Institutional comparisons—theory

Reference to Table I suggests two propositions which, if generally true, are significant: (a) that full public financing generates

15. Since families without children consume education vicariously, their price is $p_e^i = (c/B)b^i$. B is the community's base—capital assets (K) or annual money income (Y) or annual consumption ($Q = \Sigma\Sigma p_j x_j^i$); b^i is the base of the ith family unit—k^i, y^i, or q^i. Note that each family can estimate its share of every community dollar spent by estimating its share of the community's base, (b^i/B).

16. On a per child basis, this breaks down to $0.50 for families without children.

larger support for education than full private financing, and (*b*) that the community level of education is identical under each of the fully public financing institutions. While the first is plausible enough, the second is likely to be challenged strongly. But intuition is often a poor substitute for analysis. At this level of abstraction, it would seem that the second possesses greater generality than the first. Both must be examined in some detail.

Public financing substitutes a criterion other than use of educational resources as a basis for payment.[17] If, for example, the basis is capital, ownership of capital assets fixes liability. The level of education determines the amount of the liability, but not its location.

A shift from private to public financing unequivocally would induce higher education levels only if it simultaneously reduced the price of education to all economic units. This it cannot do. What public financing does is to admit the possibility of shifting part of the resource cost from some users to other users. In the Basic Arithmetic Model, the price of education to parents fell from $10.00 without subsidy to $9.00 with philanthropy to $7.50 with public financing because part of the burden was increasingly borne by families without children. For the latter, the price rose from zero to 20 cents to 50 cents per unit of community education.

In a slightly altered model, one where all families had one child, the price of education for each family would have been identical under both private and public financing. On the other hand, if the tax base had been unequally distributed, those with a less than average share of the base could have shifted a part of the resource cost to those with an above average share. At least one of the two circumstances must be present if the public and private prices of education are to differ: there must be nonusers or an unequal distribution of the tax base. Since both are typical of the real world, this requirement is not particularly onerous.

The mere presence of dissimilarities among economic units is not sufficient to guarantee a higher level of publicly financed education. The level of education uniform throughout the community is determined by the *median* preference. Under private financing, the average level of education responds to the range of private family purchases, which itself reflects differences in preferences and incomes. *A priori*, there is no way of knowing how the median public level will compare with the average level under full private financing.

17. "Use" is not to be confused with "benefit." Although all families may benefit from education of the community's children, only parents (or their children) may be properly said to use the resources.

Collectivizing education eliminates what may be an important element of competition among parents. Under any institution which permits families to choose quantities of education independently of other families, parents are forced to consider the effect of their individual choices on the child's future economic position vis-à-vis other children. Differential advantages in the form of a larger share of future community income accrues to those children whose parents are successful in securing relatively more education. To fall behind is to doom the child to a lower standard of living in future years. In effect, parents are faced with a "prisoners" dilemma.[18] For each parent, the optimal response or strategy is to seek ever more education. By imposing uniformity among children, public financing removes the dilemma and permits parents to choose lower levels of education.[19]

Public financing is more likely to increase total community support if there is a sizeable minority group of non-users (e.g., families without children) to whom parents as a group can shift a significant part of their educational burden. The greater the number of parents for whom the public price of education is below the private price, the higher is the median level likely to be. The higher the median level, the greater is the likelihood that the median public level of education will exceed the average private level. While the result in the Basic Arithmetic Model is purely fortuitous, the model well illustrates the way in which this effect may operate.

The foregoing remarks apply equally to both fully private financing institutions. No separate treatment has been required. Comparison of private philanthropy and public finance, however, does involve a special consideration. The amount of a private subsidy is entirely the choice of the subsidizers, not the subsidized. By contrast, the amount of a public subsidy is determined by the median voter who will be in all probability a parent. It is at least conceivable that the median voter will set a level of education which requires a smaller per unit subsidy than that which would have been forthcoming voluntarily from private gifts. If this should be the case, the median level of education would almost certainly decline with a change from private to public financing.

This possibility must be balanced with the "free rider—impotent giver" problem explored above. Voluntary contributions may carry

18. Cf. R. D. Luce and H. Raiffa, *Games and Decisions* (New York: John Wiley & Sons, 1957), pp. 94–97.

19. Though outside the scope of this model, this element of competition may exist between independent school districts in a multi-community society even with full public financing in each district.

with them an aura of insignificance. The stronger and more wide-spread this feeling is among potential contributors, the smaller the level of private subsidization. In turn, this would increase the probability that the level of compulsory subsidization associated with the median vote will be larger than the level achieved voluntarily.

If full public financing does not insure a higher level of community support for education, it raises the question: "What does it do?" As suggested, it may facilitate the subsidization process. It establishes a minimum level of education for each child. In terms of other criteria not included in this study, this may be much more important than maximizing the level of community education. But, as discussion will show, both goals can be achieved under institutions which combine private and public financing. Beyond this, full public financing equalizes educational opportunities among children by constraining all choices to the median. For some, this may be the most important result. It carries with it the warning, however, that in a democratic society one who supports equality must be prepared to accept this equality at the median level.

Perhaps the best way to approach the second proposition is by building on the results of the Basic Arithmetic Model. The identity of publicly financed outcomes in this model can be traced directly to the equal distribution of capital, income, and, in the absence of savings or tax discrimination, consumption. For every family, the public price of education is the same under all three tax institutions. The critical feature, however, is not the equal distribution of bases but the equality of base share for every family. This suggests a more general proposition: As between any two alternative tax institutions with identical tax structures and distributions of preferences, if every economic unit has the same share of each tax base, the median choice will be the same under both institutions.[20]

Neither case is wholly appropriate for the real world where family shares of income and shares of capital may exhibit significant variations. For any given family, the public price of education may vary considerably with the base employed. But it would be a "fallacy of composition" to conclude from this that the median choice must also be subject to wide variation. If the public price with income taxation is higher than with capital taxation for my family, it must be lower for some other family. It follows, therefore, that my preferred level of education will be lower with income taxation,

---

20. The distribution of the base among families need not be equal. It is the shares as between bases for the family, not the share of the base among families, which must be equal.

but will be higher for some other family. Though the median voter may change from base to base, the median preference may remain the same. In fact, if one base is normally distributed with respect to each level of the first, and educational preferences are normally distributed with respect to each combination of bases, the median preference will tend to be the same under both taxing institutions.[21]

This is not to deny that models can be constructed wherein the median choice would be greatly altered. But between the extremes of equal shares and normally distributed bases must lie many cases in which the median preference is unchanged. At least at this theoretical level, all general full public financing institutions would seem to generate identical levels of community support for education. All of which suggests that if differences in support levels do exist in practice, they probably stem from distorting characteristics of real world use.

Institutional comparisons—real world

Included in the base of capital asset taxation envisioned above would be all forms of nonhuman assets, net of liabilities, held by families: real tangible property (land, buildings and improvements), tangible personal property (automobiles, furniture), and intangible property (stocks, bonds, mortgages, cash). Corporate assets, rather than bearing taxation directly, would be reached through family ownership of corporate securities; noncorporate business assets would be attributed directly to their owners. Taken together there is no *a priori* reason not to assume that these assets are normally distributed with respect to family income.

In sharp contrast, asset taxation as generally applied today is a tax on the gross value of real tangible property. Intangible and tangible personal property, for quite understandable reasons of administration, is rarely taxed. There is ample evidence that asset forms are not normally distributed. Higher-income families tend to hold much larger portions of their gross assets as intangibles or as business properties. Lower-income families tend to hold most of their gross assets as tangible property. For many, their primary asset is a heavily mortgaged home on which interest payments are deductible from personal income taxation. To this must be added the fact that, during the family's life span, lower income years are likely to be associated with child-bearing and child-rearing years.

21. Note that the bases are normally, *not* equally, distributed. I offer this hypothesis after a somewhat limited investigation. Much more investigation needs to be done in this area.

It would seem to follow that, for the majority of families, their share of income will be lower than their share of taxable property. By so affecting the majority, the public price of education would be higher and the median educational preference lower with real property taxation than with income taxation.

This reckons without several conflicting considerations. The direct taxation of business property ostensibly creates a pool of non-voting taxable assets to which parents can shift a significant part of their educational burden.[22] But then so does separate taxation of corporate income. An apparent tendency to assess business properties at higher ratios than residential properties would tend to favor property taxation; a similar tendency to assess expensive residential property at lower ratios to favor income taxation. Deductibility of medical expenses and the dependents' exemptions would also tend to favor income taxation, as does the progressive structure of personal income taxation. On balance, this latter and the extent of home mortgages probably favors income taxation in the choice process of most families.

Consumption taxation involves somewhat similar details. By virtue of the ban on savings in the arithmetic model, family income equals family consumption expenditures. The two tax institutions yield identical results. In reality, substantial savings take place out of current income. Available evidence indicates that income and the average propensity to save are positively correlated. Upper income families save a larger, and hence consume a smaller, portion of their incomes. As a result, lower income families are likely to have a larger share of community consumption than of income and, quite probably, of taxable property. For a majority of families, the price of education financed by consumption taxation is likely to be higher, and the median educational preference lower, than that financed by income or property taxation.[23]

To this point, the analysis has proceeded on the basis that voting units possessed both information adequate for rational choice and a sensitive device for registering preferences. It was noted that rational choice in the setting of public financing need be no more difficult than in a market setting. In practice, it may be exceedingly

---

22. This assumes that a tax on business assets is not shifted to consumers in the form of higher prices.

23. The practice of exempting expenditures for food and services tends to reduce the relative disadvantage of consumption taxation; the progressive structure of personal income taxation tends to increase its advantage.

difficult. Neither assumption bears much resemblance to the world as we find it. Essential items of information are often difficult, if not impossible, for the average voter to obtain. Referenda are the exception rather than the rule, and never in the form presented here.

In most cases, voters are forced to make multi-dimensional choices—accepting or rejecting elected officials or multi-service budgets—in the face of preponderant uncertainty as to how relevant alternatives will affect them as individuals. Involved are problems of the shifting and incidence of taxation, the large and unsettled areas of legislative assemblies (school boards, town councils, or state legislatures), single service versus general fund financing, earmarking of revenues, measurement of outputs, and intergovernmental relations. Space does not permit discussion either of the origins of the problems or of their possible repercussions on the level of community education. One need only note that they arise whenever public financing is involved. Thus, while they may influence the rank order of institutions within classes in terms of the support generated, there is no obvious reason why they should influence the rank order of classes.

Before turning to mixed fiscal institutions, it may be of interest to observe that public financing carries with it seeds of discontent. Voting does not secure for each his preferred position. Only those for whom the community choice corresponds to their preference will be satisfied by the results. For those who would have preferred more education at the public price, the body politic will appear niggardly and irresponsible. Those who will have preferred less education will castigate the body politic for its profligate and irresponsible behavior. These reactions are generated quite apart from any consideration of the optimal level of community education. Regardless of whether the level of education is optimal, there will be all the symptoms of pervasive social imbalance in education. All too often this basic characteristic of public decision-making is overlooked.

IV. *Mixed Private Financing and Public Financing From General Revenue*

Mixed fiscal institutions combine characteristics of both full private and full public financing. One imagines that the system of schools would be much like that described under private financing. Schools may be either privately or publicly owned and operated. The needed resources depend upon the educational units made available to each pupil and upon the number of pupils enrolled. Essentially, the only difference is that some minimum level of education for each child is prescribed by the body politic.

Schools may offer the minimum program or any educational program which utilizes more resources than those required to achieve the minimum. They may not offer programs which utilize fewer resources. Parents have complete freedom to choose any program at or above the minimum. The resource cost of the minimum level of education is financed entirely by public funds. The funds required to finance any part of a program in excess of the minimum are raised by tuition charges imposed upon pupils or their parents.

Financing of the minimum level from general tax revenues may be carried out in one of two ways. Public grants may be paid directly to educational institutions on the basis of a school's enrollment. Alternatively, per pupil grants can be furnished parents in the form of educational vouchers which are surrendered to the schools upon enrollment. Analytically, the two methods are equivalent. Whether the grants are paid directly to schools or indirectly to parents, the per unit publicly financed price of education for families with children is, as before, $(cm/B)b^i$. In either case, tuition charges to parents will be zero if the school provides and the parent chooses only the minimum prescribed program. For programs above the minimum, tuition charges equal the per pupil resource cost minus the per pupil subsidy.

Decision making in a world of mixed fiscal institutions involves a dual choice for families. The community as a whole must arrive at some decision regarding the minimum level of education to be financed through taxation. As with full public financing, this is done in a community-wide referendum in which each voter indicates his preferred level of subsidy. Once the median preference is determined and the community decision rendered, each family must decide how much additional education it will finance from its post-tax income at the marginal resource cost. If, at the family's post-educational tax position, the marginal rate of substitution between education and other goods exceeds the private price, the private purchase of additional units of education will increase the family's utility. If the marginal rate of substitution is less than or equal to the private price, families have nothing to gain by adding to the subsidized level and are constrained from taking less.[24]

24. Families for which the marginal rate of substitution is less than the private price could improve their utility position if they could secure refunds at the private price for accepting less than the prescribed minimum level of education. This is a warning that, in the case of public grants to schools, schools must not be permitted to "pay" parents for enrolling children and, in the case of vouchers, schools must not be permitted to refund any part to parents.

Assuming that the tax base is annual income, the public price of education is $7.50 in the Basic Arithmetic Model.[25] At this price, high preference families would prefer that the public subsidy finance ninety-three units of education. Average preference families would prefer sixty-three units. Families without children would seek a community subsidy of about ten units per child, counting on additional private purchases of parents to raise the community total to 810 units. Given the model's population distribution, the median preference is that of an average family: sixty-three units or $630 per child.

Having achieved their preferred level, average families find that the private price of education exceeds their marginal rate of substitution. They will not wish to finance additional education. On the other hand, high preference families will seek sixteen units more than the subsidized level of education or a total of seventy-nine units. The community as a whole consumes 1,025 units of education or resources worth $10,250. This contrasts favorably with the 945 units consumed by the community under full public financing.

Institutional comparisons

By comparison with full private or public financing, the altered constraints of mixed fiscal institutions have vital repercussions on both the preferred level of public subsidization and the total level of community education. With full public financing, the family's choice is between zero education and some positive level at a price determined by its share of the tax base. There is no private price of education, no private independent choice of educational levels to be made.

With mixed financing, parents for whom the public price of education exceeds the alternative private price will prefer to finance their children's education entirely on their own. Accordingly they will favor a zero public subsidy. By contrast, under full public financing, these same families would choose some positive level of education (possibly a level above the median), even though the public price exceeds the marginal resource cost of education.

Parents for whom the public price equals the private price will be indifferent as to the subsidy level. They bear exactly the same burden per unit however education is financed. If they exhibit a preference during the referendum, it will be on other grounds, per-

25. Although all tax bases yield identical results in the Basic Arithmetic Model, the remarks concerning alternative tax institutions also apply here.

haps ideological or their interest in the education of children other than their own. Parents for whom the public price is below the private price will prefer full subsidization of whatever level of education they choose. The level they vote for will be exactly the same as the level preferred under full public financing. Finally, as long as they are indifferent to the distribution of education among children, families without children will prefer a lower level of publicly financed education under mixed than under full public institutions. Their reaction reflects the fact that some parents will privately finance education above the minimum.

This, then, provides the range of preferences recorded in the referendum. Some families will prefer no subsidy; some will be indifferent as to the subsidy level. Some will prefer the same level under either full public or mixed financing; some will prefer lower levels of subsidy. The median preference falls only if one or more families which would have expressed above-median preferences under full public financing now express a below-median preference. Ignoring those which are indifferent to the subsidy level, the most likely families to do this are those with above-average shares of the tax base. In a shift of institutions, their preference falls to zero. On the whole, however, one would expect little effect on the median preference from this source, unless there is a strong correlation between above-average tax shares and above-median levels of preference.

It seems reasonable to assume that families without children would have recorded below-median preferences under full public financing. The fact that they prefer still lower levels with mixed financing does not affect the median choice.

Even if some decrease in the level of public financing does occur, the community level of education should rise. No child can receive less than the prescribed minimum. Those families for which the marginal rate of substitution exceeds the private price can and will finance additional education. This would be typical of families with relatively high preferences for education or with relatively high income. One is confident that there are enough of these families to more than offset the minimal decline anticipated in the minimal level of publicly financed education.

In comparison to full private financing, the ability of public financing to command larger subsidies favors mixed financing. The reduced demand of families with relatively high shares of the tax base is almost certain to be more than offset by the increased demand of all other parents. One can expect mixed financing to generate larger support than full private financing.

Real world counterparts

As a practical method of financing education, direct public grants have been subjected to many special modifications. For some, the results may have hidden their essential relation to the institution described. One of the best examples of direct grants is the support of "state" universities and colleges, as well as many "private" ones. Virtually without exception, these schools levy tuition charges, often substantial charges, upon the students they enroll. Annually, their presidents appear before legislatures to justify continued or new support from the public fisc.

If these grants seem to depart from the model grants, it is because they rarely are expressed on a per pupil basis. Lump sum grants independent of enrollment clearly are a possible variation. From the standpoint of the parent, a given level of education is less expensive at some schools than at others. Alternatively, the same total tuition charge finances programs of differing quantity-quality. Description of a rational choice process by the community in this case requires a very complicated model. I suspect, however, if one were to examine the appeals of school presidents, that one would find frequent and pointed reference to enrollment trends.[26]

Perhaps a more interesting example is state grants to local public school districts. These grants are allocated to the community through a variety of ingenious formulas. But for the most part, they are based on "average daily attendance."[27] In effect, the minimum level of education is prescribed by the state, with individual communities taking the place of the independent parents of the basic model. Whatever additional public education chosen by localities is financed by taxes levied locally.

In a multi-community world, such grants redistribute resources from communities richer in the tax base to those less rich. Rationally, wealthier communities will choose to finance less education locally than they otherwise would have. Poorer communities will finance more. I see no *a priori* way of knowing whether the gains will offset the losses. As with all full public financing in any case, individual families are constrained by the median choice in the com-

26. University subsidies may also include substantial amounts of research support. Whether this is a means of inducing larger (or more efficient) instructional support could bear investigation, supported, of course, by public funds.

27. Basically, the grants are per pupil. Average daily attendance formulas encourage local authorities to enforce state attendance laws.

munity. This suggests that, independent of the state grants, local community programs should provide for the type of mixed private and public financing described above.[28]

Though the case for educational vouchers to parents has been cogently argued by Professor Friedman, their use continues to be a curiosity.[29] A few Northeastern communities pay the tuition costs of children attending independent "academies." In the State of Virginia, localities have the option of supplementing the state tuition grants available to all children enrolled in private schools. At the present time, fifteen counties and three cities have refused to participate in the State's program.[30]

The acceptance of direct grants to schools and resistance to educational vouchers is something of a mystery since the two are analytically equivalent. One apparent source of opposition to tuition grants is a widespread feeling that, "public schools are for everybody and if parents want to choose a private school for their children, they should use their own resources."[31] Specifically under the Virginia system, objections have arisen because, "parents are using this program to send their children to expensive private schools, . . . some even out of state."[32] I submit that these statements reflect a fundamental misconception about the role of public financing in supporting education.

v. *Mixed Private Financing and Public Financing Through Tax Adjustments*

The public financing discussed above took the form of a separate or easily distinguished levy on individual families in the community. The entire proceeds of the educational tax were used to support the

28. Outside the United States, some countries—e.g., the Netherlands —apparently provide public support to private schools on the same basis as that provided public schools. See the excellent survey by the International Bureau of Education titled *Financing of Education* (Geneva, 1955).

29. See M. Friedman. "The Role of Government in Education," *Economics and the Public Interest,* R. A. Solo, ed. (New Brunswick, N.J., 1955), pp. 123–44.

30. Reported by *The Washington Post,* August 26, 1964, p. D8.

31. Attributed to Arlington County Manager Bert Johnson, *The Washington Post, ibid.*

32. Attributed to Superintendent of Alexandria Schools John C. Albohm, *The Washington Post, ibid.*

training of children. Still another set of fiscal institutions exists in which public support is organized by adjusting the tax liabilities required for the provision of other public goods and services. Comprising this distinct set of institutions are tax credits and tax deductions. Because outcomes listed in Table I indicate some fundamental differences between these two, each is treated separately.

With tax credits

As a fiscal institution, tax credits alter the public price of education in much the same way as other methods of public finance. For purposes of the basic model, the tax credit presumes the following form: Parents purchase education for their children from a system of schools—privately or publicly owned and operated. A certain portion of their education expense is subtracted or "credited" against their "gross" tax liability for public goods and services other than education. If, for a given parent, the gross tax liability exceeds the tax credit allowed, the parent remits the difference to the public fisc. If the tax credit exceeds the gross tax liability, the public fisc remits the difference to the parent.[33]

The exact size of the tax credit is determined in the community-wide referendum. Whatever the amount chosen by the community, each set of parents must spend and credit that amount against its gross tax liability. Any parent may spend more on education than can be credited, but he cannot spend less. In effect, the credit prescribes the minimum level of education to be provided each child.[34]

Summed over all families, the gross tax liability minus any tax credits must yield sufficient revenue for noneducational public services. Increasing the credit necessitates a higher gross tax rate applied to the tax base. To the rational voter, the public price of education is the *increase* in his gross tax liability.

Formulated in this way, tax credits are analytically equivalent to direct subsidies and educational vouchers. The educational alternatives are the same for each and every family under all three. In particular, the gross tax liability, and hence the preferred level of minimum education, the post-tax position, and hence individual

33. Proposals to limit the maximum allowable credit to the taxpayer's gross tax liability (thereby eliminating any refunds) have no foundation in either logic or equity.

34. No community acting rationally would permit full crediting of all educational expenditures by parents. The setting of a maximum allowable tax credit is essential if the apparent public price of education to the parent is equal the actual price.

purchases of additional private education, are identical. Not surprisingly total community education is 1,025 units.

The only difference among the institutions is the method of making available public funds for education. With direct grants, all funds to finance the minimum level of education are paid into the public accounts. The public fisc then distributes these funds to schools on the basis of enrollment. With grants to parents, the fisc distributes vouchers to parents and then redeems these vouchers from schools. With tax credits, most of the public funds for education never reach the fisc. In turn, the fisc remits only to low income families with children. The only grounds for choosing one institution over another is administrative efficiency. Policing tax credits may be much more costly than policing direct grants or vouchers.

With tax deductions

Tax deductions permit parents to deduct a specified portion of their educational expenditures from gross annual income. This permits some shifting of educational costs among families by altering respective shares of taxable community income. Higher income parents and families without children have higher shares and lower income parents have lower shares. At the same time, the reduced community tax base necessitates higher tax rates to produce the revenue required for other public services.

The public price of education to any family is the family's tuition cost plus the change in the family's tax liability. For lower income parents, the tax liability change will be negative, thereby reducing the price of education. For families without children, tuition costs are zero, and the tax liability change must be positive.

To this extent, tax credits and tax deductions alter educational prices in much the same way. The difference, and it is significant, is in the magnitude of the changes produced. Educational expenditures are a much smaller percentage of annual income than of potential tax liabilities. The necessary increase in tax rates is much smaller with deductions than with credits. As a result, the potential for shifting educational costs is much reduced. Each family ends up bearing virtually the full cost of educating its children.

Predictably, the average level of education would be significantly lower with tax deductions than with tax credits and little if any higher than with full private financing. In the Basic Arithmetic Model, the median choice as to the size of the deduction is $480— sufficient to finance only forty-eight units of education. Families with high educational preferences maximize utility by spending an additional $190 (which is not deductible). The community as a whole finances 815 units or $8,150.

v i. *Public Financing of Public Schools with Optional Private Schools*

The present organization of American education has produced a fiscal institution quite unlike any of those examined so far. With rare exception, taxes are collected and directly used to finance public school operation. Public financing is confined to public schools. At the same time, education in privately financed schools is permitted and may be substituted for public school attendance. Technically, parents retain the right to choose between public and private schools.

From the standpoint of the individual parent, the choice is anything but equivalent. If the child is enrolled in public school, his contribution to education is confined to his educational tax liability, which is, for all practical purposes, independent of his choice between schools. If the child is enrolled in private school, he incurs the full cost of tuition plus his tax liability for public education. To decide between the two alternatives, the family must compare its post-tax–"free" public education position with attainable levels of private education financed from post-tax income. Expressed technically, private education is chosen only if the indifference curve passing through the family's public school position intersects the family's line of privately attainable combinations.

This fiscal institution involves the family in a process of interdependent decision-making. The level of public education which can be financed from a given rate of taxation depends upon the number of children enrolled in private schools. The number in private schools depends upon the level of public education available. As long as families retain freedom of choice, no family can know its alternatives with certainty. The more children in public schools, the less education a child enrolled there receives (a fact not lost on school boards in areas with a heavy concentration of Catholics). And the larger the proportion of children attending private schools the less attractive the private school alternative is. Nevertheless, the community should grope its way toward an equilibrium distribution of the school population, perhaps through some process of *tatonnement*.

In comparison, the option of private schools should lead to an average level of education somewhat higher than with full public financing. At the minimum, all children could be enrolled in public

schools. Since no family has reason to choose a level of private education below that available in public schools, the community
achieves the same level of education under both institutions. At the
same time, the option of private education by even one family raises
the community total.

A somewhat different picture may emerge if parents select
private schools on religious grounds. The objective indifference
curve criterion need no longer hold and families may enroll their
children in church schools which command fewer (secular) educational resources than are available to public school students. Not
only will levels of education be unequally distributed among children, but it is entirely possible that the community as a whole invests less in education.

VII. *In a Dynamic World*

Inherently, full public financing tends to introduce rigidities into
the supply of activities so organized. In a static society, this would
be of little importance. In a dynamic, changing world, it may be the
most important consideration. The appropriate institution in a static
world may be wholly inappropriate in a dynamic one. The contrast
between full public financing and mixed financing in the latter is
often sharp.

Education is a particularly appropriate illustration. The process
of adjustment of a public school system to changing circumstances
is familiar to most communities. Numerous authors have suggested
that an expanding population, rising incomes, and an increasingly
complex society leads to a sharp increase in the quantity and quality
of education demanded. Parents seek better education for their
children. Faced with growing school populations, school administrators agitate for additions to existing plant and personnel. Blue-
prints are studied and building sites discussed. The shortage of
qualified teachers at existing salary scales is pondered; new salary
scales are contemplated. Meetings are held and the cooperation of
community leaders and press is sought in an effort to produce a
consensus in favor of expansion. Bond issues and new taxes are
proposed. Gradually, the community divides itself into those in
favor and those opposed. A referendum is scheduled or the plans
become an issue in a city council or school board election. Finally,
the vote is taken, the median choice prevails.

If expansion carries the day, construction begins; new schools
are built. Salary scales rise and new teachers are hired. Bonds are
issued and new taxes imposed. If the proposal fails, administrators

will be downcast and parents indignant. No matter how highly the defeated minority may regard new schools and no matter how truly beneficial, the opposition will have prevented expansion. Perhaps more important, years may pass before a decision is rendered. The original plans may then be quite inadequate. But the fault, the failure lies in the use of an institution which requires community consensus for any changes. In short, it lies in the exclusive use of the public fisc.

The flexibility of competing markets stands in sharp contrast to that of government. Population growth increases demand for prevailing levels of education. Rising incomes increase demand for more education per child. The educational entrepreneur, anticipating and responding to these changes, makes his plans. If expansion is deemed profitable, capital markets supply the necessary investment funds. Classrooms are constructed. Salary scales are bid up by competition; more and better teachers become available. An advertising campaign quickens the interest of parents. Enrollment follows.

New schools and better schools are the outcome of independent decisions. They do not wait upon a community-wide consensus; they do not depend upon a majority. If competitive market organization had nothing else to recommend it, this flexibility in the face of changing circumstances would do so. Independent decisions by independent individuals, seeking new ways and new standards of excellence, is a powerful facilitator of adjustment.

There is great danger the question at issue will be confused. The issue is not which institution provides for more ready adjustment. The issue is not which institution can induce more support for education at a given moment in time. The issue is which is most effective in the face of both these needs. The present organization of education has led to an effective or *de facto* monopoly by public schools. The full burden of adjustment is placed upon the public school system—the very system which is least adaptable.

The difficulty here is not with public financing per se, but with its form. Public provision need not and should not preclude viable private provision. The tax money that finances public education should also be made available for subsidizing private education. A *priori*, mixed fiscal institutions—direct grants to schools, tuition grants to parents, and tax credits—should generate larger support for education over time than full public institutions. Payments per child can be based on the per pupil cost of operating public schools. With the price differential removed, private facilities will compete on equal terms with public facilities: "Let the subsidy be made available to parents regardless of where they send their children—provided only that it be to schools that satisfy specified minimum standards—and a wide variety of schools will spring up to meet the demand."[35]

VIII. *In a Multi-Community World*

The basic model is not adequate to examine institutional characteristics in a multi-community society. The subject requires a more complex model. Nevertheless, a simple alteration of this model may be indicative. Assume the community is really a nation of five identical communities—each having one family with high educational preferences, two with average preferences, and one family without children. It might seem obvious that the fiscal alternatives for each community considered separately are exactly the same as for the nation as a whole. If this were so, it would make no difference whether a particular institution is implemented at the national level or at the local level.

In fact, local implementation means that each community must treat the educational levels of all other communities as an exogenously determined variable. For the parent, who by assumption reacts only to the education of his own child, this may be of little importance. For nonparents, this may make an important difference. Because each dollar surrendered aids only three children rather than fifteen, the price per unit of public education to nonparents is higher. Whether or not the nonparent cares about children in other communities, he will seek a lower level of education in his own community than he would in a national financing institution.[36] When public financing is involved, however, this has repercussions on the total volume of education only if it changes the median preference recorded in the referendum. In any case the argument influences only the location of fiscal responsibility, not the rank order of fiscal institutions.

35. M. Friedman, "The Role of Government in Education," *op. cit.*, p. 129.

36. And if he does care, any pattern of out-migration of children at maturity will further reduce his preferred level. As Professor Weisbrod has noted, "If a community realizes that some of the benefits produced by its expenditures are reaped by persons outside, then it may fail to undertake expenditures which would be desirable from the viewpoint of the entire society." (See B. A. Weisbrod, *External Benefits of Public Education* [Princeton, N.J., 1964], p. 4.)

Similar conclusions emerge if communities exhibit differences. An unequal distribution of incomes or educational preferences may lead to considerable variation in the levels of education supported by the various communities. Public financing, whether full or mixed, provides scope for shifting of educational burdens among communities as well as among families. In so doing, it may raise the average level of education per child for the nation as a whole in much the same way as it does for a single community.

IX. *Conclusions*

Several alternative fiscal institutions have been explored in terms of a single criterion: the relative effectiveness in financing education. Using an admittedly simple analytical model, it was discovered that not one of the institutions could insure a higher level of support than the others, at least not in a static world of full informed decision-makers.

In terms of probable outcomes, however, the analysis indicated that an institution which admits mixed private and public financing— e.g., direct grants to schools, tuition vouchers to parents, or tax credits—generates more support by the community for education than full private or full public financing. This result becomes even more certain when the model is related to a dynamic world of rising incomes or educational preferences.

Unless it can be shown that real world considerations introduce opposing effects, and if the primary goal is to maximize the resources devoted to education in a democratic society, some mixed fiscal institution should receive the active support of those concerned about deficiencies in the level of education financed today.

15

Mixed Public and Private Financing of Education: Efficiency and Feasibility

Mark V. Pauly[1]

Governmental support for basic education is rarely questioned; this consensus has long been institutionalized in the American public school system which, ideally, provides each child with access to *equal* publicly supported facilities. Questions have been raised concerning the efficiency of organization, and public operation has been criticized. No one has demonstrated, however, that there are inefficiencies inherent in *equal* provision of public support to each student, whether facilities be publicly or privately operated. This paper will show that, if efficiency considerations are controlling, ethical canons of distribution being neglected, *unequal* public support is necessary under most plausible circumstances. The argument does not depend on differentiation of children according to ability to learn; in the analysis all children are assumed equally capable of benefiting from education. The argument depends critically on the distinction between marginal and inframarginal externalities.

I.

In the modern theory of public finance, a pure public good is defined to be a good every unit of which produced is equally available for consumption by all [11]. A necessary condition for optimality in the production of such a good is:

$$(1) \qquad \sum_{i=1}^{m} u_p^i / u_r^i = F_p / F_r$$

Reprinted by permission of the author and publisher from *American Economic Review*, vol. LVII, no. 1 (March 1967).
    1. The author is indebted to Professors James M. Buchanan, Gordon Tullock, and Thomas Borcherding for many helpful comments.

where the term on the lefthand side of the equality represents the summation (over all m persons in the community) of the ratios of each person's marginal utility from public good X_p to his marginal utility from some private (numeraire) good, and the term on the righthand side represents the ratio of the marginal cost of the public good to that of the numeraire good. That is, condition (1) states that the marginal rates of substitution summed over all persons must equal the marginal rate of transformation, or, more crudely, that the summed marginal evaluations must equal the marginal cost.

It is clear that such services as education do not fall under the strict Samuelson definition of a public good. Full exclusion is possible; a desk occupied by one child cannot be occupied by another. Education is provided or financed publicly, therefore, not because the technical considerations of production make it difficult to exclude others from the consumption of it, but rather because persons other than the direct consumers of education (the child, or, more generally, his family unit) derive benefit from that child's consumption of educational services.

This idea is usually expressed by saying that some kinds of education—citizenship or literacy-oriented education—generate spillover or neighborhood effects which benefit persons other than the direct recipients of the education.[2] While "everybody stands to gain from living in a more educated community," the child or his family clearly benefits more from his consumption of educational services than does anyone else.[3] The basic reason for public provision of education is not that it is impossible to exclude anyone from the consumption of educational services, but that consumption of such services by any child confers benefits on everyone else; the external economies are those arising from consumption per se.

This type of externality in consumption requires a utility function (assumed, for simplicity, to be attached to families) in which there enter as arguments not only the consumption of education and all other goods by the family itself, but also the consumption of education by *all other* families in the community. If X_{pi} represents the

2. See the discussion by Milton Friedman [5] [6, pp. 85–98] and others [10] [12]. B. A. Weisbrod also discusses spillover effects [13], but he is mainly concerned with those of a geographical nature.

3. R. A. Musgrave [9, p. 13] considers education to be a "merit want" that involves substantial elements of social wants, but it is difficult to be sure just exactly what he means by a merit want. See also Head's development [7].

amount of educational services consumed by the ith family, a typical utility function for the ith family consuming n goods plus education in a community of m persons is as follows:

(2) $$U^i = U^i(X_{1i}, X_{2i}, \ldots, X_{ni}; X_{p1}, \ldots, X_{pi}, \ldots, X_{pm}).$$

Note that the consumption of education by each one of the other families constitutes a separate "public good" in family i's utility function.[4]

Each family thus has a potentially positive marginal rate of substitution between another family's consumption of education and the goods it consumes itself. The optimality condition (similar to condition (1)) is that these marginal rates of substitution summed over all families must equal the marginal rate of transformation. That is, for the good X_{pj}, the education of the jth child, optimality requires that the following condition holds:

(3) $$\sum_{i=1}^{m} u^i_{pj}/u^j_r = F_{pj}/F_r.$$

Generally, family j will have the highest marginal rate of substitution between child j's education and the numeraire good (that is, the highest marginal evaluation of the education of child j), but other families as well may have a positive marginal evaluation of child j's education. A positive marginal evaluation for other families indicates that, if provision of child j's education is left solely to family j, marginal external benefits to other families may exist which could be obtained by some community provision of education to child j.

I I.

The procedure for conceptually determining the optimum amount of community payments for the education of any child would appear simple. Given the amount of education provided by the parents, if the rest of the community evaluates positively an additional unit of education to a child, the community should provide a subsidy for education, an addition to the parents' expenditure, until the education of that child is extended up to the point at which condition (3) above is satisfied.

4. This procedure allows all "impure" public goods and even purely private goods to be analyzed as public goods. It has been developed by James M. Buchanan [1].

Satisfying this optimality condition is far from simple, however, because the externality generated by consumption per se of education is what has been termed a "reciprocal externality" [2]. That is, the amount of benefit an additional unit of education for child j would confer on the rest of the community depends on how much education family j has already provided for its child on its own, and at the same time family j's decision whether to make expenditures for additional education for its child depends on how much the community has spent. The presence of this sort of externality raises the possibility of the nonexistence of equilibrium [4], and of the nonexistence of a uniquely optimal result. The outcome depends on the bargaining skill, the adroitness in concealing preferences, on the parts of family j and of the community.

This problem can be illustrated as follows: Suppose the community initially provides zero educational services. The family units will allocate their budgets among education and all other goods in such a way that they maximize their utility. Education will be provided for each child by his own family up to the point at which $u^j_{pj}/u^i_r = F_{pj}/F_r$. Assume that education is a normal good, and that all parents of equal income levels wish to provide equal amounts of education for their children (that is, identity of tastes as regards education), so that families with low incomes will be consuming small amounts of education, and families with large incomes large amounts. If the community now "wakes up" to the possibility of obtaining benefits from the provision of additional education, the benefit to the community (that is, the marginal evaluations summed over all families except family j) for expenditures on additional education to be provided to child j will be greater the smaller the amount of educational expenditure made by child j's parents, so long as the community's demand or marginal evaluation curve is negatively sloped. It is possible that some parents with large incomes will have made on their own large enough expenditures on education so that the community evaluates additional education for their child at zero. In such a case, though provision of education to a child confers benefit on the community, it does so only inframarginally. However, for those parents with low incomes who provided only small amounts of education (possibly zero) for their children, the public supplement will be large, and will diminish as the parents' income increases. In such a case, the externalities are marginal. But this is an equilibrium situation only if the parents continue to provide for their children the amount of education they would have provided when community expenditures were zero, which is unlikely—the education provided by the community will doubtless substitute for some of the education provided by the parents.

If, however, we suppose that all parents initially provide no education for their children, then the amount the community will provide in maximizing its utility will be the same for every child. The value to the community of one literate and patriotic citizen is about equal to the value of any other. This equal provision will be optimal only if the parents cannot or will not provide education on their own. If parents will provide supplements to the state financed amounts, to allow such payments is clearly Pareto-optimal, since only those parents making the expenditures need bear the incremental costs. If institutional arrangements are such as to make such supplementary financing extremely difficult, inefficiency clearly characterizes the result. Such a situation approximately corresponds to that of the present public school system, in which socialization of the schools (and consequent public aid only to public schools) has resulted in such high cost in terms of public aid lost to parents who would wish to supplement their child's education (and who can do so only by sending him to a nonpublic school) that most do not do so.

The inference here might seem to be that optimality could be introduced by allowing each parent who desires it to receive a voucher of value equal to the per-pupil expenditure within the public school system, which voucher would be of the same size to all parents.[5] If such vouchers were given, each family would extend its own expenditures up to the point at which its own marginal evaluation of an additional unit of education for its child (given the total amount provided by it and by the community) equalled the marginal cost. But since the community's marginal evaluation, though lower than it was when family expenditures were zero, may very well still be positive, this position may still be nonoptimal

$$\left(\text{that is, } \sum_{i=1}^{m} ME > MC\right).$$

Moreover, the community's evaluation of an additional unit of education to any family will have fallen more the more expenditure for education that family had made on its own, and the community will readjust its own payments accordingly.

5. See, for instance, André Danière's discussion [3]. A voucher system with the vouchers of equal value to all families has actually been used in the State of Virginia for several years, and is described in [15].

Whether we begin with level of parental expenditure when community expenditure is restricted to zero, or with level of community expenditure when parental expenditure is restricted to zero, removal of the restriction, and consequent increase in community expenditure in the first case, and in parental expenditure in the second, will lead to a reduction in expenditure by the other party. Hence, we can conclude that simple removal of the restriction on community or parental expenditure (by a voucher scheme, for instance) will not lead to a Pareto optimum, but will lead to a further process of adjustment and readjustment on the parts of community and parents. It is impossible to specify the optimal amount of community expenditure for any child's education without knowing the community's and the parents' choice functions, and the types of bargains struck in getting to optimality.

III.

By making some assumptions about these choice functions, and by assuming away strategic behavior, we can indicate the nature of an optimal solution. The crucial assumption here will be that the community's demand curve for education is (almost) perfectly inelastic in the relevant range. This is equivalent to assuming that families, in their capacity as members of the community, have a minimum or "target" amount of education they wish to see provided to each child—an amount which is considered (a) the minimum necessary for good citizenship and (b) the maximum amount the community would wish to provide for citizenship-oriented education at any positive price.

Refer to Figure 1 below. The solid lines are the result of the following conceptual experiment: Families at different income levels are confronted with varying amounts of community expenditure for their children's education (given as lump sums), and are allowed to adjust their own expenditure to maximize their utility. It is assumed that no family is taxed to provide education for its child, that the amount of community expenditure represents the contributions of persons other than the child's parents. The assumption that education is a normal good and that all families have the same tastes for their children's education means that families 1 through 4 are arranged in ascending order of income. These choice lines (drawn linear, though they need not be) must have an absolute slope greater than unity, since each family will doubtless wish more education when it is provided "free" by the community than when it must pay the full marginal cost of it, so long as education is a normal good.

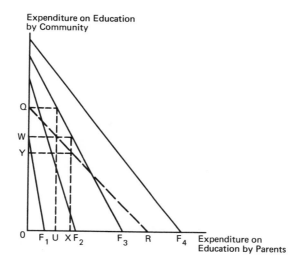

Figure 1

The dashed line QR represents the various outlays on education that will be made by the community for various outlays made by the parents. This line has an absolute slope of one, based on the a priori assumption made above of a "target" amount of education. Thus if the parents spend nothing on their own (the assumption underlying the public school system), the community will spend OQ for each child. If the community spends OQ, but the parents are allowed to provide additional amounts (the voucher system), family 3, for instance, will spend OU. But if family 3 spends OU, then the community should optimally spend only OW; if the community does in fact spend OW, family 3 will spend OX, and then the community will spend OY, and so forth. A series of adjustments and readjustments by the community and each family occurs, but it can be seen that the process is converging to an equilibrium.

The equilibrium payments by and for each family are given by the intersections of QR with the choice lines for each family. (For family 1 the community would pay the full cost of education; family 4 would pay the full cost on its own). It can be seen that the community payments will vary inversely with income. These equilibria are also optimal. At all quantities of education less than at the intersections, the marginal evaluations of the community and of the family exceed the marginal cost, so that expansion in quantity is indicated. For quantities of education above the equilibrium amounts the marginal evaluation of the community falls to zero, and that of the family is less than the marginal cost, so that optimality requires a reduction in quantity. Only at the intersections, where the marginal evaluation of the community is zero, and that of the family is equal to marginal cost, is condition (3) above satisfied. For families with incomes high enough that they provide all of the minimum basic education on their own, the community should optimally make zero expenditures.[6] For families with incomes so low that they make no expenditures on education, no matter what the community does, the optimum payment is the minimum basic amount. For families with incomes in between, the optimum community payment should vary inversely with the fraction of the minimum basic amount provided by the parents' expenditure. That is, it should vary inversely with income.

This solution, it must be admitted, arises only because of the peculiar form given to the community's choice function. But since it seems a fair conjecture that the community's demand curve for citizenship-oriented education is very elastic, if not perfectly so, and that income effects of parental expenditures are negligible, this result is interesting.

IV.

Let us consider the more general and more likely case in which the community's demand curve for education, though downward sloping and probably inelastic, is assumed to depart somewhat from perfect inelasticity, and income effects are positive. A diagram could be drawn for this case in which QR would have an absolute slope of less than unity, and it would again show a series of independent-adjustment equilibria. Again, the equilibrium amount of community provision would vary inversely with income.

But now these equilibria are not optimal. The community and the parents adjust independently until *each* of their marginal evalu-

6. E. G. West [14] seems to make the same assumption that was made here—that there is a minimum amount of education in which the community is interested, and that it has zero demand for education for any child beyond that point. He further claims that, in fact, almost all families are in the position of family 4, having incomes sufficiently large that they would provide the minimum basic amount of education if there were no community provision of education to them and if their current taxes were reduced by the amount they now pay for their child's education. He does not recognize, however, that for those who receive community payments, these payments should vary inversely with income. See also Mill's comments [8, pp. 190–91].

ations equals the marginal cost. Hence, the sum of these two evaluations exceeds the marginal cost. What is necessary to get optimality

$$\left(\sum_{i=1}^{m} u^i_{pm}/u^i_r \right)$$

is an agreement between the community and each family to share
the cost of providing additional education for each child. Unless the
cost of reaching such agreements is prohibitive, this is the typical
public good case in which the sharing scheme at optimality is,
strictly speaking, indeterminate.

Intuitively one would suppose that, since in independent-adjustment equilibrium (which can always be reattained by the community) payment by the community varies inversely with income,
if the same "kinds" of bargains are struck at all income levels, a
similar pattern will have to be exhibited at the optimal point.[7] One
possible sharing scheme which does give this result is based on the
assumption that the community's share is to be kept as small as
possible. This assumption is made for three reasons: (1) Since the
community can adjust more freely than can individual families, it
can get a bargain more in its favor. (2) The process of providing a
service through the fisc is likely to entail high tax collection costs.
(3) Most importantly, since lump-sum taxes are not likely to be
practical, almost any method of public provision through tax and expenditure involves some excess burden; any feasible tax will cause
some distortion. Hence, any reduction in the extent of public provision will reduce this burden [2].

Refer to Figure 2; the ΣD curves are the vertical summations
of the community's demand curve with the demand curves for each
family. Income effects are ignored here. The optimum quantities of
education are OQ_2 for families 1 and 2, OQ_3 for family 3, etc. (Family 1 is so poor it has no perceptible demand for education at any
positive price.) Since the community can, in effect, vary the price
per unit to the families, it can get them to make payments equal to
the area under their demand curve below its intersection with the
cost line (e.g., *OCEB* for family 2). Then the amount the community
will have to pay to get the provision of education extended up to the

7. If the parental demand curve for education were very elastic at
high-income levels, it is conceivable that, under some sharing schemes, the
community might be led to pay subsidies varying directly with income,
since a small subsidy from the community could trigger such a large increase in parental outlay that the community would wish to increase its
payments. But since all parental demand curves for education are likely
to be inelastic, this situation seems implausible.

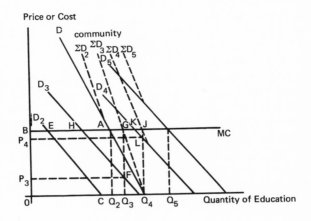

Figure 2

point at which condition (3) is satisfied is the whole rectangle OQ_2AB for family 1, area CQ_2AE for family 2, triangle FGH for family 3, triangle LJK for family 4, and zero for family 5. Note that the size of these areas varies inversely with income.

The amounts that the community should pay in an optimal situation are, of course, the result of a bargaining process, and it is conceivable, given only condition (3), that the community should optimally pay the same amount to all. But this would require a unique sort of bargaining behavior which is unlikely to occur, if the community were free to adjust. Equal community payments to all would involve more favorable bargains for those with high incomes, and less favorable bargains for those with low incomes. It is unlikely that the community would permit such bargains to be struck.

Actually attaining the optimal result may be difficult, since lump-sum payments like those in Figure 2 are only optimal if there is an explicit agreement on how much each family at each income level is to spend on education. But a scheme in which the community agrees to pay some fraction of the cost of *each unit* of education purchased by the parents could lead to optimality in the absence of explicit agreement with each family. The optimal structure of these payments is not, however, one in which the community pays the same fraction of the per unit cost at all income levels, but rather it is one in which the fraction paid by the community varies inversely with income. In Figure 2, the community would pay fraction P_3B of the cost of each unit of education family 3 purchases, and a smaller fraction P_4B of the cost of each unit bought by family 4. It would pay none of the cost for "rich" family 5, and would pay the full cost for families 1 and 2.

A matching scheme such as this, with the community's share of the per unit costs varying inversely with income, can lead to that optimality in the provision of citizenship-oriented education which cannot be obtained simply by allowing parents to supplement equal-value state tuition certificates. If, on the other hand, the assumption that the community desires every child to attain some fixed minimum level of education is accepted, then efficiency requires unequal lump-sum public payments for different families. In either case the optimum community outlay varies inversely with income.

References

1. J. M. Buchanan, *Demand and Supply of Public Goods* (forthcoming).
2. ———— and Gordon Tullock, "Public and Private Interaction under Reciprocal Externalities," in J. Margolis, ed., *The Public Economy of Urban Communities*, Washington, 1964, pp. 52–73.
3. André Danière, *Higher Education in the American Economy.* New York, 1964.
4. O. A. Davis and A. B. Whinston, "Externalities, Welfare, and the Theory of Games," *Jour. Pol. Econ.*, June 1962, 70, 241–62.
5. Milton Friedman, "The Role of the Government in Education," in R. A. Solo, ed., *Economics and the Public Interest*, New Brunswick, N.J., 1955, pp. 128–35.
6. ————, *Capitalism and Freedom.* Chicago, 1963.
7. John Head, "On Merit Goods," *Finanzarchiv* (forthcoming).
8. J. S. Mill, *On Liberty*, 2d ed. London, 1859.
9. R. A. Musgrave, *The Theory of Public Finance.* New York, 1959.
10. A. T. Peacock and Jack Wiseman, *Education for Democrats.* London, 1964.
11. P. A. Samuelson, "The Pure Theory of Public Expenditure," *Rev. Econ. Stat.*, Nov. 1954, 36, 387–89.
12. W. C. Stubblebine, "Institutional Elements in the Financing of Education," *So. Econ. Jour.*, Suppl., July 1965, 32, 15–35.
13. B. A. Weisbrod, *External Benefits of Public Education.* Princeton 1964.
14. E. G. West, *Education and the State.* London, 1965.
15. *Report on the Virginia Plan for Universal Education*, Thomas Jefferson Center for Stud. in Pol. Econ. Occas. Paper 2, Charlottesville, Va., 1965.

16

Paradoxical Results in a Public Choice Model of Alternative Government Grant Forms

Charles J. Goetz and Charles R. McKnew, Jr.[1]

The theory of government expenditure is gradually receiving a degree of attention more nearly commensurate with that traditionally accorded the theory of taxation. In the development of theorems about expenditure decisions, however, it has perhaps been overly tempting to apply familiar models within a context where they do not strictly apply. The discussion below employs a multiperson, government-decision model to show how the extension of traditional consumer demand analysis to a public choice context leads to an erroneous generalization about the response of government demand in the face of different types of grants. Specifically, we disprove the generally accepted[2] and intuitively plausible rule that matching grants allow the grantor government to stimulate the recipient government's provision of a particular public good by more than an unconditional grant of the same amount. Our results are intended to be as much a methodological exercise in the results of "public choice"

1. Goetz's research on grants was initiated under a grant from the Relm Foundation.
2. This theorem, which is explained more specifically in the text below, is so widely accepted and taught that it is difficult to cite published attempts to formally establish its basis. A recent exception is the controversy in the *National Tax Journal*: Lester C. Thurow, "The Theory of Grants in Aid," *National Tax Journal*, Vol. 19 (December 1966); Alan Nichols, "Unconditional vs. Matching Grants," *National Tax Journal*, Vol. 20 (September 1967); Lester C. Thurow, "A Reply," *ibid.*; John Cotton and Thomas O'Brien, "Unconditional vs. Matching Grants: Further Comment," *National Tax Journal*, Vol. 21 (March 1968); and Thurow, "A Further Reply," *ibid.* Thurow, who had originally questioned the universality of the theorem, appears to substantially concede in the latter article.

models as they are a revelation of a seeming paradox in the theory of grants.

In Section I, the standard proof of the grant theorem is discussed. Section II outlines an appropriate public choice budgetary model from which a counter-example of the grant theorem is generated in terms of specific numerical examples. Finally, Section III discusses the implications of the results in general terms.

I. *Basis of the Orthodox Theorem*

Figure 1 summarizes the orthodox basis for the belief in the superior stimulative efficacy of matching grants.[3] Good B is the public good which the grantor government wishes to stimulate. Line AB represents the original community budget constraint. Line AB_m is the modified budget constraint if a 50 percent matching grant is given for the purchase of B. Select any point e on AB_m as the postgrant equilibrium. Then the horizontal distance ge is the cost of the grant to the grantor government. An unconditional grant of the same amount would result in the budget constraint A_uB_u. Assuming that e was originally a tangency point under the matching grant, and that the relevant preference function satisfied the usual convexity conditions, the equilibrium for the unconditional grant must be on A_uB_u and to the left of e. Hence, it is contended, the matching grant must always result in a higher quantity of Good B than the unconditional grant of equivalent cost.

Our alternative model presented below will be a four-good model, with two public goods and two private goods. Note, however, that the argument of the Figure 1 diagram can still be defended as applicable to this four-good case on the basis of the Hicks composite-good theorem, since the relative prices of all goods other than the subsidized one remain invariant. The only modification is that Good A must, therefore, be reinterpreted as a composite consisting of the remaining public good and the two private goods.

II. *A Public Choice Model of General Funds Budgeting*

The model we present below is an unorthodox one, involving majority rule and the separate determination of government budget size and government budget composition. This model, however, has been designed to reflect exactly the customary government practice of

---

3. See, for instance, the essentially identical analysis of Cotton and O'Brien, *op. cit.*

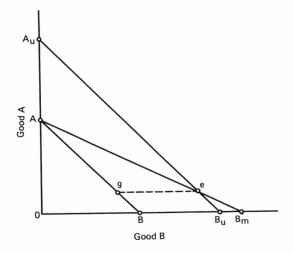

Figure 1

voting separately on taxes and expenditures under so-called "general funds" financing.

To describe the decision-making process in detail, we assume a grant-recipient political unit governed by three voters.[4] These three budgetary decision-makers may be interpreted as citizen-voters of a direct democracy or, perhaps more realistically, as legislators in a representative democracy. Since the type of model used is not amenable to general mathematical statements of solution, we propose to develop an example using specific functional forms which were chosen to facilitate the exposition. For purposes of illustration each voter is therefore assigned a utility function of the same general functional form. The utility function can be separated into a C.E.S.-type branch for two public goods, X_1 and X_2, and a Cobb-Douglas branch for the private goods, X_3 and X_4[5]:

$$(1) \qquad U(X_1, X_2, X_3, X_4) = z(aX_1^{-c} + bX_2^{-c})^{-1/c} + dX_3^e X_4^f$$

4. This simple case may, of course, be extended to greater numbers.

5. The usual restrictions on the parameters are adopted: $X_1 \geqq 0$, $X_2 \geqq 0$, $a > 0$, $b > 0$, $Z > 0$, $c \neq 0$, and $-1 < c < \infty$; $X_3 \geqq 0$, $X_4 \geqq 0$, $d > 0$, $0 < e < 1$, $1 < f < 1$, and $(f + e) < 1$. The separable "branches" simplify our exposition but do not affect the results. Such branches are described in Robert Strotz, "The Empirical Implications of a Utility Tree," *Econometrica*, Vol. 25 (April 1957).

In the public goods branch, let E signify the vote-determined level $\overline{M}$ of expenditure on X_1 and X_2, constrained by the sum of the individual's incomes

$$(2) \qquad E = \overline{M} \qquad \begin{aligned} & X_i = X_1, X_2 \\ & E \leq \sum_j Y_j \end{aligned}$$

For private goods, E will denote the individual's disposable income given his tax share, β_j, of the cost of public expenditures:

$$(3) \qquad E = (Y_j - \beta_j \overline{M}) \qquad \begin{aligned} & X_i = X_3, X_4 \\ & \sum_j \beta_j = 1 \end{aligned}$$

Then the *desired* demand of an individual for each good may be reduced to the form:

$$(4) \qquad X_i = K_i E \qquad i = 1, 2, 3, 4$$

where K_i is a "mix coefficient" indicating how many units of X_i are desired per unit of expenditure when the expenditure level E is appropriately defined (as in [2] or [3]) for X_i's branch. Explicitly, the desired mix coefficients of individual j are:

$$(5) \qquad K_{1j} = [p_2(p_2 a_j/p_1 b_j)^{1/-c_j-1} + p_1]^{-1} \text{ and}$$
$$(6) \qquad K_{2j} = [p_1(p_1 b_j/p_2 a_j)^{1/-c_j-1} + p_2]^{-1}$$

for the public goods X_1 and X_2.[6] Also, by substituting into the group's public goods budget equation, $M - p_1 X_1 - p_2 X_x = 0$, either coefficient may be expressed in terms of the other. Therefore, by using the relation

$$(7) \qquad K_{1j} = \left(\frac{1 - p_2 K_{2j}}{p_1} \right)$$

we can express voter j's desired "mix" of the public goods for any budget M by

$$(8) \qquad \frac{X_2}{X_1} = \frac{K_{2j}M}{K_{1j}M} = \frac{p_1 K_{2j}}{(1 - p_2 K_{2j})}$$

At this point, we wish to strongly distinguish j's *desired* budgetary composition between X_1 and X_2 from the *actual* majority-determined composition which as [8] indicated, may be expressed

---

6. The private goods coefficients are:

$$K_{3j} = (p_3 + p_3 f_j/e_j)^{-1}$$
$$K_{4j} = (p_4 + p_4 e_j/f_j)^{-1}$$

These relations are not important in the present application.

as a function of $\overline{K}_2$, the *actual* mix coefficient for X_2. How is $\overline{K}_2$ determined?

Figure 2 contains "lines of optima" for each individual when the parameters of the utility function [1] are as listed in Table 1 and the economic parameters have values as given in Table 2. In par-

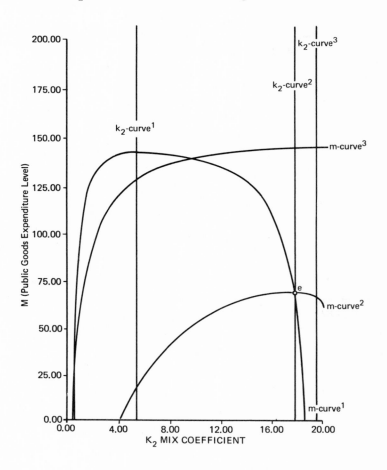

Figure 2

ticular, the labelled k-curves are desired values of K_2 for the individuals identified by the superscripts, given alternative levels of public goods expenditure M. Of course, since M does not appear in the underlying equation [6], these k-curves are vertical lines in the special case of our chosen utility function [1]. Under simple majority rule, moreover, the politically determined mix will be that corre-

Table 1

Values of Utility Function Parameters

Values	Individual One	Individual Two	Individual Three
a	9.27000	5.92000	5.66000
b	0.86000	9.99000	9.82000
c	5.07000	−0.56000	−0.70000
d	49.78200	13.415×10^5	848.42000
e	0.02686	0.00878	0.56291
f	0.25262	0.05068	0.06897
z	1.00000	1.00000	1.00000

sponding to the middle k-curve because this is the median preference.[7] To anticipate our discussion slightly, it should be clear that any grant which alters the effective price p_2 in [6] will shift the k-curves and thereby alter $\overline{K}_2$.

We are interested in the ultimate decision on the quantity of X_2, to which a stimulus is desired by the grantor government. Therefore, as [4] indicates, the completed model must show the voting determination of the actual budget size $\overline{M}$. In our "general funds"

Table 2

Economic Parameters for Illustrative Examples

p_1, p_3, p_4	0.10
p_2 (Matching Grant)	0.05
P_2^*(Block Grant)	0.10
Y^j (j = 1, 2, 3)	50.00
β^j (j = 1, 2, 3)	1/3
G (Block Grant)	61.18

voting model, the individual seeks to equate the marginal utility of private expenditure (disposable income) with the marginal utility of U_j with respect to M where

$$(9)\, U_j(M) = z_j \left[a_j \Big([(1 - p_2\overline{K}_2)/p_1]M \Big)^{-c_j} + b_j(\overline{K}_2M)^{-c_j} \right]^{-1/c_j}$$
$$+ d_j[K_{3j}(Y_j - \beta_j M)]^{e_j} [K_{4j}(Y_j - \beta_j M)]^{f_j}$$

has been derived by substituting [2], [3], and [7] expressed in vote-determined values of K_2 into [4], and then substituting [4] in [1]. Thus, j's utility-maximizing public expenditure level is

7. On the pivotal role of the median preference, see Duncan Black, *The Theory of Committees and Elections* (Cambridge, 1958).

$$(10) \qquad M_j = \frac{1}{\beta_j}$$

$$\left[\left[\frac{-z_j(a_j[(1 - p_2\overline{K}_2)/p_1]^{-c_j} + b_j\overline{K}_2^{-c_j})^{-1/c_j}}{\beta_j d_j K_{3j}^{e_j} K_{4j}^{f_j} (e_j + f_j)} \right]^{1/e_j + f_j - 1} + Y_j \right]$$

Note that M_j is a function of $\overline{K}_2$.[8] Hence, for each voter we can add to Figure 2 lines of optima, labelled m-curves, which relate an individual's desired value of budget size to the expected budget mix implied by K_2. The actual value $\overline{M}$ is the median M_j along the $\overline{K}_2$ vector; i.e., where the median m-curve cuts the median k-curve. The equilibrium value of X_2 is $\overline{K}_2\overline{M}$, the units of X_2 per dollar spent multiplied by the public goods budget.

It is crucial to note that there is no necessity for the median m-curve and median k-curve to belong to the same individual; in our example based on Table 1, they in fact do not. Our contradiction of the standard theorem on the stimulative effects of grants depends critically on this fact and its relation to the familiar theory of tie-in sales. The budgetary composition implied by $\overline{K}_2$ must be regarded by the median budget-level voter as a tie-in constraint since it fixes the ratio in which X_1 and X_2 must be purchased through the public sector, as indicated by [8]. Since the m-curves are not monotonic, there is a range of tie-in values of $\overline{K}_2$ which increase M_j and another range of $\overline{K}_2$ values which actually decrease M_j. We apply this fact in the analysis of Figure 3.

Figure 3 reproduces only the median m-curve and the median k-curve from Figure 2. The equilibrium point e is cut by a rectangular hyperbola according to the relation

$$(11) \qquad\qquad MK_2 = \overline{X}_2$$

where $\overline{X}_2$ is the equilibrium value corresponding to e. Then all points to the right of this "iso-X_2 curve" correspond to higher levels of X_2 provision and all points to the left of it correspond to lower levels. Based on the parameters in Table 2, Figure 3 depicts the situation with a matching grant sufficient to make the effective price of X_2 equal to one-half the normal market price p_2^*.

To examine the case of the block grant, we change p_2 to p_2^* and give a compensating equal-value block grant of $G = .5p_2^*\overline{X}_2$, where

8. The general logic of our results holds if the private goods branch is raised to a power of h ($o < h < 1$) if the reader wishes "declining marginal utility" in each branch. We do not use such a case for illustration since it does not permit a closed-form solution similar to [10].

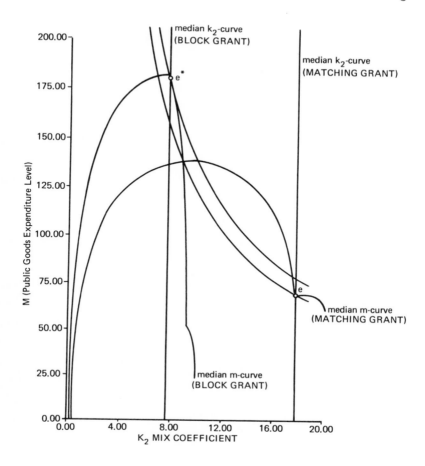

Figure 3

$\overline{X}_2$ is the quantity chosen with the matching grant at the rate of $.5p_2^*$. According to equation [6], all of the k-curves now shift leftward to reflect the higher price of X_2. Also, the m-curves each shift upward because of the income effect of transfer G raising each Y_j by the amount β_jG. The new values of the m-curves and k-curves are plotted in Figure 4, the analogue of Figure 2. The decisive median $\overline{K}^*$ and $\overline{M}^*$ curves are also transferred to Figure 3, where it may be observed that e^* corresponds to a *higher* value of X_2 than under the matching grant of equal value. This result clearly contradicts the standard theorem developed in Section I. Exact numerical results corresponding to Figures 2 through 4 are summarized in Table 3.[9]

Table 3

Public Good Results in Illustrative Example

| Individual | Matching Grant | | Block Grant | |
	Desired K_2	Desired Budget	Desired K_2	Desired Budget
1	5.495	64.22	4.033	180.25°
2	17.762°	68.88°	7.666°	61.27
3	19.387	145.26	8.626	184.60

Note: X_2 under Matching Grant = 1223.48
    X_2 under Block Grant   = 1381.77
° Indicates median choice forthcoming under majority rule.

III. *Implications and Conclusions*

How can the results of our counterexample be reconciled with the standard analysis embodied in Figure 1? As noted in the discussion in Section I, the Hicks "composite good" convention is necessary in order to apply Figure 1 to a world of more than two goods.[10] We will, however, show how the composite good convention cannot reliably be applied to a general funds voting model of the type we have employed, even though it is perfectly correct for most familiar purposes.

In utilizing the composite goods convention, the composite good must be understood as measured in units of expenditure on its constituent goods. The slope of the indifference curve at a given point in Figure 1 with coordinates h and $\overline{X}_2$ is therefore

$$(12a) \qquad \frac{\partial U/\partial h}{\partial U/\partial X_2} \qquad \begin{matrix} h = p_1X_1 + p_3X_3 + p_4X_4 \\ X_2 = \overline{X}_2 \end{matrix}$$

when the values of X_1, X_3, and X_4 are optimized within the expenditure constraint defined by h. In the public choice model, however, the values of X_1 and X_2 are not free to fluctuate independently. From [8] above, we must append to [12b] a third side-condition which fixes the "mix" of X_1 and X_2 according to the politically-

9. On request, the senior author will supply other sets of parameters yielding similar results or a Fortran IV computer program designed to generate such cases from random parameter selections.

10. J. R. Hicks, *Value and Capital*, Mathematic Appendix, Sec. 10.

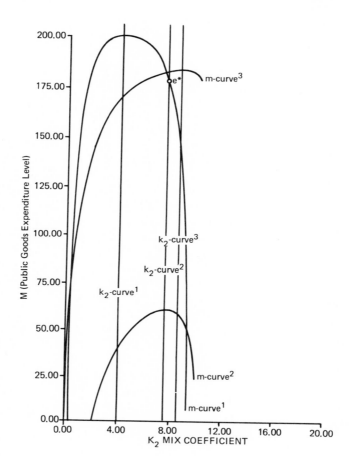

Figure 4

determined public budget composition. Hence, the public-choice model's version of a composite good indifference curve slope is

$$
(12b) \qquad \frac{\partial U/\partial h}{\partial U/\partial X_2} \qquad \begin{aligned} h &= p_1X_1 + p_3X_3 + p_4X_4 \\ X_2 &= \overline{X}_2 \\ X_2/X_1 &= (p_1\overline{K}_2)/(1 - p_2\overline{K}_2) \end{aligned}
$$

where K_2, is, by equation [6], a function of p_2. Except for the median man in the "budgetary mix" dimension, for whom $\overline{K} = K^j$, the formulas [12a] and [12b] are therefore not equivalent. Thus, unless an individual has the median desired K_2 under *both* the matching and the block grants, the indifference curves of Figure 1 must actually be redrawn as the price of X_2 is modified. That is, at the coordinates (h, X_2), the slope of the indifference curve is not, in general, invariant with the price of X_2. Figure 1 is, accordingly, not an appropriate analysis under the more realistic circumstances of general fund budgeting as we have attempted to incorporate them into the analysis of government response to grants.

The common-sense of our alternative model arises fairly straightforwardly out of the theory of tie-in sales.[11] Under the normal set of relative prices for the public goods, Individual 1 is the decider of budgetary size by virtue of his median preference on desired level. This pivotal individual also prefers relatively less of X_2 than the "mix" majority in the persons of 2 and 3, so that he is faced with an effective tie-in between the quantities of the two public goods. Although this tie-in exists under both grant forms, it becomes much more unfavorable under the matching grant, since Individual 1 has a price-inelastic demand for X_2 while 2 and 3 have elastic demands.[12] Consequently, when the matching grant lowers the price of X_2, the divergence between the mix reduces 1's desired budget level such that 2 takes over as median man at a budget level which declines by more than X_2's proportionate increase in each dollar spent. That is, the matching grant causes $\overline{M}$ to decrease by more than $\overline{K}_2$ increases. The result is a lower value of X_2 under the matching grant than under the block grant. By contrast, the standard anaylsis implicitly assumes that each individual equates his own desired budget level M to his own desired mix K_{2j}, in which case—as the intersections of M_j and K_{2j} in preference model is not an appropriate conceptualization of the government decision process, that it is methodologically incorrect because of the tie-in aspect.

Our present analysis has a close affinity to other counter-intuitive results produced by Buchanan[13] and Goetz[14] in which the tie-in effect across the two dimensions of general funds budgeting

11. There is not a copious literature on tie-in sales, although the topic is of considerable theoretical interest. However, see M. L. Burstein, "The Economics of Tie-in Sales," *Review of Economics and Statistics*, Vol. 42 (February 1960).

12. It will be recalled that, in the C.E.S. function, the utility function parameter c determines price elasticity: $-1 < c < 0$ is the elastic range and $c > 0$ is is the inelastic range. Cf. Hans Brems, *Quantitative Economic Theory* (New York, 1968), pp. 26–27.

13. J. M. Buchanan, "The Economics of Earmarked Taxes," *Journal of Political Economy*, Vol. 71 (October 1963).

14. C. J. Goetz, "Earmarked Taxes and Majority Rule Budgetary Processes," *American Economic Review*, Vol. 58 (March 1968).

also plays a key role. Our use of standard, homogeneous utility functions to illustrate the application of a public choice model to the theory of grants was dictated by expository considerations. The general rationale is, of course, applicable to a much wider range of cases than the overdrawn, highly simplified one presented here. For instance, although the analysis becomes enormously more complicated, the possibilities for counter-intuitive results are greatly expanded when nonhomothetic utility functions are employed.[15]

The exercise presented here is principally one of pure theory and cannot be used to comment on the empirical probability of the effects whose possibility we have demonstrated. Nonetheless, the results do indicate the methodological dangers in analyzing multi-person, public choice decision processes with the standard models of consumer choice theory.

15. These results will be explored in a more general paper: Charles J. Goetz, "Some Anomalies of Group Demand" (in process).

17

Some Institutional Considerations in Federal-State Fiscal Relations

Kenneth V. Greene

Presumably, in a federalism the majority of the populace has an interest in preserving a certain division of functions and activities between governmental levels. At least a majority of the nation, *ceteris paribus*, would prefer certain functions to be financed and provided on the state-local level. They place a positive value on this decision.

This paper attempts to discover whether economic interests could cause, under various circumstances, a majority of the nation to transfer some functions which could be performed as efficiently on the state-local level to the federal authorities. Emphasis is placed upon the economic factors involved in the supply and financing of collective services.

Albert Breton [1] has contended that "from an economic point of view . . . how it (the division of functions between governmental levels) changes when it changes is of no great interest." But if the welfare of the members of a society is affected by this division, as apparently it is when a federalism exists, then the forces behind such a change *do* have economic relevance. This paper interprets any existing division of functions as the result of rational collective decision-making. It seeks to determine how economic institutions can cause such a division to change without any change in the population's taste for decentralization. This is a question of considerable interest and it is amenable to economic analysis.

It is of considerable interest in the United States because there has been a trend for more and more services to be performed or

Reprinted by permission of the author and publisher from *Public Choice*, vol. IX (Fall 1970).

The author has benefited greatly in the formulation of the ideas contained in this paper from the guidance of Professor James Buchanan. Needless to say, any errors are solely the author's responsibility.

financed on the federal level. Morton Grodzins [7] is probably correct when he notes that there has never been a clear-cut division of functions in the American federal system. But if one follows his analogy comparing the system with a marble cake it must be admitted that the mix with which this cake has been baked has changed considerably over the years. There has been an ever increasing proportion of federal ingredients.[1] In large measure, this weakening of the relative position of the state governments has been affected by a loss of some degree of their fiscal autonomy rather than by outright usurpation of their traditional functions. The conditional grant has been the primary means used to accomplish this shift of authority.

It is a moot point whether or not these grants destroy or strengthen the federal system. Surely many of these grants were designed to correct for interstate benefit spillovers. Yet judging by the considerable interest shown by both economists and politicians in alternative solutions to the "fiscal dilemma" of the states, it must be concluded that both professional and public opinion has concluded that conditional grants tend to impose upon the autonomy of state and local governments. Surely the widespread endorsement of federal revenue-sharing with the states by many political figures indicates that many politicians feel that conditional grants programs have restricted state and local autonomy in certain areas and may destroy it in the future.

Economists have offered two basic explanations for the straits that the state-local governments find themselves in. Appeal is often made to the low income elasticity of state-local versus federal tax revenues. The contention is that this puts the states at a competitive disadvantage because the subjective costs of collecting taxes is higher when tax rates must be raised than when new tax revenues automatically fill the coffers of the collecting agency. Therefore, the states just cannot raise the revenue necessary to finance their traditional activities and the federal government must fill the gap.

The "states' dilemma" argument implies that the states are in an n-person prisoner's dilemma-type setting. Each would prefer to raise taxes to finance needed expenditures. But since there is little interstate cooperation, each finds that its rational course of action is to keep its rates low no matter what the other states do. The reason is potential tax based migration.

1. Undoubtedly, in the fifties and sixties, state and local expenditures have increased more rapidly than have Federal expenditures. Yet, in many areas, these increases have been accompanied by Federal prodding and the Federal government has moved into new fields such as aid to higher education.

Each of these rationales for the "fiscal dilemma" in which states find themselves is open to a fundamental criticism. Low income elasticity of tax revenues is obviously a superficial difficulty. If this were the only problem, tax rates could obviously be increased sufficiently to finance the needed expenditures. But are not the high subjective costs of raising taxes a barrier to increased rates? Perhaps they are, perhaps the more or less automatic federal personal income tax increases as the economy expands result in a preference for federal provision and/or financing. But such a line of reasoning runs aground on the usual assumption that the personal income tax involves less fiscal illusion than any other major form of tax and on the assumption that large federal taxes are presumably perceived more readily than relatively smaller state tax levies.[2] The argument that a state cannot raise its rates as much as it would like because of the fear that this will cause some of its tax base to emigrate also has a weak link. The argument may have some plausibility if it is imagined that corporate income and business taxes are the only feasible form of state financing. It is less than convincing to argue that base migration is an important hindrance to the adoption and extension of personal income taxes, sales taxes, or to any other tax that is used to finance expenditures which benefit the taxpayers. The fully rational consumer-taxpayer will consider both sides of the fiscal account. If he can derive a net benefit from a state-financed expenditure, why should he vote against the measure? The fantastic number of new major state taxes and major state tax increases in recent years also seems to belie this contention.

The thesis here is that there may be some more basic economic circumstances that can help explain the states' needs for federal help. The institutional infrastructure of a federalism, specifically its interstate income distribution and its tax institutions, is examined to see whether it might motivate a federal majority to opt for a federal program for a collective service which could be provided most efficiently at the state-local level.

One political theorist has observed that the federal grant programs are:

> . . .an outcome of the loose coalition which resorts to a mixed federal-state program because it is not strong enough in individual states to secure its program and because it is not united enough to achieve a wholly federal program against the opposition which a specific program would engender.[3]

2. For a summary of the literature on "fiscal illusion" see James Buchanan [2, pp. 183–89.]
3. Moneypenny, [8, p. 15.]

He may have distilled the essence of the forces behind the proliferation of federal conditional-grant programs. Part I of this paper explores why this could be so even in a federation with purely proportional tax structures. Part II explores the possibility when the federal tax structure is more progressive than the state structures, as is the case in the United States.

I.

Since the purpose is to discern whether interstate income distributions and tax institutions in a federalism can encourage the transfer to the federal level of functions which tradition and economic efficiency criteria dictate ought to be performed by the states, some sort of collective decision-making model is necessary. This model must explain how expenditure levels on various services and how the division of functions between governmental levels are determined. The individualistic pure democracy models employed by Downs [5] and Buchanan and Tullock [3] will be used here. A consumer-voter is assumed to be fully rational, self-interested, subjectively certain of what his own benefits are from every unit of a collective service and also subjectively certain of the tax prices per unit of service on the different governmental levels. He will vote for an expanded level of provision whenever his tax price falls short of his marginal evaluation of the additional unit of service. A majority voting rule is assumed so that more of a collective good or service will be forthcoming whenever a majority would benefit thereby.[4]

The governmental level of provision of the service is assumed to be determined in the same way. If a majority in the federation finds that federal provision and/or financing either alone or combined with the amount of service that can then be financed at the state level makes them better off than the level attainable solely through state auspices, then a federal program will be adopted.

Interstate benefit spillovers from the activity or service in question are assumed away. Undoubtedly, spillovers are widespread in many state activities stimulated by the central government through means of conditional grants or jointly supplied by both central and state governments. The question under examination here is not whether there is an economic justification for federal supervision or partial provision on such grounds. It is whether in the absence of such spillovers, a federal majority might find it beneficial to opt for

4. Obviously the United States political system is a far cry from this direct democracy.

full or partial federal provision and/or financing despite the fact that such federal provision is less efficient and even though there are no barriers preventing the states from financing additional service levels.

The collective good or service in question is assumed to be a quasi-public one. One production unit is equally available to all of a limited number of consumer-voters. The average costs of production are assumed constant. If $x provides one consumption unit for n people, then $2x must be spent to provide one consumption unit for $2n$ people. Since there are no economies of large scale in provision, a people valuing decentralization would, *ceteris paribus,* prefer state control over the service.[5] Defining the unit of production as yielding a consumption unit to a limited number of people means that larger political jurisdictions have no inherent cost advantages as would be the case with goods purely public over the entire nation. Aside from their interstate benefit spillovers, services such as education, public employment agencies, public housing, and public parks may roughly fit the requirements.

Note then that the objective costs of federal provision of n units of the service are the same as the objective costs of n states each providing one unit. Federal provision is inefficient, however, in the sense that there is a subjective cost involved in federal provision that is not present in state provision. The populace places a positive value on the principle of subsidiarity.

Further simplifying assumptions are that, (a) there are only three types of individuals in each state; these types are identified by income class ("rich", "middle" and "poor"); (b) every individual in the income class has the same income; (c) all individuals in the same income class have the same preferences so that only those people with different incomes will have different marginal evaluations of various provision levels and hence income groups will tend to vote as blocs; (d) that preferences for the good or service while varying in the designated manner intergroup do not differ interstate.[6]

5. The constant average cost assumption is not vital. Our subsequent analysis could easily be modified to take account of declining and rising average costs. Rising average costs would fortify the tendency toward retention of control at the state level and falling average costs would weaken it.

6. The equal preference assumption can be defended on the grounds that, in a large-number setting, taste differences within an income group will tend to cancel out. See for instance, James Buchanan [2, pp. 157–58.] The assumption of interstate invariability of tastes must be modified in a realistic description of the United States, especially with reference to "distaste" for federal control.

Now the tax structure and income distribution in a federalism could foster the transfer of a service or its financing to the federal level for one of two basic reasons. First, it might be the case that a majority in the federation actually faces lower tax prices per unit of service on the federal level. Even if there is a discount applied to the benefits derived from federally provided services, the differences in tax prices might be sufficient to overcome this discount and encourage federal provision and/or financing. On the other hand, perhaps only a minority of the people in a federation would pay a lower per unit tax price on the federal level. Others, however, dissatisfied with the present level of state provision might be willing to support a federal program despite the fact that it would involve higher personal tax prices, if they could thereby obtain a greater level of provision than that which is obtainable on the state level. These two minority groups might then form a successful majority coalition.

To illustrate the second possibility, suppose that all tax structures, state as well as federal, are purely proportional. An individual with twice as much income as another, would pay twice the latter's share of any given tax bill. In such a case if the states had the same average incomes, the federal and state tax prices per unit of service of the type assumed would be identical for each and every individual. If the individuals valued decentralization, they would retain complete control over the function at the state level.

But what if the states differ in their income distribution and average income levels? For instance, suppose there are only two states.[7] In rich state A, there are four upper income taxpayers, each with an annual income of $12,800, four middle income taxpayers, each with an annual income of $6,400 and two lower income taxpayers, each with an annual income of $3,200. In poor state B, suppose the rich, middle, and poor taxpayers number two, four, and four respectively. If a unit of a given service which serves ten people costs $12,000, then obviously the per unit tax prices confronting individuals with identical incomes will be higher in the poorer state. If the service were provided and/or financed on the federal level, the federal per unit tax prices would be higher than the state per unit tax prices in the rich state and lower in the poor state. These tax prices are shown below.[8]

7. This assumption is not at all restrictive. It is meant only as an heuristic device. The analysis could easily be extended to the *n*-state case.

8. In interpreting these prices note that if we multiply the number of people in each income group in a constituency by the per unit tax price shown, the sum of these multiplications would show the total cost of providing each person in that constituency with a unit of service.

Tax Prices per Unit of Service

	State A	State B	Federal
Rich	$1,846.16	$2,400.00	$2,123.08
Middle	923.08	1,200.00	1,061.54
Poor	461.54	600.00	530.77

It would seem then that since the poor state does not constitute a federal majority, federal provision and/or financing would not be forthcoming.[9] Such a conclusion, however, is not necessarily correct because it assumes that the level of provision is necessarily fixed. It assumes the individual's choice is only between federal and state provision or financing given a specific provision level. This is not necessarily true. It is possible that some individuals in the rich state could possibly agree to federal provision if they could thereby attain a more desirable level of provision.

Assume the following set of marginal evaluation schedules for units of the service in question:

Marginal Evaluations of Different Income Groups

	1st Unit	2nd Unit	3rd Unit
Rich	$2,600	$2,500	$1,800
Middle	1,500	1,400	900
Poor	1,000	800	700

Since the marginal evaluation of the second unit exceeds the per unit tax price for each income group in each state, two units would be unanimously approved in each state. A motion to provide three units at the state level would be rejected, for only the poor in each state would reap a net benefit from the extended provision. Two units are then provided in each state.

Suppose that a proposal is made to transfer provision and financing to the federal level and to expand provision to three units. Consider the net addition to each person's tax bill involved. The rich in the rich state, for instance, pay $3,692.32 for two units provided by the state. Since their federal per unit tax price is $2,123.08, the marginal cost of replacing two units of state with three units of federal provision is $2,676.92 ($[3 \times \$2,123.08] - \$3,692.32$). The other marginal costs of the transfer are listed below:

9. If the poor state were larger, it might exploit the rich state. This would make for an unstable sort of federalism. Nigeria may have been a good example of this.

Marginal Costs of Three Units Federally Provided

	State A	State B
Rich	$2,676.92	$1,569.24
Middle	1,338.46	784.62
Poor	669.23	392.31

Note that these marginal costs fall short of the marginal evaluation of the third unit of provision for every income group in poor state B and for the lower income group in rich state A. Thus, even if there is some discount applied to the benefits derived from the federally provided services, there is room for a successful interstate coalition to transfer provision, or at least financing to the federal level. A majority would derive a net benefit from doing so.

Such an example is clearly unrealistic. It is meant only to illustrate the possibility of an interstate coalition pushing successfully for federal provision of a service which by efficiency principles ought to be performed by state (or local) communities.[10] One of its major drawbacks is that it is constructed so that the equilibrium level of state provision is the same in each state. In reality the level of provision would generally be greater in the richer state.[11] Complete transference of the activity or its financing to the federal level would be less common. In order to obtain a greater level of provision in such a manner, any group in a rich state desiring such an expansion would have to pay the higher federal tax price over a larger number of inframarginal units. Partial federal financing with requirements of partial maintenance of previous service levels may be a way to permit minority groups in rich states to pay the higher price only on a fraction of the total provision level.

The example is also deficient in that it discusses only two states. In a multistate federation, states will range from those with

10. Both Charles Tiebout [10] and Alan Williams [11] argue that on efficiency grounds a function should be financed by the lowest level of government within a multilevel system that can internalize its benefits and can attain all possible economies of scale in provision.

11. The rich state will always have a greater provision level provided that, (*a*) marginal evaluations are decreasing functions of provision levels; (*b*) tastes do not vary between states; (*c*) no single group in any state contains a majority of the state's population (otherwise the income group with the controlling preferences could be different); (*d*) the income elasticity of marginal evaluations is positive and constant; (*e*) state tax and expenditure decisions are made by a purely democratic majority voting rule; and (*f*) production units are infinitely divisible.

per capita incomes relatively far above the national average to those far below it. Whenever all states have identical tax structures, then the closer a rich state's average income is to the national average, the more likely, *ceteris paribus*, that the minority group therein desiring a greater level of provision would be willing to pay the higher federal tax price over a given number of inframarginal units in order to obtain some extramarginal units.

This may be true for two reasons. First, the less rich the rich state, the smaller its level of provision and, hence, the greater the dissatisfied minority's marginal evaluation of an additional unit of provision.[12] Also, the closer will be the state tax price to the fixed

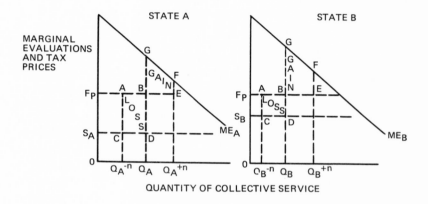

Figure 1. The Relative Size of Inframarginal Losses and Extramarginal Gains in States with Different Average Incomes.

federal tax price and hence the smaller the inframarginal loss. This is illustrated in Figure 1. Q_A is the richer state's equilibrium level of provision. Q_B is that of the poorer state. $Q_A > Q_B$ because the income group with the controlling vote will be the same in each state, but it will face a lower tax price per unit of service in the richer state.[13] The figure depicts the identical marginal evaluation curves of an individual in an income group in each state that feels that the state

12. Provided the assumptions of footnote 11 hold true and given identical state tax structures.

13. The richer state will have a greater provision level provided the assumptions detailed in footnote 11 are fulfilled. It must be emphasized that these assumptions are not needed to support the main thesis of this paper: that institutional factors may help explain the desire for increased federal financing and provision of certain traditional state functions.

provision level is too small, because at the state equilibrium level his marginal evaluation exceeds his tax price.

Suppose the federal per unit tax price for this income group is F_p. This is necessarily higher than the state tax price in state B, S_B, because all tax structures are identical and state B has an average income above that of the national average. The state tax price in State A is lower than that in State B because state A is richer.

Consider then a federal program expanding provision in each state by n units and replacing n units of state by federal provision. One can readily see that the extramarginal gain, BGEF, exceeds the inframarginal loss, ABCD, in state B. The reverse is true in state A. Individuals in this income group would approve of the federal program in state B and would reject it in state A.

So far the two states have been assumed to be equal in terms of population. The effect of the sizes of the rich and poor states on the possibility of a successful federal coalition of the type described is ambiguous. Obviously the larger the rich states, the smaller the positive differential between federal tax prices and tax prices in the rich states. Hence, it is more likely for this reason that minorities in the rich states will opt for federal provision. If, however, all tax structures are proportional, only minorities in the rich states will be interested in joining such coalitions because of the belief that state provision levels are suboptimal. The larger the rich states as a percentage of the nation's population, the smaller the percentage of the nation's populace that are potentially such dissatisfied minorities, but the more likely that they will join such a federal coalition.

Before leaving the pure proportionality case, a few comments are in order. First, unless the poor states are larger, it is impossible when all tax structures are purely proportional (or, for that matter, all identical) for a majority of a federation to favor federal provision and/or financing because tax prices are lower on that level. Secondly, the example detailed, in which the lower income group in the rich state was shown to be in favor of federal provision if some additional services could be provided, was chosen arbitrarily. Even if it is assumed that marginal evaluations for any given provision level are monotonically increasing functions of income, there is no more reason to predict that the lower income groups would enter such coalitions than to predict that the rich would do so. Each particular service would have to be considered in isolation and one would have to try to infer from the nature of the activity exactly which group in the rich state would be interested in extended provision.

Finally, an important question arises regarding why, when the rich state is no smaller than the poor (as in the example), the income groups in the rich state which are injured by the federal program cannot act to make themselves better off by agreeing to provide more units of the service at the state level. After all, given any particular provision level, they would be better off if it were financed at the state level. In the case of an isolated service, institutional barriers to the return of the service to state governments which might make such an action prohibitively costly are a possible answer. Once the machinery of federal provision and administration is established, the "sunk cost" involved in the federal bureaucracy and the vested interest in that bureaucracy might prevent such action.

But surely if the same situation arises time and again, will not those groups in the rich state that are made worse off by federal financing and/or provision of a greater level of the service realize that they are better off bowing to the wishes of the minority within their state? Such might be the case if time and again it was recognized that a particular minority group entered into successful federal coalitions to obtain extended provision levels. But even then the majority in the rich state might be uncertain about the outcome of federal votes until after the fact. There would undoubtedly be cases where minorities might agitate for extended provision, but would be unable to obtain it on the federal level. Thus, if the majority groups in the rich states always tried to appease the minority, they might agree to state extension when, in fact, federal extension would not be forthcoming.

Moreover, there is no reason to presume that the same income group would consider the state level of provision suboptimal for all services. The "learning process" for majority groups might not be as repetitive and, therefore, as effective as might first appear.

II.

Although it is possible to imagine federations in which all tax structures are proportional, this is not the case in the United States. Here the federal tax structure is dominated by a progressive income tax, while most of the state financing devices are either roughly proportional or purely regressive.[14] When tax structures are different at dif-

<hr/>

14. A liability concept of progression is employed here. See Richard A. Musgrave and Tun Thin [9]. A tax structure is deemed purely progressive only if the ratio of tax bills for any given pair of individuals with different incomes is greater than the ratio of their incomes. Pure regressivity prevails if the size of the ratios are reversed. Therefore, a proportional tax structure would levy $2 of taxes on a man with an income of $12,800 for every $1 levied on a man with income of $6,400.

ferent government levels a new factor enters the analysis. For in such a situation some income groups in the rich states may actually face lower per unit tax prices on the federal level. In fact, it is conceivable that a federal majority may face lower tax prices on the federal level.

Thus, suppose that the federal income distribution is 40% upper income taxpayers each with an annual money income of $12,800, 40% middle income taxpayers each with an annual income of $6,400, and 20% lower income taxpayers each with an annual money income of $3,200. Suppose that the liability ratios through a federal income tax are: 7.0: 3.1: 1. That is, for every dollar of tax paid by the lower income unit, the middle income unit pays $3.10 and the upper income unit pays $7.00. If the cost per physical unit of a service which provides ten people with a consumption unit is $12,000, then the federal tax prices per unit of provision are:

Federal Tax Price per Unit of Service

Rich	$1,981.14
Middle	877.36
Poor	283.02

Assume that this federation is composed of two equal-sized states with the following income distribution:

State A		Average Income	State B
% of Population			% of Population
Rich	45%	$12,800	35% Rich
Middle	45%	6,400	35% Middle
Poor	10%	3,200	30% Poor

If the service in question is financed in each state by a tax containing the liability ratios: 2.1: 1.7: 1 for the three income groups, then state tax prices per unit of provision are:

State Tax Prices per Unit of Service

State A		State B
$1,392.26	Rich	$1,546.02
1,127.07	Middle	1,251.54
662.98	Poor	736.20

One can readily see that the lower and middle income groups in both states face lower per unit tax prices through means of federal financing. In toto, they also constitute 60% of the federation's populace and, therefore, have the power to transfer the provision and/or the financing of the service to the federal level.

Presume, however, that the middle income individuals in State A have such a strong distaste for federal control that they would refuse to support any sort of federal financing or provision scheme. Still and all, it is conceivable that some sort of federal program could obtain the support of a majority coalition if, for instance, the upper income classes in each of the states consider their state provision levels to be suboptimal.

In this case the upper income group in the poorer State B might join with the other members of the state in support of a federal grant program which would extend provision and, perhaps, displace some state financing with federal financing. These groups together with the poor in the rich state who get a very large tax break on the federal level and who might, therefore, support such a scheme constitute 55% of the federation's populace. In any case, a federal majority might vote in favor of an expanded level of provision of a collectively-provided good or service solely because of differences in state and federal tax institutions and differences in interstate income levels.[15] The institutional infrastructure of the federalism could be at the root of the problem.

But do the assumed tax liability ratios have any relationship with reality? Are they at all an approximation of the tax liability ratios that prevail in the United States with any tax instruments? The following table shows the effective tax rates for the federal income tax for different family personal income brackets in 1961:

Table 1

Federal Personal Income Tax, Effective Tax Rates by Family Personal Income Class, 1961

Family Personal Income (before income taxes)	Effective Tax Rate
Under $2,000	2.3%
2,000- 2,999	4.7%
3,000- 3,999	5.5%
4,000- 4,999	6.4%
5,000- 5,999	7.4%
6,000- 7,499	8.4%
7,500- 9,999	8.7%
10,000-14,999	9.6%
15,000 and above	17.9%

Source: Adapted from Jeannette M. Fitzwilliams, "Size Distribution of Income in 1962," *Survey of Current Business* 43, (April 1963), Table 12, p. 13.

15. Again, in a federation with a large number of states each with identical tax structures, the "transference hypothesis" will predict greater support for such federal programs the lower the state's average income level as long as the conditions specified in footnote 11 are fulfilled.

These statistics indicate that the average tax paying unit with a $3,200 pretax personal income paid approximately $176.00 in personal income taxes in 1961; one with a $6,400 pretax personal income paid approximately $537.60 and one with a $12,800 pretax personal income paid $1,228.80. These imply tax liability ratios for these income groups of 6.98: 3.054:—the assumed ratios rounded to the first decimal.[16]

On the other hand, a 1959 study by David G. Davies [4] of effective tax rates by money income class for sales taxes in ten large cities where the applicable tax included food in its base and in eleven large cities where the tax base excluded food revealed the following:

Table 2

Sales Taxes, Effective Tax Rates
by Money Income Class

Income Class	Effective Tax Rate When Food is Taxable	Effective Tax Rate When Food is Exempt
Under $1000	2.141%	2.697%
$ 1,000 and under 2,000	1.430	1.403
2,000 and under 3,000	1.374	1.198
3,000 and under 4,000	1.326	1.202
4,000 and under 5,000	1.297	1.212
5,000 and under 6,000	1.261	1.243
6,000 and under 7,500	1.114	1.241
7,500 and under 10,000	1.045	1.087
10,000 and over	.69	.99

Source: David G. Davies, [4], p. 74.

This reveals that a family unit in a state which taxed the sale of food with a money income of $12,800 would pay $88.32 in sales taxes, that with a money income of $6,400 would pay $71.30, and the family with a money income of $3,200 would pay $42.43. Therefore, the tax liability ratios for these groups are 2.081: 1.682: 1—the assumed ratios when rounded to the nearest tenth.

Although these figures are, at best, rough approximations, they do reveal some broad generalities. Thus, it is apparent that the percentage of the total tax bill collected within a state that is collected

16. Obviously family personal income and money income are not the same. But the difference is small enough to be ignored for the purposes here.

The effective rates after the passage of the Revenue Act of 1964 were probably only very slightly different. The nominal tax rates themselves indicate a higher ratio of the tax price of the middle both to that

from the middle and lower income classes therein will be smaller when the tax bill is collected through means of an income tax with the designated liability ratios than when it is collected through means of a sales tax with the designated liability ratios. Since, for any level of provision, the total tax bill for the inhabitants of a poor state will be lower when the provision level is federally financed (the average tax rate would be lower since the national per capita income is higher), it follows that the lower and middle income classes in relatively poor states would always face lower tax prices per unit of provision when the provision is financed by the federal income tax than when it is financed by a state sales tax which taxes food.[17]

It is readily apparent, moreover, that this may also be true for the lower and middle income classes in some of the richer states in the federation. The average tax rate under federal financing will be higher in these rich states than with state financing, but these groups would pay a smaller percentage of the greater tax bill collected within their state.

Simply because they face lower tax prices on the federal level does not necessarily mean that these groups will favor federal provision or financing combined with expanded provision levels. The members of the middle class, for instance, may feel that even the state level of provision is excessive. But there might be a program of

---

of the rich and that of the poor, but generally the measures in the bill tending to reduce the tax base benefited this middle class.

Although their study referred to after-tax money income classes and employed an income concept more or less equivalent to net national product, the Tax Foundation's estimates of the percentage of total income paid as Federal income taxes in 1961 and 1965 as:

After Tax Money Income Class	1961 Average Effective Tax Rate	1965 Average Effective Tax Rate
$ 3,000- 3,999	4.5%	4.9%
6,000- 7,499	6.9%	7.5%
10,000-15,000	10.0%	10.9%

Note the 1965 rates are practically constant multiples of the 1961 rates. For the remainder of the rates which display this constant multiple aspect in all but the lowest income classes, see *The Tax Foundation, Tax Burdens and Benefits of Government Expenditures by Income Class, 1961 and 1965* (New York, 1967) p. 20 and p. 24.

17. This will also be true for a sales tax which exempts food, for the liability ratio relevant to the same income levels for such a tax would be 3.3: 2.1: 1.

federally financed expansion and displacement of some previous state financed provision levels which would meet with their approval. This could be true even if there is a discount applied to federal benefits.

On the other hand, if the upper income groups in the wealthier states are dissatisfied with state provision levels and desire more of the service, then they, too, could conceivably opt for a federal program even if they are forced to pay a higher tax price per unit of service. Of course, the greater the mere displacement of state by federal financing and/or provision, the fewer the number of such rich groups that would enter the federal coalition.

It may be more realistic to assume that the choice confronting the consumer taxpayer is not between federal financing through means of the progressive personal income tax vs. state financing through a sales tax, but rather between the progressive federal tax institution and the entire state tax structure. Thus, the individual may feel that additional state expenditures will be financed in such a way that the interpersonal distribution of tax burdens within the state remains the same. That is, if the state presently collects 50% of its nonearmarked tax revenues from a progressive income tax and 50% of its nonearmarked tax revenues from a sales tax exempting food, then the consumer-taxpayer may feel that an additional state expenditure of, say, $10 million will be financed by a $5 million increase in both sales and in personal income tax revenues. So that if an individual with a $12,800 income formerly paid $700 in state taxes, and an individual with a $6,400 income formerly paid $400, and one with a $3,200 income formerly paid $250, now they would pay, say, $770, $440, and $275, respectively.

But granted this is the case, it has been shown elsewhere that when the distributions of total state nonearmarked major taxes are classified according to the concept of liability progression, only 24% of the state structures show any degree of progressivity, none show a degree of progressivity as great as the federal income tax, and only another 10% show rough proportionality.[18] Thus, the idea that large proportions of most state populations would face lower tax bills if a project costing a given amount of money in each state were financed by federal income tax revenues than if it were financed through state auspices remains basically sound. In fact, in New York, one of the richest states in the nation, with one of the most progressive tax structures in the country, approximately 49% of the

18. For the procedure by which state tax structures were classified, see Kenneth V. Greene [6].

total population was in such a position in 1961. In Illinois, a state with a regressive tax structure but a per capita income level well above the national average, it was estimated that about 84% of the state's populace found itself in such a position. Needless to say, in poor states with regressive tax systems practically everyone faced lower tax prices at the federal level.[19]

The mere recitation of a few relevant statistics does not prove that the "transference hypothesis" can explain the tremendous proliferation of federal grant programs in the United States in the 1960s. If it can be presumed, however, that economic man is operative in the choice between federal and state financing and between provision levels of collective goods and services, then it may have some explanatory potential. If the "economic theory of democracy" has any substance, then the existence of these tax price differentials must be presumed to be important enough to take into consideration in any study of federal economic relationships.

It may be exceedingly difficult to discern the workings of the institutional forces that have been emphasized here. The existence of significant interstate benefit spillovers in some areas stimulated by federal grants cannot be denied. This certainly clouds the picture. People may be motivated to support some federal conditional grant programs both because of interstate externalities and the factors emphasized here. Moreover, in the United States, there are interstate differences in distastes for federal control. These would be difficult to quantify. It would be difficult to determine whether, for instance, Alabamians would vote against a federal grant program for vocational education, despite the fact that their per unit tax prices are considerably lower on the federal level, simply because they place a substantial value on state autonomy or because the "transfer hypothesis" does not apply. Precise testing of the hypothesis may be impossible. Ideally, precise knowledge of the tastes of different income groups in different states would be necessary for precise empirical tests, but even if reasonable and simplified assumptions are made to get implications (such as the implication that greater support for federal programs will be found in the poorer states), these implications cannot be tested precisely. To do so would require data on national direct referenda so that the percentages of the population supporting a measure in each state could be discerned.

If the hypothesis offered here is relevant, however, it would offer an additional rationale either for unconditional federal grant programs or for unlimited federal personal income tax credits for

19. *Ibid.*, pp. 186–92.

state taxes paid. The adoption of an unlimited federal credit scheme would assure that the state programs could be financed at federal tax prices. As emphasized, groups might support federal conditional grant programs with extended provision levels only because they face lower tax prices and so would reap an inframarginal gain on the units formerly financed by the states. Insofar as this is true, one of the sources of support for these programs might be eliminated by the federal credit device. The individuals in the states could then decide their optimal provision levels for various collective goods and services solely on the basis of these federal tax prices and without regard to the differential advantage that might be garnered by entering into the types of coalitions discussed. It is conceivable, however, that many collective goods and services provide interstate benefit spillovers which are not recognized by the states' inhabitants. If this is true, the federal tax credit scheme could result in a lack of support for conditional grant schemes which might be positively harmful in its allocational effects unless provisions were made to correct for this defect.

A federal revenue-sharing program based simply on per capita income or the federal taxes collected in a state may not be very effective in thwarting the type of phenomenon that has been discussed. It would leave the underlying rationale for the preference for federal financing and/or provision unchanged. Insofar as it would permit greater state provision levels of certain goods or services, it might, however, diminish the number of minorities who will join a federal coalition even though they will have to pay higher per unit tax prices on the federal level. A federal revenue-sharing program connected in some way with increased state tax and expenditure levels, such as presumably would be the case with the Pechman scheme, might be quite effective in that it would more or less impose federal tax prices for additional state expenditures and would eliminate support for federal conditional grants based solely on the hope of some federal displacement of formerly state financed provisions. The interstate competition among states for a fixed sum of block grant monies might also help correct for the possible underprovision of certain goods and services with significant interstate benefit spillovers.

References

1. Breton, Albert, "The Provision of Public Goods and the Stability of Federalism," an unpublished manuscript.
2. Buchanan, James, *Public Finance in Democratic Process*. Chapel Hill, 1967.

3. ————, and Tullock, Gordon, *The Calculus of Consent.* Ann Arbor, 1962.
4. Davies, David G., "An Empirical Test of Sales Tax Regressivity," *Jour. Pol. Econ.* 67 (Feb. 1959): 72–78.
5. Downs, Anthony, *An Economic Theory of Democracy.* New York, 1957.
6. Greene, Kenneth V., "Tax Institutions, Income Distributions and The Transfer of Functions in a Federalism," unpublished doctoral dissertation, Charlottesville: University of Virginia, 1968.
7. Grodzins, Morton, "Centralization and Decentralization in the American Federal Systems," *A Nation of States,* ed. by R. Goldwin. Chicago, 1963.
8. Moneypenny, Phillip, "Federal Grants-in-Aid to State Governments, A Political Analysis," *Nat. Tax Jour.* 13 (March 1960), 1–6.
9. Musgrave, Richard M., and Thin, Tun, "Income Tax Progression, 1929–48," *Jour. Pol. Econ.* 56 (Dec. 1948): 498–514.
10. Tiebout, Charles, "An Economic Theory of Decentralization," *Public Finances: Needs, Sources, Utilization.* ed. by James Buchanan, Princeton, 1961.
11. Williams, Alan, "The Optimal Provision of Public Goods in a System of Local Government," *Jour. Pol. Econ.* 74 (Feb. 1966): 18–33.

18

Earmarked Taxes and Majority Rule Budgetary Processes

Charles J. Goetz[1]

Earmarking of tax revenues is a practice whose condemnation by political science and public administration theorists has been joined almost universally by economists.[2] Either explicitly or implicity, the criticisms of earmarking usually arise out of the analogy with consumer demand theory where the imposition of additional constraints frequently produces an inferior budgetary choice. J. M. Buchanan [2] has recently pointed out the inappropriateness of the consumer demand analogy in the analysis of group choice. Arguing that budgeting practices must be analyzed as alternative modes of resolving the conflicts between divergent individual budgetary preferences, he provides an analysis which depicts earmarking as actually superior to general funds budgeting in certain respects.

This paper adopts Buchanan's important methodological advance wherein a group rather than an individual decision model is employed. It also confirms his conclusion that earmarking is not necessarily an inadvisable practice. By relaxing Buchanan's simplifying assumptions, however, the analysis presented here suggests that his original model (1) depends on a peculiarity of the individual preference functions and (2) introduces what may be regarded as a "bias" in the normative implications. An alternative rationale for earmarking is developed within a modified model where, however, the normative conclusions about earmarking become less determinate.

Reprinted by permission of the author and publisher from *American Economic Review*, vol. LVIII, no. 1 (March 1968).

1. The author is indebted to Case M. Sprenkle for his comments on an earlier draft.

2. Examples of the "standard" criticisms are cited by J. M. Buchanan [2, p. 475n]. For some recent empirical observations, see E. Deran [4].

1. *The Buchanan Argument*

The essence of Buchanan's argument is that earmarking provides a means of adjusting both the size and the composition of public expenditure via a separate cost-benefit calculus for each public good. By contrast, general fund budgeting permits an individual decision-maker, whether citizen or legislator, to "vote" only on the aggregrate outlay for "bundles" of public services whose composition is predetermined by the budgetary authority. Thus, the general fund case is represented as an analogue to the private-sector practice of "tie-in" sales where sale units consisting of heterogeneous products are employed to extract part of the buyer's "consumer surplus" by forcing him into an "all-or-nothing" type of choice.

Among the basic assumptions of the supporting analysis are the following:

1. The ratio allocating any general fund budget between the public goods in Buchanan's simple two-good model is predetermined by a "budgetary authority."

2. For both the general fund and earmarking cases, the distribution of taxes, and, hence, the marginal tax-prices of public goods to each individual have been determined outside the model.

3. There exists one voter-taxpayer-beneficiary possessing a median set of preferences about each expenditure decision to be considered. This convention of selecting a voter-taxpayer-beneficiary with a median set of preferences is applied in order to concentrate attention on what is in effect the determining decision-making element in the group.[3]

A relatively simple pair of cost-benefit models embodying, in turn, the general fund and earmarking budgetary institutions is then employed to analyze the alternative outcomes as reflected in the pivotal median individual's choice calculus.

Given an understanding of the basic premises, it is unnecessary to repeat the details of Buchanan's analysis. It should be obvious that a pivotal individual, who by assumption casts the decisive vote for all budgeting decisions within the earmarked system, will regard the fixed general-fund mix of expenditures as an additional constraint on his previously unconstrained choice. This additional constraint

3. If preferences among the outcomes meet the condition of "single-peakedness," the median individual becomes decisive in simple majority-rule models. See Duncan Black [1]. The limitations of this "median man" convention as applied to government budgeting analysis are discussed below.

therefore normally forces him into an inferior budgetary decision. As Buchanan points out, there is but one special case when the additional constraint becomes, in effect, inoperative: when the general fund ratio between the public goods happens to be the same as the ratio which would be freely chosen under the earmarking scheme. "Tie-ins" linking the expansion of one good to that of another may thus have the effect of distorting the collective decision.

Within its framework as set out above, Buchanan's line of reasoning does not seem subject to serious exception. This paper indicates some important aspects of the problem which change when the key assumptions cited above are relaxed.

II. *Analysis of Assumptions*

An initial question may be raised concerning the assumed predetermination of the general funds expenditure allocation by a governmental authority which apparently is unresponsive to individual preferences exerted via the voting process. If the "median voter" successfully imposes his preference in the (legislative) budget-size decision, should his influence over the (executive-bureaucratic) budget decision be less? And since the median voter's preferences do govern in the legislative assembly, what circumstances render the legislature incapable of modifying unsuitable budget guidelines formulated by the bureaucracy? Buchanan's brief footnoted allusion to such factors is, unfortunately, somewhat cryptic.[4] Moreover, it is essential that this line of objection be met since only imperfect response can explain why the general funds budgetary composition would diverge from the special case wherein the earmarking and general funds results coincide.

Lack of political responsiveness on the budgetary composition decision may or may not be a realistic hypothesis. Since, however, a modified model can establish a rationale for earmarking even in the absence of bureaucratic unresponsiveness, the analysis developed below employs the weaker assumption that the same decisionmakers

---

4. Buchanan [2, p. 459n]. "Control over the budgetary allocation, at one stage removed, does exist through the voter's ultimate power to remove public officials through electoral processes. And, even for the budgetary allocation as presented, legislative power to modify the allocation of funds among the separate public service outlays is normally exercised. However, these powers to change the uses to which general-fund revenues may be put do not modify the basic "tie-in" features of the model until and unless the tax structure is simultaneously considered in the same decision process."

determine both the budget mix and the budget size. Not only does this make any general funds "inefficiency" completely endogeneous, but it also adopts what some will prefer as a closer approximation to real-world decision-making conditions.

The second assumption to be relaxed is that of exogenous determination of the tax system. In the original Buchanan model this assumption merely rendered the analysis less complex. Elimination of assumptions (1) and (3) above makes variation of the tax system a pivotal point in the alternative model which this paper presents.

Finally, relaxation of the "median voter" convention is perhaps the most important step to be taken. Applied to a multidimensional series of decisions, this device is a much more restrictive one than is immediately evident, since it assumes that the *same* voter has the median preference in *all* of the relevant dimensions of budgetary adjustment. The small likelihood of this condition actually being met is better appreciated if the various dimensions of budgetary adjustment are explicitly enumerated. The set of suboptimization decisions includes:

1. *Choice among general fund alternatives:* (*a*) The *composition* of the general funds budget for any given budget size; (*b*) the *size* of the general funds budget, given the composition and the tax costs to each voter; and (*c*) the *tax distribution* used to finance alternative sizes of general funds budgets.

2. *Choice among earmarking alternatives:* (*a*) The *levels* of provision for each good provided through earmarking, given the earmarked financing method for each good; (*b*) the *earmarked taxes* for each good provided via earmarking.

3. *The institutional choice between earmarking and general funds budgetary procedures.*

Buchanan's model excludes 1(*c*) and 2(*b*) above since the taxes are determined exogenously. The neatness of his conclusion, however, depends on the important implicit assumption that the representative individual being examined has the median preference—and therefore casts the controlling vote—for all movements in the remaining dimensions 1(*a*), 1(*b*), 2(*a*), and 3. Satisfaction of this condition imposes extremely strong restrictions on the set of individual preference functions in the collectivity.

What difference does it make if, in fact, there exists no reference individual who possesses the median preference in each of the listed dimensions? In a model with a universally pivotal voter such as Buchanan's median man, any departure from the adjustment attained under unconstrained voting is necessarily a movement away from the perfect personal optimum which the pivotal reference voter could otherwise select. By contrast, the absence of an individual who is decisive in each budgetary dimension implies that there does not exist *any* reference individual who will achieve his full optimum when the collective decision-making process operates in unconstrained fashion. In the latter case, while the imposition of a new constraint (such as one on the budgetary mix) will normally "distort" the original result, it becomes impossible to say whether this "distortion" moves the solution toward or away from any particular individual's budgetary optimum.[5] This is an important qualification of the Buchanan model in that it removes any presumption that the elimination of constraints exogenous or otherwise, makes the choice process more "efficient."[6]

III. *An Alternative Analysis*

This section develops an earmarking rationale on grounds which are independent of those assumed by Buchanan. Thus, the present approach may be regarded either as a supplement to or as an alternative for his original model, depending on one's assessment of the limitations outlined above.

The simplest model appropriate for the analysis is one which permits an expenditure choice between two public goods, X_1 and X_2, and a financing choice between two tax systems, T_1 and T_2. These variables may be thought of as pairs of single goods and single taxes, respectively, or as composite goods and composite financing media defined with reference to specified "mixes." For simplicity, the prices of X_1 and X_2 are assumed to be equal and also identical with the amount of revenue provided via unit increments in either tax system T_1 or T_2. The analysis is framed in terms of a particular incremental adjustment of the public budget, but the principles involved can be applied to discrete changes. Following Buchanan, it

---

5. This observation has a basis parallel to the "Second Best" theorem of K. Lancaster and R. Lipsey [6].

6. Buchanan's identification of earmarking as more "efficient" for the reference individual is perhaps open to misinterpretation. His usage does not imply "betterness" in the sense of increased "social welfare." An interpretation of this type would be at variance with Buchanan's individualist-positivist methodological position. The real contribution of his analysis is a rationale for the widespread use of what many reject as an inefficient practice.

is further assumed that income effects do not modify individual evaluations of the alternative expenditures and taxes.[7]

Table 1

Incremental Evaluations of Expenditure and Tax Increases

Preference I		Preference II		Preference III	
X_1	+6	X_1	+4	X_1	+14
X_2	+12	X_2	+3	X_2	+12
T_1	−4	T_1	−5	T_1	−16
T_2	−7	T_2	−6	T_2	−4

Members of the decision-making group are represented by three different preference systems. These preferences may be interpreted as corresponding to three single individuals or to three homogeneous groups of equal size.

Table 1 lists incremental evaluations of the expenditures and taxes for each of the three preferences in the group. The decision matrices of Table 2 include all possible tax-and-expenditure decisions achievable via the incremental moves described. For expository convenience, particularly in the discussion of uncertainty below, the index of preference may be regarded as a cardinal one. It is only the *ordinal* relationships of Table 2, however, which are really necessary for the basic effects described.

The status quo involves the choice of the purely symbolic "nonexpenditure" and "nontax" variables X_0 and T_0. Bracketed elements in the matrices are excluded as possible decisions on either of two grounds: (1) tax increases without accompanying expenditures (i.e., X_0T_1 and X_0T_2) would unanimously be ranked lower than the option of no change at all, represented by X_0T_0; (2) expenditure increases without tax increases (i.e., X_1T_0 and X_2T_0) are economically inconsistent with the requirement of budget balance.

In analyzing budgetary decisions within this framework, a key point is that general funds budgeting implies separate decisions on the expenditure allocation and the financing distribution. Although the following discussion may be reversed, the tax decision will be treated as always coming first in time.[8] Suppose, then, that a tax in-

7. Although reasonably realistic for small changes, this assumption is strictly a device to avoid the clumsiness of providing different sets of illustrative evaluations for each change in the accompanying decision variables.

8. Decisions in each separate dimension depend only on the ordinal preferences in that dimension. Hence, no matter whether taxes or expenditures are determined first, precisely the same pair of subdecisions will determine the overall budget decision in which we are interested.

crement is proposed in the Table 2 situation. Movement from the status quo at X_0T_0 requires that a majority attribute positive value to that element of the matrix which corresponds to the (column) tax decision about to be taken and the anticipated decision on the (row) expenditure allocation to be furnished out of the new revenues.

Table 2

Decision Matrices Derived from Individuals' Preferences

	Preference I				Preference II				Preference III		
	T_0	T_1	T_2		T_0	T_1	T_2		T_0	T_1	T_2
X_0	0	[−4]	[−7]	X_0	0	[−5]	[−6]	X_0	0	[−16]	[−4]
X_1	[+6]	+2	−1	X_1	[+4]	−1	−2	X_1	[+14]	−2	+10
X_2	[+12]	+8	+5	X_2	[+3]	−2	−3	X_2	[+12]	−4	+8

If additional taxes are to be raised for a budgetary increment, the preferences of the voters between T_1 and T_2 are independent of the expected decision about expenditure composition. Thus, the majority prefers T_1 over T_2 regardless of the matrix row. Nevertheless, no tax at all (i.e., T_0) will be chosen unless the value of the expected expenditure allocation exceeds the tax costs. Hence a voter's tax preferences are *not* independent of the expected expenditure pattern.

This can be illustrated via the Table 2 situation. If the members of the group have reasonable knowledge about other voters' ordinal preferences between alternative expenditure compositions, an individual contemplating his tax decision will expect the X_1 pattern to be purchased out of any revenue increment since X_1 ranks highest for a majority. The majority tax preference T_1 would therefore lead to decision X_1T_1, which involves a negative payoff for a majority. Nor is it possible for one of the majority tax preferences (I and II) to gain a positive payoff for a majority by a compromise vote in favor of T_2, since X_1T_2 is still negative for two persons. So long as X_1 is the expected expenditure, therefore, the majority will choose T_0 and reject any budget expansion.

A key to the use of earmarking is suggested if we observe that a positive payoff *does* exist for a majority (I and III) at X_2T_2. Why are these majority gains not exploitable under general funds budgeting? The answer is that an analogue to the Prisoner's Dilemma prevents Preference I from voting with Preference III for tax T_2 in exchange for III's voting with I on the expenditure choice of X_2. The dilemma is that Preference III may be expected to renege on his part of his logrolling operation since, once the tax column is fixed,

III's gains are always maximized by choosing the X_1 row in alliance with Preference II. What is required here is an enforcement mechanism to insure a Preference I voter that his attempt at cooperation will not result in III's chiselling and the negative payoff X_1T_2 in lieu of the gains achievable at X_2T_2.

A binding exchange of proxies would, for instance, permit the necessary cross-dimensional trade of votes between I and III. Explicit vote-trading, however, frequently appears to be regarded as impractical either because it is costly, time-consuming, or not sanctioned by some persons. In these cases, despite the existence of potential majority gains, the budgetary process becomes "struck" at the status quo unless an alternative trading mechanism can be used.

Clearly, any impasse resulting from general funds budgeting in the Table 2 situation is avoidable if integrated budgetary decisions are substituted for the fragmented suboptimization process. If the tax and expenditure mixes are determined jointly, the coalition between I and III can be *enforced* by earmarking tax T_2 for use on expenditure X_2. While the enforcement problem was not dealt with explicitly by Wicksell, earmarking is obviously closely related to his suggested simultaneous determination of taxes and expenditures [10].

Coalition solution X_2T_2 is not, of course, necessarily a stable result. For instance, II should be willing to minimize losses by joining a counter-coalition for either I's maximum at X_2T_1 or III's maximum at X_1T_2, giving rise to the possibility of majority cycles. No attempt to deal with the n-person game-theoretic implications will be undertaken here. This paper purports to show only that circumstances exist where earmarking actually increases the achievable range of solutions for the group.

The "efficiency" of earmarking as a practice is then most easily evaluated if one imagines the illustrative group to be confronted by the choice between a budgetary constitution which permits earmarking and an alternative decision rule which prohibits it.[9] If the rule is considered one for a one-shot budgeting "game" with payoff matrices similar to those of Table 2, a Preference II voter should always seek to prohibit earmarking since it implies potential losses. For this reason, earmarking cannot qualify as a welfare improvement in the sense of a Pareto-move. By contrast, either I or III can insure themselves against losses by joining with II to constitute a majority for

9. This is by no means a purely academic question. Constitutional prohibitions against earmarking are frequently advocated. For instance, see [7] and [8].

prohibition of earmarking. If they do *not* do so, the implication is that the expected value of the earmarking result is positive for each of them and, hence, preferable to the zero payoff from general funds budgetary adjustments. The illustrative data may be used as a case in point. Based on Table 2, the expected value of the solution is positive for both I and III if each result is regarded as equally probable.

Changing the context to a multitrial game where the Table 2 matrix is only the current state of a varying payoff function, the earmarking scheme may actually win unanimous support and meet the Paretian welfare criterion. This would occur if, for instance, the passage of time shuffles the identities of relatively intense "winners" and relatively indifferent "losers" in a fashion which is sufficiently random for the distributional aspects to wash out. Again, Table 2 may be used as an illustration. If future circumstance were expected to assign the I, II, and III-type payoff matrices randomly on future budgetary "plays," the "game" can be converted to one with positive payoffs for each participant when earmarking is permitted. If earmarking increases net gains to the group at each point in time, it would then become the more efficient means of maximizing each individual's long-run gains from operation of the public budget.[10]

Modification of this model to allow a high degree of uncertainty about the preferences of other voters cuts two ways. On the one hand, earmarking may become more appealing because it can eliminate the uncertainty of the tax decisionmaker about the subsequent disposition of the funds he contemplates making available. On the other hand, the resultant fixity of the expenditure pattern makes it more difficult to readjust if the economic conditions foreseen at the time of the original earmarking "contract" alter. This problem of erroneous expectations is, however, common to any type of agreement which must be discharged in the future.

Thus, while the consequences of permitting earmarking are dependent on a host of empirical factors, it is possible to indicate circumstances where the general funds method of adjustment may actually be inferior, either for a majority of the group or even by unanimity. There is certainly no a priori reason for economists to reject earmarking out-of-hand as an "inefficient" device within the context of a majority-rule decision process.

10. This possibility that distributional effects will wash out in the long run merely re-echoes a point made by many in the welfare economics debate between the actual compensationists and the hypothetical compensationists. See, for instance, J. R. Hicks [5, p. 111]. Of more direct relevance to the distinction between Pareto-optimal rules and Pareto-optimal outcome is Buchanan's essay on the relevance of Pareto optimality [3].

IV. *Conclusions*

This paper suggests an alternative or supplement to Buchanan's explanation of earmarking. Under certain conditions, the only possible budgetary adjustments which yield majority gains may require logrolling between members of the majority coalition on tax adjustment. General funds budgeting is a suboptimization process wherein incentive to chisel and lack of enforceability render cooperation between factions unlikely. By contrast, earmarking provides an enforceable "tie-in" between the tax concessions and expenditure concessions necessary to achieve a majority gain under certain circumstances.

This theory is consistent with the "benefits" character of most earmarked taxes since concession of an expenditure adjustment in favor of a particular interest group might be expected to be "paid for" by concession of a tax adjustment against that group.[11] Earmarking of gasoline taxes for highway expenditures is one of the abundant and relatively obvious examples which meet these conditions. The link between the tax preference and the expenditure preference need not be so direct, however. For instance, advocates of a progressive income tax and higher educational expenditures might logroll with advocates of a sales tax and higher welfare expenditures. The outcome could then be either a sales tax largely earmarked for education or an income tax largely earmarked for welfare expenditures.

The welfare implications of this analysis should be interpreted with extreme caution. Nevertheless, earmarking can be recognized as a perfectly rational strategic tool for majority coalitions, a conclusion sufficient to explain its frequent empirical practice. Earmarking may even meet the Paretian welfare criteria if it is evaluated as a long-run process. Of course, the logrolling rationale outlined above applies only to the extent that strategic dilemmas of the type described are empirically probable descriptions of the conflicts between legislative interest groups.

References

1. D. Black, *The Theory of Committees and Elections.* Cambridge, 1958.
2. J. M. Buchanan, "The Economics of Earmarked Taxes," *Jour. Pol. Econ.*, Oct. 1963, 71, 457–59.

11. A description of the characteristics of earmarked state taxes in the United States during fiscal 1963 can be found in the Tax Foundation's latest study of earmarking [9].

3. ————, "The Relevance of Pareto Optimality," *Jour. Conflict Resol.,* Dec. 1962, 6, 341–59.

4. E. Deran, "Earmarking and Expenditures: A Survey and a New Test," *Nat. Tax Jour.,* Dec. 1965, 18, 354–61.

5. J. R. Hicks, "The Rehabilitation of Consumer's Surplus," *Rev. Econ. Stud.,* Feb. 1941, 8, 111.

6. K. Lancaster and R. Lipsey, "The General Theory of the Second Best," *Rev. Econ. Stud.,* 1956, 24(1), 11–32.

7. New Jersey State Chamber of Commerce, *Revenue Dedication in State Government.* Trenton, N.J., 1954.

8. C. Sprenkle and W. Habacivch, "Earmarking," in *Report of the Commission on Revenue, State of Illinois,* Springfield, Ill., 1963.

9. Tax Foundation, *Earmarked State Taxes.* New York, 1965.

10. K. Wicksell, *Finanztheoretische Untersuchungen und das Steuerwesen Schweden's.* Jena, 1896.

19

Budget Size in Democracy

J. Ronnie Davis and Charles W. Meyer[1]

In a democracy collective decisions are made by partnerships or coalitions of individuals. Virtually all collective decisions have an effect on the budget of the public sector, and under majority rule partnerships of any size greater than one-half of the voters can control the composition, hence the size of the budget.

Although the budgetary consequences of democracy have been discussed by several contributors to the developing economic theory of democracy, there is little hint of a consensus among them. Downs concludes that the budget is too small[8]. Tullock [18, p. 578] and Johnson [10, p. 12] agree that some parts of the budget are overextended while other parts are underextended, but they do not agree on which components to include in each category. For example, Tullock argues that national defense will be slighted; Johnson, that it will be overextended. Each bases his conclusion on the same contention that defense benefits the entire population rather than particular groups. Finally, Buchanan and Tullock [6, Chapter 11, esp. p. 169] argue that the budget will be overextended unless both taxes and benefits are distributed generally among all voters [also, cf. 3, p. 91n; 4].

Obviously, any discussion of the proper size of the budget hinges on some conception of the "correct" budget. In this paper, we derive our own definition of the correct budget from benefit-cost analysis. Using our concept of the correct budget as a starting point, we proceed to analyze the budgetary outcome of the democratic process. Here, we rely heavily on modern game theory and

Reprinted by permission of the authors and publisher from *Southern Economic Journal*, vol. XXXVI, no. 1 (July 1969).

1. We are indebted for helpful comments on earlier drafts to D. K. Bose, James M. Buchanan, Joe R. Hulett, Gordon Tullock, and the anonymous referees of this *Journal*.

collective decision-making theory. We find that, even under conditions of perfect knowledge of costs and benefits, the budget in democracy is *larger* than the budget norm. When "rational ignorance" is introduced, we find that the budgetary excess can still be too large.

I. *The "Correct" Budget*

Coalitions are potentially effective as long as expected benefits exceed expected costs for each member of the coalition. Since a coalition can obtain net benefits for its members only if it is large enough to "win," the incentive to add members exists until the coalition is just large enough to control the vote; it has no incentive to offer benefits to additional members once this size is reached [15, pp. 32-46]. Therefore, under simple majority rule, nearly half the voters will be potential net losers on any budgetary vote.[2]

Using the terminology of game theory, participants in collective decision making may play games which are positive-sum and negative-sum from the point of view of the population as a whole. Negative-sum games are possible once a less-than-unanimity voting rule is adopted. Obviously a unanimity rule would prevent the playing of a game in which any voter in the population experienced negative net benefits. Of greater interest is the question of how negative-sum games can be played under majority rule. If costs exceed benefits for the population as a whole, it would appear that the losers in the population could cut costs to themselves by paying the winners not to play the game.[3] Should this happen, however, the winners would be using the democratic process as a means of eliciting transfers from the losers. We shall examine this process in more detail after considering our criterion for the "correct" budget.

Any individual, i, has an incentive to participate in a coalition as long as he expects that the gains from coalition activity (b_i) will exceed the losses (c_i). For a coalition of n members, therefore, there is an incentive to play any game for which

2. Coalitions including more than the minimum number of voters needed to win might come about if, when the coalition is being formed, there is uncertainty about the outcome of the voting process. Also, indivisibilities in the consumption of goods provided by government might lead to coalitions that are larger than the required minimum. Finally some public goods, especially those of the Samuelson type [16], may provide net benefits to nonmembers.

3. It would appear, for example, that consumers could cut losses to themselves by paying producers not to insist on protective tariffs.

(1) $$\sum_{i=1}^{n} b_i > \sum_{i=1}^{n} c_i.$$

In equation (1), costs include not only the tax cost of the benefits to the coalition members but also organizational costs as well. We assume that tax costs are allocated in accordance with a tax structure that is general in nature and chosen independently of expenditure decisions.[4] By tax structure, we mean the share of total tax revenue collected from each individual. Hence, rates and tax revenues are allowed to vary, but relative tax shares remain constant. Organizational costs refer to the bargaining costs associated with the requirement that the several coalition members reach a single agreement [6, p. 68; 13, pp. 46-47]. An index of the magnitude of benefits in this case is the minimum payment which a member would accept in lieu of playing the games individually.[5]

Coalitions will not play games that are, from their point of view, negative-sum.[6] It does not follow, however, that a game which is

4. Constitutional law typically prevents majorities from using the taxing power to exploit minorities. Although tax legislation normally must apply uniformly to all members of a community or population, there is typically no corresponding restraint on the *expenditure* side [Cf. 5, pp. 181–82; 17].

5. The Bowen-Lindahl criterion [2, 12] for allocative efficiency of collective goods requires equality between marginal (tax) cost and marginal benefits for each taxpayer. This condition cannot ordinarily be satisfied under a general tax structure even if the demand schedules for public goods are known for each individual. Our criterion is based on each individual's evaluation of total benefits, not marginal benefits. The individual will be in disequilibrium if the Bowen-Lindahl condition is not met, but he will prefer to play a game so long as net benefits are positive, i.e., so long as some taxpayer's surplus remains.

Essentially, we limit costs to pecuniary outlays (in the flow sense) in the manner which is consistent with incidence theory. Benefits to an individual from the playing of a game may be positive, zero, or negative. Collective goods often yield negative benefits for some individuals, as in the case when a noisy freeway is routed through a once quiet residential area. Negative (or positive) benefits may also be of a more ideological nature, e.g., moralists are offended by welfare payments to mothers of illegitimate children and pacifists object to military expenditures. (Note the affinity with external diseconomies generated by some private expenditures.)

6. If logrolling is allowed, this need not be the case when "games" are narrowly defined. A game can be defined more broadly to include what amounts to a series of games, in which case playing a narrowly-defined, negative-sum game becomes an additional cost of playing a broadly-defined, positive-sum game (or series of games for which the summation is positive).

positive-sum for a coalition will be positive-sum for the population as a whole. The games which coalitions play may be either positive or negative when the costs and benefits are summed over a population of p members, i.e., for every coalition of n members, as defined in equation (1), either

$$(2) \qquad \sum_{i=1}^{p} b_i > \sum_{i=1}^{p} c_i$$

or

$$(3) \qquad \sum_{i=1}^{p} b_i < \sum_{i=1}^{p} c_i.$$

This distinction can serve as a basis for defining the "correct" budget. Our criterion of the correct budget is limited to those games that are positive-sum for the population as a whole. Stated in terms of the democratic process, therefore, the "correct" budget includes positive-sum games that coalitions will play, i.e., for which

$$(4) \qquad \sum_{i=1}^{p} b_i > \sum_{i=1}^{p} c_i \text{ and } \sum_{i=1}^{n} b_i > \sum_{i=1}^{n} c_i.$$

The size of the "correct" budget is the dollar value of all such games.[7] Our definition of the correct budget is, of course, dependent on the distribution of income.[8]

II. *Games People Play*

A game will not be played unless it secures the support of a majority. Under what conditions is this requirement satisfied? The simplest case is the game which is positive-sum for both the coalition and the population. This game will be played because the compensation necessary to dissuade the coalition from playing the game exceeds the potential losses to the minority if it is played. In other words, games such as

7. We have ignored zero-sum games. The existence of such games is largely accidental. If they are played, the sole result is to redistribute income. Our criterion leaves open the question as to whether or not they should be included as part of the "correct" budget.

8. Distribution is important not only because of considerations of equity, but also because of the interrelationship, through income effects, with the set of potential positive-sum games. Substitution effects can also be important. A particular game may be positive- or negative-sum, depending on what other games are played and the "order" in which they are played.

(5) $\sum_{i=1}^{p} b_i > \sum_{i=1}^{p} c_i$ for which $\sum_{i=1}^{n} b_i > \sum_{i=1}^{n} c_i$

will always be played.[9]

It is conceivable, however, that not all positive-sum games will meet the conditions stated in equation (5). Some games that are positive-sum for the population might not be positive-sum for any majority coalition, i.e.,

(6) $\sum_{i=1}^{p} b_i > \sum_{i=1}^{p} c_i$ for which $\sum_{i=1}^{n} b_i < \sum_{i=1}^{n} c_i$.

This may occur if, for example, benefits are concentrated on a minority group that is unable to form a coalition large enough to attain a majority.

Although it appears that positive-sum games of this type will not be played, they can be if compensation takes place through the public sector. By compensation we mean transfer payments made through the tax-expenditure mechanism. If the public sector can be used to channel tax revenues to specified individuals as well as to provide public services, the opportunities for forming winning coalitions are extended. Unless the number of beneficiaries from a game described by equation (6) is very small, compensation must be channeled through the public sector. Collection of funds for the transfer could not be accomplished voluntarily, because the transfer possesses the characteristics of a public good for those who benefit from the game.

The fiscal institutions of a democracy will determine the manner in which the transfer will take place. If the tax structure is of a general nature, as we have assumed, it will be necessary to have a higher level of taxes and transfers than would be required under a strict system of benefit taxation. This is so if the tax increase applies to those who are added to the winning coalition via the receipt of

9. The formation of coalitions is a key feature of "negotiable games." In the von Neumann-Morgenstern tradition [21], the solution to an n-person game is likely to be a *set* of imputations (payoffs imputed to coalition members). In terms of the stability of a given coalition, in other words, the von Neumann-Morgenstern solution is weak. We accept a modified Vickrey strong solution [20]. A strong solution is one where the following sequence (1) an imputation in the solution, (2) a change to another imputation, and (3) a return to another imputation in the solution, involves a potential net loss to one of the players participating in the original deviation [14, pp. 291–292]. In our argument this means that all of the members of a majority coalition must be compensated not to play a game, not just enough members to make it a minority.

transfers, since their gross receipts must be sufficiently great to offset the cost of higher taxes. In this case, therefore, the budget is larger under taxes of a general nature than it would be under strict benefit taxation.[10]

Once we introduce the possibility of cash transfers through the budget, games that are otherwise negative-sum for any majority can be made positive-sum through compensation (t_b). We must now reconsider our definition of the correct budget, as stated in equation (4). Should the budgetary outlays required to play positive-sum games such as those described by equation (6) be included? If our criterion is to be applied, all positive-sum games should be played. Therefore, any transfer costs (t_c) needed to play positive-sum games should also be included in the correct budget, i.e.,

$$\sum_{i=1}^{n} (b_i + t_{b_i}) > \sum_{i=1}^{n} (c_i + t_{c_i}) \quad \text{for which} \quad \sum_{i=1}^{p} (b + t_b) > \sum_{i=1}^{p} (c + t_c), \quad \text{where} \quad \sum_{i=1}^{n} t_{b_i} > \sum_{i=1}^{n} t_{c_i} \quad \text{and} \quad \sum_{i=1}^{p} t_b = \sum_{i=1}^{p} t_c.$$
(4′)

On the other hand, games which are positive-sum for a coalition might very well be negative-sum for the population as a whole. This is typically the case, for example, when special interest groups manage to use the democratic process to secure for themselves benefits financed by taxpayers in general [cf. 17]. These games clearly violate the "correct" budget criterion defined in equation (4′). Insofar as negative-sum games are successfully played by coalitions, therefore, the public sector is overextended by the dollar amount of such games.

At the same time that there are incentives for a majority to play some games which are negative-sum for the population as a whole, there are also incentives for the minority in each case to compensate the majority for not playing the games. The payments the minority would have to make to dissuade the majority members are less than the tax cost of the game if it is played. These payments must be made through the budget when large numbers are involved. If the negative-sum game is played, the budget is too large by the amount of the tax cost of the game; if it is not played because the majority has been dissuaded by a cash transfer, the budget is too large by the amount of the transfer.

10. An additional cost, not considered above, can arise under fiscal asymmetry. If taxpayers are taxed to pay a transfer to themselves, the transaction will have announcement effects that result in an excess burden.

III. *The Budgetary Consequences of Ignorance*

Our discussion in section II is based on the assumption that voters have perfect knowledge of their share of the costs and benefits of budgetary expenditures. It is more realistic, however, to assume that they are not perfectly informed. As Downs [7, 8] and Tullock [19] point out, some degree of ignorance about actual and potential government programs is rational. Information cannot always be obtained without cost, as was assumed in the discussion in section II. An individual may decide that the benefits from being informed are not likely to be worth the cost of acquiring information about those government programs and policies having a limited impact on him.[11]

On the cost side voters may fail to inform themselves about the expected costs of proposed expenditure programs. Furthermore, uncertainty about which tax or other source of revenue is marginal and about the incidence of various revenue measures contributes to miscalculation of costs. Some voters can be expected to overestimate costs, while others will underestimate them. We see no reason why, in the aggregate, ignorance should lead to cost estimates that are biased in either direction.

Similarly, on the benefit side we see no reason why ignorance should lead to an upward or downward bias in estimates. It is true that voters are more likely to be well informed about the magnitude of benefits to be obtained from programs that affect them greatly. Thus, in most cases members of producer-oriented coalitions are more likely to be well informed than members of consumer-oriented coalitions. This is because most or all of the income of an individual is usually obtained from a single source, and anything that affects that source is likely to be more important to him than programs that affect one or a few of the multitude of his consumer activities.

The major effect of differences in knowledge about the net benefit attributable to different programs would appear to be on the amount of *variance* of estimates around those that would prevail given perfect information. Again, contrary to Downs [8], we see no apparent reason why the estimates should be biased upward or downward by differences in knowledge.[12]

11. Ignorance may also arise because of the inherent difficulty of measuring the benefits from some programs. For example, the benefits from police protection are a function of the number of crimes *not committed,* but this may be impossible to measure.

12. The effect of better information, which is more likely to be acquired where the payoff is high relative to the cost of acquisition, would be to reduce the *variance* of benefit estimates around the perfect information level, not to *bias* them.

We conclude, therefore, that ignorance may cause some persons to favor proposals that they would oppose if they had perfect information about costs and benefits. Similarly, ignorance might convert some proponents into opponents. The number who switch positions may be greater in consumer-oriented coalitions than in producer-oriented coalitions. On balance, however, there is no a priori reason to conclude that the set of games played will be altered significantly as a result of ignorance. Thus the results derived in section II appear to be unaffected by relaxation of the assumption of perfect knowledge.

I V. *Concluding Remarks*

A. *The Definition of the "Correct" Budget*

We have concluded that the budget in a democracy is too large in terms of our definition of the "correct" budget. Our definition is, like all others, based on a value judgment, viz., that only positive-sum (or zero-sum) games should be played. This is tantamount to the view that government programs should be undertaken only if benefits are greater than or equal to costs. The chief criticism of this view is that it fails to take into account the distributional consequences of public spending.

Our definition of the correct budget is by no means the only one. The Bowen-Lindahl-Samuelson definitions call for equality between the summed marginal rates of substitution (ΣMRS) and the marginal rate of transformation (MRT) of any pair of public and private goods. Equality between ΣMRS and MRT is required if resources are to be allocated efficiently in an economy with both private and public goods. Lindahl [12] and Bowen [2] assume that a proper state of distribution exists. Samuelson [16] assumes a social welfare function (social ranking) that selects an optimum (highest ranking) distribution on the utility frontier. Since the information needed to determine whether the Bowen-Lindahl-Samuelson conditions are satisfied cannot be obtained because there is no institutional arrangement that will force people to reveal their true preferences for public goods, this approach does not provide a useful guideline for determining whether the budget is too large or too small.

Downs, on the other hand, defines the "correct" budget as "the one which would emerge from the democratic process if both citizens and parties had perfect information about both actual and potential policies" [8, p. 80]. If negative-sum games are played under perfect information or if they are prevented by zero-sum transfers,

Downs would include them in his definition of the correct budget. Thus, Downs' definition, like ours, is subject to criticism on distributional grounds. In addition, he is required to *defend* the playing of negative-sum games should this occur in a democracy.

Among the definitions of the correct budget cited above, only the Bowen-Lindahl-Samuelson type is an equilibrium model. Even if the budget is correct in the Davis-Meyer or Downs sense, many voters are in disequilibrium. Many in a Davis-Meyer world would consider the budget "too small," and many in a Downs world would consider it "too large." The best-known complaint of disequilibrium is found in J. K. Galbraith's *The Affluent Society* [9]. Professor Galbraith bases his case on what he calls "the theory of social balance." He argues that the public sector has secured too small a portion of the rising output resulting from economic growth. Advertising and emulation cause us to scramble for more private goods, while we overlook the pressing needs for a variety of public services.[13] Galbraith and those who share his view find themselves in disequilibrium. They would prefer higher taxes, more public goods, and less private consumption. Many fiscal conservatives also appear to be in disequilibrium; they would prefer fewer public services, lower taxes, and more private goods. We should not be surprised that fiscal "extremists" are discontent. Duncan Black has clearly demonstrated that, in a democracy with a pattern of single-peaked preferences, the preferences of the median individual will be adopted [1, pp. 14-16].

B. *The Assumptions*

The assumptions we make about the differential effect of ignorance on some coalitions is admittedly arguable. Downs, in particular, argues that there are simultaneously tendencies toward "smaller" budgets because of "relative unawareness of certain government benefits in relation to their cost" [8, p. 81] and toward "larger budgets" because producer coalitions are more aware of benefits than of costs of those government policies which directly affect their sources of income [8, pp. 90-93]. The *net* result, Downs "believes," is that the actual budget will be smaller than the "correct" one "because even indirect taxation is much more apparent than many remote government benefits" [8, p. 93]. The Davis-Meyer assumption is the

13. An issue here is the effect of advertising on the private-public mix. Evidence seems to indicate that Galbraith greatly overstates the effectiveness of advertising [cf. 11, pp. 58–61]. Much of the effect of advertising is confined to the private sector, e.g., switching from Crest to Gleem. Katona's [11] main point is that advertising is more effective in influencing decisions that are of little consequence.

same as Downs' for the tendency toward a "larger" budget, but our assumption is different from his regarding the tendency toward a "smaller" budget.

We would agree that benefits of some programs are often difficult to identify, tend to be interrelated with the benefits of other public and private programs, often carry indirect effects, and frequently register an impact only over an extended period in the future. We would also suggest that the costs of government programs are similarly difficult to identify, similarly interrelated with costs of other public and private programs, similarly levied indirectly, and (due to the possibility of shifting) similarly register an impact only over an extended period in the future. For this reason, we have assumed that, for voters as a whole at least, the values for benefits (and costs) are equally distributed above and below the perfect knowledge estimate and that better information would only reduce the variance of net benefit estimates around the perfect knowledge level and not bias them (as Downs suggests).

Our assumption regarding ignorance would not preclude a feeling on the part of most voters that the budget is too large relative to the benefits being derived.[14] For example, our assumption would not preclude the typical voter from feeling that his income taxes are too high in relation to the benefits he is receiving from government. Voters cannot reduce the size of the budget, however, without eliminating particular programs. This makes budget reduction extremely difficult, because of the "revolving majorities" phenomenon [8, p. 85]. A governing party can offend voters who think the budget is too large because they are in the minority regarding *particular* programs, their intensity of feeling is not as great as the feeling of those who favor *particular* programs, and their hostility can often be placated by other *particular* programs which favor them.

C. Summary

We have defined the "correct" size of the budget in a democracy as the dollar value (including any transfer costs necessary to form a majority coalition) of "games" that are positive-sum for the population. The actual budget tends to be larger than the correct budget. This tendency does not appear to be affected by ignorance of actual costs and benefits on the part of voters. The tendency to play negative-sum games under democracy is perhaps best thought of as a cost inherent in the democratic means of conflict resolution.

14. Perfect knowledge also would not preclude such a feeling.

References

1. Duncan Black, *The Theory of Committees and Elections* (Cambridge, 1958).
2. Howard R. Bowen, "The Interpretation of Voting in the Allocation of Resources," *Quarterly Journal of Economics,* 58 (November 1943), 27–43.
3. James M. Buchanan, *Public Finance in Democratic Process* (Chapel Hill, 1967).
4. J. M. Buchanan, "Simple Majority Voting, Game Theory and Resource Use," *Canadian Journal of Economics and Political Science,* 27 (August 1961), 337–48.
5. James M. Buchanan, *The Public Finances* (Homewood, Ill., 1965).
6. James M. Buchanan and Gordon Tullock, *The Calculus of Consent* (Ann Arbor, 1962).
7. Anthony Downs, *An Economic Theory of Democracy* (New York, 1957).
8. Anthony Downs, "Why the Government Budget is too Small in a Democracy," *Private Wants and Public Needs,* ed., Edmund S. Phelps (New York, 1965), pp. 76–95.
9. John Kenneth Galbraith, *The Affluent Society* (Boston, 1958).
10. Harry G. Johnson, "The Economic Approach to Social Questions," *Economica,* 35 (February 1968), 1–21.
11. George Katona, *The Mass Consumption Society* (New York, 1964).
12. Erik Lindahl, "Just Taxation—A Positive Solution," *Classics in the Theory of Public Finance,* eds. R. A. Musgrave and A. T. Peacock (New York, 1958), pp. 168–76.
13. Mancur Olson, Jr., *The Logic of Collective Action* (Cambridge, Mass, 1965).
14. A. Rapoport and C. Orwant, "Experimental Games: A Review," *Game Theory and Related Approaches to Social Behavior,* ed. Martin Shubik (New York, 1964), pp. 283–310.
15. William H. Riker, *The Theory of Political Coalitions* (New Haven, 1962).
16. Paul A. Samuelson, "The Pure Theory of Government Expenditure," *Review of Economics and Statistics,* 36 (November 1954), 387–89.
17. David Tuerck, "Constitutional Asymmetry," *Papers on Non-Market Decision Making,* 2 (1967), 27–44.
18. Gordon Tullock, "Problems of Majority Voting," *Journal of Political Economy* 67 (December 1959), 571–79.
19. Gordon Tullock, *Toward a Mathematics of Politics* (Ann Arbor, 1967).
20. W. Vickrey, "Self-Policing Properties of Certain Imputation Sets," *Contributions to the Theory of Games,* eds. A. W. Tucker and D. Luce (Princeton, 1959), pp. 213–46.
21. J. Von Neumann and O. Morgenstern, *Theory of Games and Economic Behavior* (3d ed., Princeton, 1953).

20

The "Dead Hand" of Monopoly

James M. Buchanan and Gordon Tullock

There is apparently some sort of common agreement, one presumably based on observation, that firms possessing and exercising monopoly power in varying degrees do in fact exist in many local, regional, national, and international markets. And by analytical definition the exercise of such monopoly power violates the necessary conditions for optimum "efficiency" or, more technically, for "Pareto-optimality" in resource use. By inference, then, there must necessarily exist some unexploited "gains-from-trade" between the monopolist, on the one hand, and his consumer-customers, actual and potential, on the other. Why, then, do we not also observe, especially in local-ized markets, more efforts on the part of consumer-organized "co-operatives" to secure control of the monopoly firms through ordinary market purchase or acquisition? Casual observation suggests that such attempts are rare indeed.[1]

This set of circumstances can be "explained," of course, on either one of two familiar grounds. It can be argued, first, that the pervasiveness of "emerging competition" is such that monopoly power, where it exists, is *always on the way to being dissipated.* Thus, in this view, the dynamics of the competitive process itself are such that monopoly is not really a serious problem at all, and the absence of consumer-cooperative attempts at market control is merely evidence of this fact.

Reprinted from *Antitrust Law and Economics Review,* Summer 1968.

1. See John S. McGee, "Patent Exploitation: Some Economic and Legal Problems," *Journal of Law and Economics,* IX (October 1966), 148: "It *is* true that intelligent, self-coerced consumer organizations, if created at low cost—or [by] the state acting in their behalf—could outbid the monopolist, producing net benefits and yet paying off the investor. But little has been said of this possibility in the reform literature."

A second line of reasoning partially contradicts and partially supplements that first one. Monopoly power can, it is admitted here, be a serious problem, and major inefficiences can and do exist because of those monopoly restrictions. Consumers, however, cannot be expected to organize to exploit the resulting gains-from-trade because of the *cost of organization*. Consumers of the monopoly firm's product are likely to be many, and any attempt on their part to secure joint action would run into prohibitively high cost barriers. Thus, even in the presence of a significant degree of monopoly exploitation, it still might not be feasible for consumers to organize themselves, or to submit to the activities of entrepreneurs seeking to organize them, and enter into market-like negotiations to buy out the monopolist.

There is doubtless some measure of validity in both of these arguments. But they nonetheless tend to gloss over and conceal an important aspect of the whole monopoly issue, namely, the fact that the *current* owners of monopoly firms may not in fact be earning more than a competitive return on *their* investment, that all present and future monopoly profits may have already been "capitalized" and removed by former owners of the firm. Thus we might still fail to observe such units being formed even in the presence of what seem to be really serious cases of monopoly power and even if the *costs* of organizing such effective consumers' cooperatives were absent or, say, fully subsidized from federal funds. In one sense, however, our analysis here can be incorporated into the "cost" argument, since we also demonstrate why individual consumers would be reluctant to enter into such arguments.

1. *The Welfare Triangle*

Consumer Gain—Social Gain

Consider a single consumer of a monopolist's product, as, for example, the one depicted in Figure 1. For the sake of simplicity, assume that all of the many consumers of this product are identical and that the monopolist himself is secured in his position i.e., freed from the threat of entry by potential competitors by, say, patent rights. The costs of producing the good, including a normal rate of return on market-valued assets, are known to be $1.00 per unit and these are constant over a wide quantity range. The price charged by the monopolist is $1.50 per unit, at which price each of his consumer-customers purchases 5 units per period, for a total outlay of $7.50. At a price of $1.00 (the normal or "competitive" price), the consumer would purchase 10 units, for a total expenditure of $10. The measure of the gain that would accrue *to this consumer* by abolition of the monopoly is shown by the familiar triangle, shaded in Figure 1, *and the profit rectangle to its left.* Arithmetically, this amounts to $3.75 in this example and, of course, $2.50 of this is a pure "transfer." *The measure of the welfare gain to society would be $1.25 per buyer, i.e., $1.25 multiplied by the number of consumers of the product* (all of whom are assumed to be identical).

Recapturing the "Welfare Triangle"

This simplified example suggests that the consumer should, rationally, stand willing to offer *up to $3.75* ($2.50 plus $1.25) for the privilege of being allowed to purchase freely at a normal or competitive price of $1.00. The monopolist should, on the other side of such a potential exchange, stand willing to provide the consumer with this privilege *at any sum over and above $2.50.*

Note that, if we confine the discussion to one customer, there seems to be no reason, at least in the conventional economic analysis of this problem, why the monopolist and the customer should not in fact make a mutually profitable arrangement here. The monopolist himself, for example, could form a "discount club," one selling the right to buy the commodity for $1.00 to all customers willing to pay the present value of an income stream of, say, $2.90 per year. This would *recapture the welfare triangle ($1.25)* and thus benefit *both* the monopolist and the customer. (Under monopoly pricing, *neither* gets it.) And this opportunity for mutual profit would not appear, at least at first glance, to be confined to abstract models. If we consider only the traditional arguments, we should also expect such bargains to be struck in the real world, as can be readily demonstrated if we consider the problems of the real monopolist who wishes to maximize the *present* value of his *future* income stream. Clearly he could not sell the right to buy unlimited quantities at the competitive price, but putting limits on the quantities purchased should not pose any major problems for him. The prices charged for entry into the "discount club" could be a simple multiple of the number of units purchased in the year before it was organized.[2]

Capitalized Value of Monopoly Firm

This scheme, it will be seen, immediately obviates one of the major reasons normally given for the absence of such efforts by customers to buy out monopolists. There is no need here for agreement

---

2. Note that there is no effort here to obtain the "consumer's surplus" above the original monopoly price. Further, there is no need to get *all* of the customers to join the discount club. Membership would be offered on a nondiscriminatory basis to anyone who wanted to pay for it.

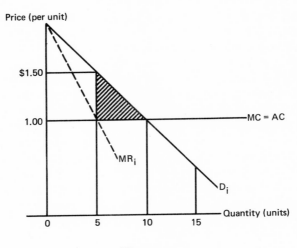

Figure 1

among all the customers, although we might well expect all of them to buy into the discount club and hence eliminate the monopoly altogether. The real question, then, as noted, is the reason for the extreme shortage of such arrangements in the real world. (Dr. Ferdinand Levy has suggested that the sale of "repair warranty" contracts by manufacturers of consumer durables (e.g., automobiles) may be an example.) For this purpose, let us return to our earlier model, one in which each of the customers is equal, and consider the bargaining situation when a sequence of time periods is explicitly taken into account. Protected by a patent monopoly in this example, our monopolist will sell his right to exploit any customer for any sum above [$2.50/r], where r is the appropriate rate of "discount" (corrected to reflect risk premiums). Assuming consumers estimate the monopolist's risks to be the same as he estimates them, they should then be willing to pay for the whole operation any sum up to a maximum total of [$3.75/r]. Gains-from-trade continue to exist in terms of capitalized values.

Capitalized Value of "Consumers' Surplus"

Consider, however, the position of the single consumer who may be asked to buy into this permanent discount club. Suppose that the monopolist has set a selling price of [$3.00/r] for membership. If the consumer expects his individual demand for the good to remain stable for a sufficiently long period of time, a subjective capitalization of prospective consumer's surplus in subsequent periods may yield meaningfully high present values and the consumer may, in this case, express a willingness to buy. Rarely, however, will the individual consumer actually expect his demand to remain stable over such long periods of time and, even if this should be the case, the limitation of life spans would doubtless interfere to prevent the full capitalization of the consumer's surplus the above computation suggests.

This failure of the individual to capitalize fully his prospective consumer's surplus on his own account may not prevent his joining the club under certain conditions, however. Even if he expects his personal demand to be highly unstable and acts on the basis of a very limited time horizon, he may nevertheless express a willingness to buy in if, in exchange for his investment, he can secure a readily *marketable,* transferable asset. In the prospective exchange between the monopolist and the consumer, however, there is an asymmetry in that, for his part, the monopolist secures a currently liquid asset, while the consumer, on his part, secures the present value of an "expectation" only, his own expected consumer's surplus, an intangible that cannot so readily be transformed into current liquid assets.

Suppose, for example, that an exchange is made on the terms suggested and that, after a few time periods have elapsed, the consumer seeks to market his membership. It is possible, of course, to imagine several institutional arrangements that could make such a marketing of individual shares reasonably efficient, but these arrangements would in every case be costly in themselves. The individual who either enters the market or leaves it entirely can probably be taken care of without too much difficulty, but it is hard to see how the consumer who wishes to reduce his consumption (perhaps as a result of a change in technology) could get his capital back. If, for example, individual consumers (and/or the monopolist) could yearly buy and sell the right to purchase one unit, then the real cost per unit to the individual purchaser would return to what it was before the discount club was organized. The best alternative would probably be to sell the original memberships at a price that not only discounts the monopolist's view of changes in his market, but the individual consumer's view as to whether or not he will remain a part of that market. New customers could buy in, but old customers could not sell out; they would simply lose their capital when they moved out of the market. This would of course sharply reduce the desirability of entering the club in the first place, however, thus suggesting that the individual, as a consumer, might well be reluctant to capitalize his prospective consumer's surplus in such a highly uncertain world.

11. *Monopoly Profits, "Deadweight" Debt, and "Future Generations"*

The "Time-Dimension" Problem

The difficulty in organizing exchanges where consumers can secure fully marketable assets stems, in turn, from the more fundamental problem raised by the *time dimensions* of the exchanges, a problem that is almost wholly ignored in orthodox analysis. The welfare gains that might possibly be secured from the elimination of monopoly output restrictions accrue largely to consumers in periods of time *subsequent* to that in which an institutional exchange of the sort discussed above might take place. Consumers in any *current* period may be reluctant to enter into such purchase agreements because of this feature alone, a fact that immediately suggests the analogy with the retirement of "deadweight" public debt. In this latter situation, current taxpayers may be very reluctant to retire outstanding issues of deadweight public debt for the simple reason that the *beneficiaries* of this action will be taxpayers living in time periods *subsequent* to the retirement operation, *i.e.*, "future generations." Only to the extent that they, themselves, expect to be members of such future taxpaying groups will current taxpayers willingly retire such deadweight public debt, and there are perhaps very few who will be sufficiently Ricardian in their outlook to carry out the full capitalization required to make such a decision wholly rational.[3]

"Burden" of Monopoly

The suggestion here is that the "burden" of existing monopoly restrictions is similar to that involved in carrying public debt of this type. The latter consists in the *interest charges* on the debt and, within any single period of time, these charges may be small relative to some appropriate national output measure, e.g., gross national product (GNP). Similarly, the "burden" of monopoly, a loss approximated by the welfare triangle, may be small relative to GNP in any single period, as indeed recent attempts at empirical measurement have tended to suggest.[4] Neither of these conclusions should

3. For the theory of public debt upon which this discussion is based, see James M. Buchanan, *Public Principles of Public Debt* (Homewood, 1958); for subsequent discussions by both supporters and opponents, see James Ferguson (ed.), *Public Debt and Future Generations* (Chapel Hill, 1964).

4. See A. C. Harberger, "Monopoly and Resource Allocation," *American Economic Review*, 44 (May 1954), 77–87.

imply, however, that major public benefits would not be produced by the elimination of the burden-producing debt instruments and monopolistic institutions. Effective retirement of outstanding dead-weight debt would produce definite *present-value* benefits, the magnitude of these being measured by the capitalized annual interest charges. And elimination of monopoly restrictions would also produce substantial *present-value* benefits, the size of these being measured by the capitalized current welfare losses (approximated by the welfare triangle in Figure 1). It is these present-value *benefits* that must be placed alongside the *costs* of taking such action in any rational cost-benefit calculus.

Monopoly-Creation "Models"

The analogy with deadweight public debt can be applied also to the *creation* of monopoly. The monopolization of an industry previously competitive in structure is, in the absence of technological change, analogous in effect to the issuance of public debt to finance *wholly worthless* public outlays. The *net wealth of the community is reduced* in either case, with wealth being properly measured to include present values for future tax liabilities, in the one case, and present values of foregone consumers' surplus, in the other.

As an alternative model, consider a monopoly that emerges coincident with a technological innovation, say, through a conferred patent right. The wealth of the community may well increase, and the monopolist's valuation of his patent right should be included in any measurement of national wealth. In addition, some consumers' surplus may also be produced, despite the prospects of monopoly restriction. (This is represented, in Figure 1, by the *upper* triangle above the monopoly-profits area.) And conceptually, at least, the present value of *this* stream of prospective consumers' surplus should also be included in any measurement procedure. This latter monopoly model thus becomes partially analogous to an issue of public debt to finance a public project that is *more than marginally productive*. Hence, net *national wealth is in fact increased* to some extent. The claims that public creditors, internal or external, have against the community in the form of the debt instruments is thus in some respects similar to the "claim" of the monopolist, as measured by his valuation of his patent right. The differences between the two cases here stem from the different *locations* of the wealth-creating activity. In the monopoly case, new wealth is presumably brought into being by the monopolist, this act of creation justifying or validating his "right" to a claim against the community. In the debt-issue case, new wealth is also presumably brought into being, but by an act of the community as a whole. The net worth of the creditors who lend funds for the activation of the new project is not changed; instead, the increase in net worth is distributed over all citizens in accordance with their expectations of "beneficiaries' surplus." Aside from this essentially distributional difference, the two cases differ also in that the proper valuation of the debt-financed project will include a full measure of prospective "beneficiaries' surplus," the whole of the area under the "demand curve," with no expected monopoly restriction. In other words, the welfare triangle will be included in this measure.

A third model of monopoly-creation lies somewhere between these first two. The introduction of a technological innovation, for example, even if it causes or allows a previously competitive industry to become monopolized in the process, might well leave the country's net *national wealth unchanged*. In this instance, the monopoly output restriction might do no more than *just offset* the technological gains introduced. Hence the appropriate analogy in this case would be that of a public debt issue employed to finance a project that is *just marginally productive*.

Monopoly Profits "Capitalized" at "Moment of Creation"

Attention to the various analogies between monopoly-creation and public-debt issue produces what should be an obvious conclusion but one that, in our view, has not been sufficiently emphasized before. *The benefits of monopoly tend to be capitalized at the moment of creation,* at least to the extent that marketable assets (e.g., stocks) are brought into being. And insofar as such capitalization does in fact take place, "future generations," in the aggregate, must bear the monopoly burden in terms of the offsetting losses in consumers' surplus.

Suppose that, in some "base" year t_0, an individual is granted a monopoly right to produce the good depicted in Figure 1. The present-value of this right, over and above the market value of the assets used to produce it, is measured at [$3.00n/r]. This is a marketable asset, and the individual monopolist enters this on the left-hand side of his balance sheet, offsetting it with a similar increase in net worth on the right-hand side. On the national balance sheet, therefore, there will appear an increment to or increase in the wealth of the economy. We assume that the capitalized value of consumers' surplus, measured by the upper triangle, is not computed.

Suppose now that, in a later period t_1, the individual who owns the monopoly right sells out to a purchaser at a price approximated by [$3.00n/r]. To the purchaser, this investment must be roughly equal in yield to his alternative investment prospects. And, to the seller, competition among prospective purchasers will insure that the yield is equal to that on alternative investments of roughly the same risk. The purchaser of his monopoly right, in t_1, thus writes up this asset on his balance sheet and writes down some other asset. His net worth remains unchanged, save for the possibility of marginal adjustments. Having acquired the monopoly right, however, the net worth of the new owner *now depends on the continuation of the existing and expected monopoly output restrictions.* If through governmental action or otherwise, his monopoly "right" is now eliminated, he suffers a capital loss. *His* net worth is reduced, while the *net worth of the original monopolizer remains unchanged.* To make our example dramatic, we can allow the latter to die between t_1 and t_2, with the monopoly restriction eliminated only in the latter period, after his death.

No Monopoly Profits for Current Owners

Thus it may be quite literally true that existing monopoly restrictions do not differentially benefit *current* owners of monopoly firms, save in some opportunity-cost sense, but, rather, that these benefits have long since been capitalized by monopoly entrepreneurs of generations past. The "evil of monopoly" lies in the period of creation, and the "ill-gotten gains" may now be enjoyed by third-generation playboys who cruise the Riviera and live off gilt-edge coupons, quite beyond the reach of any antitrust order. These gains thus remained untouched by any efforts to break up and eliminate the monopolies existing at any particular moment in time, leaving the unfortunate current owners of the monopoly rights as the ones singled out for "unjust" public treatment.

It is of course widely recognized that monopoly restrictions do not necessarily imply monopoly profits. It is perhaps less widely acknowledged that the existence of monopoly profits, in the ordinary sense, does not imply that any current owner of a monopoly firm earns more than a normal rate of return of his own *personal* investment. The *physical* assets of the firm will be employed in such a way as to yield more than a normal return, but the current owner, in *purchasing* these assets, may have transferred to the *former* owners the fully capitalized value of all expected *future* monopoly returns.

III. *Implications for Public Policy*

The monopoly problem is thus seen here as a blend of simple capitalization theory, simple accounting, and a recognition of the analogy with the problem of "deadweight" public debt. Once these separate elements of the analysis are seen, the general conclusions are fairly self-evident. Mention might be made here, however, of a number of practical policy suggestions presented by this analysis.

"Prevention" Versus "Cure"

Both equity and casual observation of the collective or political decision-making process suggests the importance of concentrating on the *prevention* of monopoly, rather than upon its elimination after it has already been created. The social "evil" of monopoly tends to be *concentrated in the moment of creation* and, once this "original sin" is committed, the effects are capitalized or "frozen" into the system. And while it is of course true that monopoly-creation can be, and probably is in many cases, a continuous process that grows over time, the more instantaneous phenomenon is nonetheless sufficiently real to warrant a shift of emphasis toward the prevention rather than the attempted cure of monopoly problems.

"Compensation" for Current Monopoly-Owners?

Equity considerations alone suggest the desirability of providing appropriate *compensation* to current stockholders when long-existing monopoly restrictions are eliminated by express governmental action. These restrictions having probably been long since capitalized by former owners, the *current* owners may well be realizing, as noted, no more than the normally-expected gains from their individual investments. Simple norms of justice would thus suggest that those current owners of shares in monopoly firms be considered no more "guilty" than nonowners and hence that any monopoly-elimination without compensation would amount, in such cases, to a particularly discriminatory "tax" on current shareholders, one that, if placed on that group openly, might well fail to win legislative approval or even constitutional sanction by the judiciary.

"Political" Barriers to "Compensation"?

Despite these acknowledged equity considerations, however, even cursory attention to democratic decision-making processes suggests that public policy would rarely attempt to eliminate any existing monopoly positions if compensation was in fact tied to the elimination measures. To pay compensation requires an outlay of public funds, and it would doubtless be very difficult to persuade current-period taxpayers (as represented in legislative assemblies) that *they* should support such outlays today when the prospective beneficiaries of their sacrifice would be consumers of *future* periods. The policy solution is almost implied in the question: The appropriate *method of financing* such compensation would be one involving the use of special issues of public debt instruments, a solution that would of course allow for an appropriate balancing-off, in a temporal sense, of anticipated costs and anticipated benefits, making the suggested outcome plausible for a rational democratic choice while at the same time securing reasonable equity in results.

Thus at least two specific applications of these principles come immediately to mind. First, if a collective decision should be made to shift a long-standing private monopoly to public or national ownership for the purpose of eliminating its monopoly output restrictions, this analysis clearly suggests that the funds to be used for compensating existing owners should be financed by debt issue, not by taxation.

Patent Policy—Free Licensing

Perhaps a more important practical application, however, lies in the realm of patent policy. If the award of monopoly rights is considered essential to insure the continuation of adequate incentives for invention, research, and development, this analysis suggests that many of the undesirable side-effects of patent monopolies could be eliminated by a combination of the instructional devices noted here. Thus an individual or firm could be granted full patent rights on new products, but once those rights were established at market values, public purchase (financed by debt issue) could be undertaken, accompanied by an arrangement for *free licensing*, a solution that would allow public purchase of the patent right without implying public purchase or ownership of producing assets.

21

On the Incidence of Tax Deductibility

James M. Buchanan and Mark V. Pauly

Who gains and who loses from tax deductions? Economists have considered this question to be so elementary that a specific answer is not required. The introduction of a deduction is presumed to shift some part of the cost of the activity subsidized to the general tax-payer regardless of his income. The gainers are allegedly those who take advantage of the deductibility feature. In this paper, we challenge these conclusions. We shall demonstrate that those who take advantage of tax deductions may lose and some general taxpayers may gain. This apparently paradoxical conclusion is attained by the incorporation of political feedbacks in the analysis.

I.

Tax deductions are quantitatively important. In fiscal 1967, American taxpayers reported $82 billion in deductions on adjusted gross incomes of $505 billion. Itemized deductions made up $60 billion of the $82 billion total. The four significant categories of itemized deductions, in decreasing order of quantitative importance, are: State and local taxes, interest, contributions, and medical expenses. Each of these could be examined in detail, and, as we should expect, several arguments could be advanced in support of each. In summary, however, deductions find their logical justification either in "adapting the income tax to individual circumstances" or in "advancing socially important objectives."[1] Under the first of these, the income base criterion, taken alone, is deemed insufficient evidence for determining horizontal equity. Specific deductions from income are

Reprinted by permission of the publisher from *National Tax Journal*, vol. XXIII, no. 2 (June 1970).

1. Richard Goode, *The Individual Income Tax* (Washington, 1964) p. 156.

allowed in order to make the definition of "equals" for tax purposes more meaningful. The medical expenses deduction, from among the four main categories, perhaps fits this description best.

The second objective for tax deductions is that of encouraging specific kinds of private activity deemed to be in the "social interest." Here the charitable deduction provides the best example. The effect of this deduction is to cause individuals to increase their contributions to eligible nonprofit organizations[2]—those performing charitable, religious, and educational activities that are generally thought to be desirable. Presumably, the deduction is permitted because the activities yield benefits to others than those who make the contributions; they generate external economies.

The recent revival of tax reform proposals aimed, at least in part, at reducing the scope for eligible deductions has been accompanied by an offsetting discussion of an extended use of the tax structure to promote specific objectives via the mechanism of deductions and tax credits. The basic difference between the tax deduction and the tax credit should be kept in mind. A deduction allows the prospective taxpayer to reduce the base upon which the tax is levied; a credit allows the taxpayer to reduce the tax that has already been computed on a determined base. So long as the taxpayer confronts a marginal rate of less than 100 percent, a dollar's worth of tax deductibility is worth less than a dollar's worth of tax credit. For the very reason that marginal rates of tax differ as among persons, however, tax deductions are not uniform as among persons; tax credits of given amounts are, by contrast, normally uniform in this sense. Empirically, deductions are much more important than credits. Aside from the investment credit enacted in 1962, tax credits are more talked about than enacted.

As suggested, the widespread notion has been that deductibility tends to shift a part of the cost of the activity for which a deduction is allowed onto the shoulders of the general taxpayer. Due's statement is typical:

> For persons in higher tax brackets the net cost of making contributions is greatly reduced by the tax (deduction) . . . the principle of deductibility has widespread support even though primary direct benefit concentrates in the higher income groups.[3]

2. There seems to be some disagreement as to the predicted elasticity of contributions with respect to the tax deduction feature. The directional effect of the deduction is, however, clear.

3. John Due, *Government Finance: Economics of the Public Sector* (Homewood, 1968), p. 408.

Implicit in this statement, and other similar ones, is the assumption that tax rates will remain the same with and without the deduction in question. But it is important to examine the reasonableness of any such *ceteris paribus* assumption. If the removal of the deduction should, through the increase in revenues generated, allow a general tax-rate reduction, it seems quite possible that the rich, as a group, might pay no higher and perhaps even lower total taxes than they pay before the change. The deduction need not reduce the "net cost of making contributions" to upper income groups generally, nor need it provide direct benefits to higher income groups.

In general, once it is recognized that removal of a deduction option implies some readjustment in tax rates and, further, that tax rates are determined by voters-taxpayers in a political process, any blanket predictions as to the distributional consequences of tax deductions become more difficult to make. In this paper, we shall develop a theory of tax deductions which incorporates behavioral readjustments through the political-decision process. When such feedbacks are introduced, distributional implications are often quite different from those that emerge implicitly and explicitly from the more limited standard approach. We shall show, for example, that the groups which save relatively more taxes by a deduction feature are not necessarily the groups that gain, relatively, from the existence of the deduction. It is possible that, as between two groups, one of which takes advantage of a tax deduction while the other does not, the group which uses the deduction is made worse off in a welfare sense. Finally, we shall examine the prospects for specifying an optimal set of deductions in the presence of external economies.

The argument proceeds through the construction of a series of simple models. We first consider a case where a deduction is permitted for individual expenditures on activities that yield no spillover benefits of the ordinary sort. Equity-motivated deductions can be considered as examples. Next, we develop two models in which deductions are allowed for private activity which yields some public or collective benefits but which does not substitute for currently-provided public goods. We show how this sort of deduction can be adjusted so as to satisfy the necessary conditions for optimality. The last section contains our conclusions.

Our method is strictly that of comparative statics, but with a difference. This difference is that we go beyond adjustments in market equilibria to treat adjustments in political equilibria. Those who choose to defend the orthodox approach may deny the relevance of political equilibrium as a meaningful tool for analysis. Anticipating this sort of criticism, we should state at the outset that the relatively restricted usefulness of political adjustment models can be acknowledged at the same time that the comparative advantages of such models in pointing toward pressures for political change are stoutly defended.

II.

Consider a situation where a tax deduction is introduced for spending on a good or activity that yields no benefits to others than the taxpayer who utilizes the deduction. This deduction could be considered to be introduced because of political trading or because of some newly discovered equity norm. Before the deduction is introduced, the economy is in full equilibrium, both in the supply of private goods and public goods.

It is useful to discuss the model in a two-person context. This allows us to treat in simple terms an analysis that can be extended without difficulty to apply to the many-person situation. Suppose there are only two spending units, A and B, with A's income being higher than B's. Each individual is assumed to adjust parametrically to tax-rate changes; that is, he does not consider the effects of his private behavior on the tax rate. This assumption seems to violate criteria for rational behavior in the strict two-person setting, but it is fully acceptable when we accept the two-person setting only to the extent that it yields conclusions applicable to the many-person case. In the latter, of course, such parametric behavior is fully rational.

Let us suppose, further, that the existing equilibrium is generated through the use of a proportional income tax, the proceeds of which are employed to finance a purely collective or public good. The equilibrium is complete in the Pareto-Wicksellian sense; each person is paying a marginal tax-price that is equal to his own marginal evaluation of the good. Tax-price is also assumed to be uniform over quantities of the public good, and for each individual. The public-goods equilibrium is depicted in Figure 1, where D_A and D_B are the two demand curves, and where ΣD is their vertical summation.[4]

We now introduce a deduction for a purely private good, say, good X. Assume that only individual A will take advantage of the

4. We can treat these as orthodox demand curves here, and, in this way, no problem arises in their vertical summation. This is facilitated by the simplifying assumption that tax-price is constant over varying quantities to each person. Without this assumption, marginal evaluations of the good would be dependent on how costs are shared over inframarginal ranges. Unique demand curves would, in this case, be impossible to derive.

deduction. The orthodox analysis would suggest that A secures an increase in disposable real income because of the net reduction in taxes that he pays for the public good. A's taxes will fall by tp_xX dollars, where t is the marginal tax rate, p_x is the price of X, and X is the number of units that A purchases after the deduction. These conclusions arise, however, only because the analysis is not extended beyond first-stage reactions.

If tax collections at some initial proportional rate, t_o, were just sufficient to cover the total cost of providing Z_o units of the public good, the introduction of the deduction would have three separate effects: (1) a shortfall in total tax collections at rate t_o below that which would be required to provide Z_o units of public good; (2) a reduction in A's tax base from Y_a to $(Y_a - t_o p_x X)$; (3) an increase in

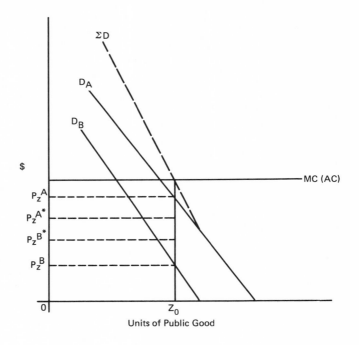

Figure 1

A's purchases of X in response to the lower effective price. These effects will set in motion forces leading to some new equilibrium.

If the community attempts to return the quantity of public goods financed to the initial level Z_o, and if it attempts to do so through increases in the existing proportional income tax, the new tax price-per-unit of the public good that A will confront must be less than his initial tax-price. This is necessarily true because of the tax-base reduction generated by the deduction. In the two-person model, this means that the tax-price to B must be higher than in the initial equilibrium. Suppose that the two new tax prices required to produce-supply Z_0 are P_z^{A*} and P_z^{B*}; these imply a new tax rate, t_1 and a return to the previous public-goods quantity, Z_0.

A glance at Figure 1 is sufficient to show that equilibrium could not prevail at this new situation. A would desire an increase in the quantity of public goods; his marginal evaluation would exceed the marginal tax-price that he confronts. On the other hand, B would now desire to reduce the quantity of Z below Z_0. In the new position, his marginal evaluation of Z would fall below the marginal tax-price that he faces. It becomes clear from the construction that some new equilibrium in public-goods supply will be attained, if at all, only when the tax structure has been altered so as to confront A with a tax rate higher than t_1 and B with some rate lower than t_1. In other words, equilibrium will be attained only by some shift from a proportional to a progressive tax on the effective income base. The equilibrium tax-prices per unit of the public good, Z, would have to return to P_z^A and P_z^B, since these are the only prices that can possibly satisfy the necessary conditions for optimality. In terms of rates of tax on the income base, A will now pay a rate on his income minus his deduction which will be less than the rate that B will pay on his total income. Since we have assumed that marginal tax-price remains unchanged over varying quantities of the public good, the new equilibrium is identical with the old one, except for the change in nominal tax rates.

This conclusion arises only under the restriction that tax-prices remain unchanged over varying quantities of the public good. If this restriction on the model is dropped, the analysis becomes considerably more complex, but the basic elements of the result are not changed. The precise quantity of public goods provided may be different in the two equilibrium positions because of the operation of income effects, and, in the net, distributional gains from the deduction may be secured by one party. However, it remains true that the amount of tax reduction continues to overstate the gains to A and, also, that at the margin, tax rates must shift against A to attain the new equilibrium.

Under the simplified conditions outlined, and without the complexities just mentioned, it can be shown that A will suffer a welfare loss. The tax deduction has the effect of lowering the effective market price of X, from P_x to $(P_x - tP_x)$. As a result of this price reduction, he will purchase more X. As we have shown, however, his total tax bill in the new equilibrium will be the same as before the deduction was introduced. Figure 2 will be helpful at this point. The abcissa measures units of the private good, X. As shown, Mr. A extends his purchases from X_o to X_e in response to the deduction. There is a welfare loss from this extension that is approximately measured by the area FGH. This loss arises because the price reduction is illusory rather than real. In the market for good X, the price remains at P_x. The individual acts as if he confronts a lower price because he expects that he will secure the public good on more advantageous terms. On balance, the effect of the deduction for the person who uses it becomes similar to the granting of a per unit subsidy on an item of consumption combined with the levy of an offsetting lump-sum tax.

The argument places the whole notion of using tax deductions to secure horizontal equity norms in a new light. Insofar as individuals are able, through their own behavior, to change the quantity of the particular good or activity for which the deduction is allowed, whether this be medical care or borrowing at interest, there must arise an excess burden of the sort indicated. There will be a welfare loss involved in trying to achieve further equity; the efficiency-equity conflict appears in yet another form.

It becomes relatively easy to extend the model to allow both persons to utilize the deduction. The basic conclusions are not modified. A more relevant shift in the model involves the starting

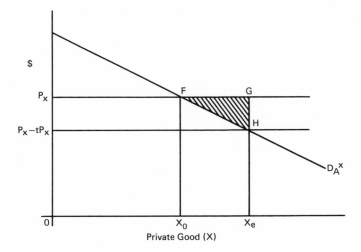

Figure 2

point. If we should commence with full public and private goods equilibrium, *with* the tax deduction, the model could be employed to analyze the effects of removing the deduction. Descriptively, this is applicable to some of the current discussion of tax reform. If an existing deduction is removed, the results will not necessarily be to subject the groups currently utilizing the deduction to relatively larger tax shares. But if the existing deductions are such that only particularized subgroups, within income categories, can effectively utilize them, the orthodox analysis comes into its own.

I I I.

We shall now consider two cases in which a deduction is allowed for private outlay on goods which are close substitutes for public expenditures. First, suppose that a pure public good is being provided in Pareto-Wicksellian equilibrium, so that the necessary conditions for optimality are fully satisfied. Let the cost-price of this good, whether to public or private buyers be $1.00, and let the publicly supplied quantity be Z_0. Suppose that a deduction is introduced which allows the individual to reduce his tax base one-for-one with private purchases of Z. An individual will take advantage of this if his marginal tax-price (which is, in equilibrium, equal to his marginal evaluation of the good) exceeds one minus the marginal tax rate that he confronts. (Note that if the marginal tax rate t is less than 50 percent, there can, at most, be only one person who could use a deduction since, at most, only one person could have a marginal evaluation which exceeds $.50. Similarly, if t is 90 percent, there can at most be only ten persons who will use the deduction. This restriction insures that the model here is useful largely in providing the groundwork for more realistic models in which the good provided publicly is not Samuelsonian pure.)

Suppose that the initial public-goods equilibrium includes marginal tax-prices of $.67 and $.33 for A and for B, these being equal to marginal evaluations. Public-goods units are measured in "dollar's worths." The deduction is introduced, and suppose that only A takes advantage of it. He will make private outlays on the good, Z, because he will think that, in so doing, he can improve his own position. By expending $1.00 privately on Z, A's tax bill is reduced by $.67; hence, the apparent price per unit of Z falls to $.33. In taking this action, A presumably ignores the erosion of the tax base and also the perfect substitutability of the good as between private and public provision. At the old tax rate, funds will no longer be sufficient to allow the public purchase of the previously existing supply. This decline will be less than the increase in private outlay, however, since taxes are reduced by only some fraction, t, of private outlays on Z. In our numerical example, tax revenues fall by $.67 whereas private outlay goes up by $1.00.

In the parametric model of behavior, the other person, B, will treat the collective-consumption good provided by A's private purchase (and, by definition, equally available to both A and to B), as an exogenous increase in his real income along a single dimension. Hence, B will be thrown out of equilibrium at the old tax rate. The tax-price that he pays for a unit of the good that is purchased publicly will have increased because of the fall in total tax base; B will, therefore, want less than the Z_0 units provided in the previous equilibrium. He will find, however, that he is being provided with *more* units than before, when he considers both public and private supply. Tax-rate readjustments or readjustments in the quantity of public supply are required in order to bring B back into some new equilibrium.

When we look at A's position, however, tax-rate adjustments which would satisfy B are ruled out. The marginal evaluation for A, as well as for B, will be lower than in the initially prevailing equilibrium because of the increase in gross quantity of Z. A would, therefore, be unwilling to accept any higher tax-share for publicly supplied units. Any approach toward an equilibrium that would satisfy both parties must involve cutbacks in the quantity of the collective-consumption good that is publicly supplied. The net results of the tax deduction can be seen in their starkest form if we neglect possible income effects. In this case, we should expect B to be satisfied only after the public supply is reduced by precisely the amount of the private supply increase. In our numerical example, B then secures the same quantity of Z with a total tax bill that is $.33 lower than before. A secures the same quantity with a total outlay, tax bill plus private purchase, that is $.33 more than before. The person who has taken advantage of the deduction has been trapped by what we may call a "tax deduction illusion."

To this point, we have analyzed only the effects of a discrete and initial usage of the deduction option. We have not traced through the behavioral adjustments that would produce a new equilibrium. Rigorous analysis becomes difficult here because of the necessity to allow for income-effect feedbacks on marginal evaluations. As A expands his private purchases of Z under the tax-deduction illusion, he transfers real income to B. This will reduce A's marginal evaluation and increase B's, so long as Z is a normal good. Even when income effects are incorporated, it remains possible that equilibrium is attained only when all public supply of the good is eliminated, the whole supply being purchased privately by A. There seems to be nothing in the behavioral adjustment process that generates movement toward a position that would satisfy the conditions for optimality. In the new equilibrium, the total supply of the collective-consumption good may be above or below that of the optimal public supply before the deduction is introduced.

I V.

Again we want to consider a two-agent model, but in this case we assume that the public good is initially supplied by some combination of public and private expenditure.[5] For example, families may be making some outlay on the college education of their children at the same time that this education is being financed also by the community at large. Assume, as before, that family A's income is greater than family B's income, and that only family A takes advantage of the tax deduction when this is offered.

We assume that a pre-deduction equilibrium exists, but in this respect this model differs somewhat from those considered earlier. *Given* the outlay that is made by the family, it will be true that equilibrium prevails in the Pareto-Wicksell sense. Similarly, *given* the outlay made by the community, the position of the family is in equilibrium concerning its own private supplements. Since, however, each of these interacting units, the family and the community, reaches its equilibrium position independently of the actions of the other, the final equilibrium will not fully satisfy conditions for Pareto optimality. Under the circumstances outlined, the gross supply of the good will generally be sub-optimal.

We now permit a tax deduction for *additional* private expenditures on college education. Only family A takes advantage of this option. Orthodox theory suggests that family A benefits from this new feature in the tax law while family B does not benefit directly, and benefits indirectly only to the extent that there remain external marginal benefits from the extension in the education of A's child. As in the earlier models, we can show that this line of reasoning is in error.

When family A is permitted to deduct from its tax bill (which finances supplements to other families' children) its own incremen-

5. This model is described in more detail in M. V. Pauly, "Mixed Public and Private Financing of Education," *American Economic Review*, LVII (March 1967), 120–30.

tal outlay on education, the effective price of education is reduced. A will, therefore, extend its private purchases. This will, in turn, cause the rest of the community (B in the limited two-family model) to reduce the collectively-financed supplements to child A's education.

In addition to this feedback, there will be a second effect. Because of the deduction, A's taxes will no longer be sufficient to finance the contribution to B's education that A desires. A will be agreeable to an increase in its tax rate to return to some sort of equilibrium with respect to the community's purchase of education for child B.

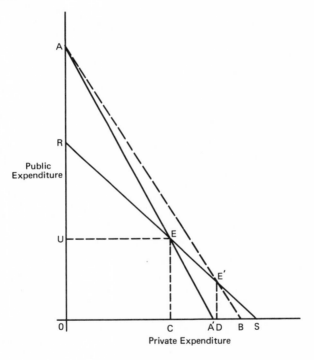

Figure 3

In sum, who benefits from the deduction? Family A has not reduced and may have increased its tax payments for child B's education, but it has been induced to increase its own private outlays on its own child's education. There has been a net loss to family A, the only family in the model that took advantage of the tax deduction. The model can be illustrated diagrammatically in Figure 3.

We measure private expenditures by Family A on the education of its own child on the abcissa; we measure the collectivity's outlay on the education of Family A's child on the ordinate. The line AA' indicates the expenditure levels preferred by Family A for every level of public supplement; RS indicates the similar locus of preferred outlay for the collectivity. The independent adjustment equilibrium is found at E; here, Family A spends CC privately and the community supplements this with a spending level of OU.

The deduction has the effect of changing Family A's locus of preferred combinations from AA' to AB. A new equilibrium is shown at E'. Family A is induced by the deduction option to make additional expenditure in the amount CG because of the expected reduction in its tax burden. But, as the analysis has indicated, the tax bill for A remains the same or rises so that Family A suffers a net welfare loss because of the "tax deduction illusion" as in the earlier models. Overall efficiency in the community may, however, be increased in this model, by contrast with the earlier ones examined. This is because we specified that the initial equilibrium was one in which the gross quantity of the good or activity was suboptimal. Family A's increased outlays resulting from the deduction illusion generate welfare gains to Family B, and these may more than offset the net welfare losses suffered by Family A.

v.

The main point developed in the several simplified models discussed has been one of demonstrating that the predicted distributional effects of tax deductions may be different from those which the orthodox analysis implies. When the concept of political equilibrium is introduced, and when full readjustment through the political-decision structure is incorporated in the models, some of those who seem to gain from the introduction of tax deductions may lose.

In this section, we shall consider the possible use of the tax deduction as a means of satisfying the conditions for optimality in the presence of external economies. Suppose that taxes are paid for a public good, but that there exists another good or activity that is not provided publicly which would yield significant marginal external benefits to all members of the community. Let us assume, for simplicity, that the two goods are not close substitutes and that private *production* of the unprovided good (as distinct from private provision) is as efficient or more efficient than public production. A practical example might be the activities of churches or religious organizations which, for constitutional reasons, are not carried out publicly, but which are alleged to yield external economies, at least to large numbers of citizens.

The introduction can lead individuals to increase the activity to the point at which an optimal quantity is generated. With a given tax rate t, a tax deduction is equivalent to a cut of t percent in the effective price of the eligible activity. There will exist some pattern of price cuts which will cause purchasers to expand provision out to the optimal amount. Distributionally, the effects will remain as we have indicated earlier. But, if distributional considerations are neglected, efficiency in the provision of externality-generating goods can be secured through the deduction illusion.

At this point, it may be useful to contrast the deduction, as a means of securing efficient quantities of such goods, with more direct methods. It is sometimes argued that the use of tax deductions avoids public or collective control which follows upon direct public expenditures.[6] Such an argument is largely invalid, however, because it will generally be possible to provide governmental funds *directly* to individuals to spend as they please, through earmarked part-or full-payment vouchers. Instead of being allowed a deduction for medical expenses, individuals could receive part or full payment of their expenses, as is indeed now in practice for those over 65 through Medicare. There need be no change in the degree of public control. Ordinarily providing full-payment vouchers to all regardless of income would not be very efficient in encouraging expenditures on particular goods or services; such vouchers would take the form of income supplements and would induce offsetting reductions in private outlays on the parts of the recipients. What is needed for efficiency is a pattern of effective price reductions varying with incomes. Vouchers which will provide *partial* payment for desired quantities of the particular good or services are equivalent to excise subsidies.

A tax deduction is behaviorally equivalent to an excise subsidy. And it is useful to contrast these two devices. Under an excise subsidy, individual purchasers of an externality-generating good are faced with net price reductions which will cause them to expand their rates of purchase. In this case, the results are identical with those that can be secured with tax deductibility. With the excise subsidy, however, revenues for the subsidy must be collected through an explicit increase in taxes. The tax deduction feature accomplishes an expansion of purchases without the necessity of this step. This

6. Goode, *op. cit.*, pp. 170–71; Due, *op. cit.*, p. 408.

may have major advantages in terms of political strategy, but, more importantly, the distributional results are different. Under the tax deduction device, those who are existing and potential purchasers of the externality-generating good may be deluded into paying substantially all of the net cost of internalizing the external economy. Those who are neither actual or potential purchasers of the good but who secure the external benefits from the extension of its usage or provision, may, through the deduction, secure something for nothing.

We have made no attempt here to present a complete theory of tax deduction when the political as well as the market structure is conceived as being modified by individual choice behavior. What we have done is to suggest that the incorporation of political adjustments modifies the standard predictions about the effects of deductions. We have demonstrated our analysis in terms of very simplified models. The analysis was necessarily abstract, and, as is usually the case, the assumptions will need to be examined and conclusions qualified if the results are to be applied. Nevertheless, these models should provide the basis for developing more complete models which might then be used for the derivation of empirically testable hypotheses.

22

The Political Economy of the Military Draft

Robert D. Tollison[1]

Economists have given considerable attention to the allocative and distributive effects of the military draft.[2] The common trademark of these studies is the acceptance of the draft as a given political institution which has a predictable opportunity cost impact on the individual and when aggregated on society. This approach is methodologically analogous to the neoclassical treatment of tax institutions which was characterized by the lack of expenditure considerations and more generally by the lack of consideration of the political origin of fiscal institutions.[3] Modern public finance scholarship has abandoned this asymmetrical and simplified methodology. The theoretical integration of tax and expenditure processes and the political origin of fiscal institutions are now problems of the first order of concern. The object of this paper is to analyze the military draft using this more modern methodology. Particular emphasis will be placed on the development of a model which explains in a very simplistic way the political origin and stability of a military draft in a democratic setting.

The paper is divided into four parts. Section I presents an individualistic choice model of the draft in a referendum-type de-

Reprinted by permission of the publisher from *Public Choice*, vol. IX (Fall 1970).

1. Professors James M. Buchanan, Roland N. McKean, James C. Miller III, Roger Sherman, and Gordon Tullock contributed valuable criticism and advice in the development of this paper. Responsibility for any errors, of course, remains with the author.

2. For representative works, see Oi [8], Pauly and Willett [10, 11], Davis and Palomba [4], and Fisher [6].

3. This statement excludes Wicksell and the Italian tradition in public finance.

mocracy. Section II relaxes the assumptions of the model to show how the introduction of more realistic collective conditions tends to reinforce the choice process depicted in the model. Section III discusses the distributional implications of eliminating the draft and what these implications in turn imply for the political adjustment process required to abolish the draft. Section IV concludes with mention of other implications of the model.

I. *The Model*

The immediate task is to set forth the assumptions of the analysis which serve to simplify the collective environment of the model to manageable proportions. As will be noted, however, the divergencies between the individualistic model and the world are not large. The model should possess explanatory power.

First, a referendum-type democracy where each issue must be considered by the voters is assumed. Individuals in the model base their voting behavior on how they expect the draft issue to affect their present wealth positions. Second, individuals can discount perfectly the present wealth impact of the draft issue. This discounting condition applies to the tax-in-kind associated with being drafted and to the potential subsidy generated by lower budgetary outlays for manpower under a draft system.[4] Third, it is initially assumed that the voting population is rectangularly distributed by age. Fourth, it is assumed that the draft issue is the only issue facing the collectivity and that all costs of collective decision on this issue are negligible. This assumption rules out complications of logrolling and political decision-making costs at this point. Fifth, it is assumed that the right to vote exists for the draft-age group of the population (18- to 20-year olds).[5] This rules out any explanation of the draft in terms of institutional rigidities in the system, e.g., an age requirement for voting. Also, those qualified in the draft-eligible group of any period's 18- to 20-year old group are assumed to be sufficient to meet the military's demand for manpower. The latter two conditions assure that the incidence of the draft is general for the draft-eligible group and

---

4. This two-sided aspect of the effect of a military draft on a budget system is recognized clearly in Altman and Fechter [1, p. 31]; Hansen and Weisbrod [7, especially pp. 396–97]; Pauly and Willett [10, p. 55]; and Willett [13].

5. This admittedly begs the question of why the 18- to 20-year olds were selected as the draft-age group. The answer, however, is inherent in the analysis to be developed. The delineation of a draft-age group here simply provides a convenient starting point for the analysis.

that the age range of the draft-eligible group is constant over time.

Into this setting the issue of whether to draft military manpower (as opposed to paying market wages) can be introduced in some initial voting period. The potential present wealth effects of the issue will determine individual choice and need to be elaborated. For those voters beyond draft-age, the issue represents a potential addition to present wealth in the form of a discounted stream of future tax savings on military manpower.[6] Under the terms of the model, this group will support the issue. Draft-age individuals must calculate the net present-wealth impact of the issue. This would be the balance of the foregone income suffered while a draftee and the subsidy received in future budget periods as a veteran (assuming the draft is still in existence). Let it be assumed for the moment that this balance is negative, i.e., that $w_t > w_s$, where w_t is the discounted and negative present wealth impact of being drafted and w_s is the expected subsidy, also discounted. The draft-age group in the model would thus vote against the issue.[7]

It is easily demonstrated that under these conditions that the draft issue will be passed under a wide range of voting rules. Indeed, the issue could be passed under very restrictive voting rules since a preponderant majority of the rectangularly distributed voting population lies outside the draft-age range. The lined area in Figure 1 represents those supporting the issue in the initial period.

The voting process for the initial period represented in Figure 1 can be altered if other possible net wealth balances are struck by the draft-age group and other than a rectangularly distributed voter-age distribution is introduced. The remaining wealth balances that the draft-age group could face on the issue are $w_t < w_s$ and $w_t = w_s$. Both conditions have conceptual plausibility, particularly if the military experience is associated with some form of post-draft annuity (veterans' benefits) or other possible return, perhaps non-pecuniary in nature (patriotism). Under either condition all voting rules, in-

6. This result assumes that the budgetary saving associated with drafting military manpower is not reflected in increased defense expenditures for non-manpower purposes or increased non-defense spending of some form.

7. Throughout the following analysis, the entire draft-age group will be assumed to face given choice conditions. This is done only for the sake of exposition. Different segments of this group could strike different wealth balances on the issue leading to a diversity of choice behavior and attitude on the draft issue among members of the draft-age group. The effects of viewing the draft-age group in a non-homogeneous manner should be apparent as the discussion proceeds.

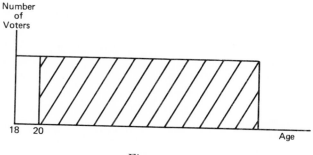

Figure 1

cluding unanimity, would pass the issue. All voters obviously support the issue where $w_t < w_s$ holds. Where $w_t = w_s$ holds, the draft-age group is indifferent on the issue and allows the other members of the collectivity to vote affirmatively for them.

Figures 2 and 3 illustrate the initial voting period with other than a rectangular voter-age distribution.

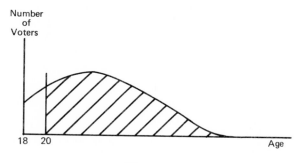

Figure 2

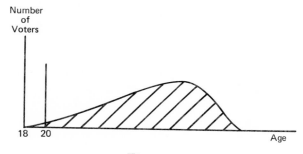

Figure 3

Figure 2 represents a "younger" voting population with a greater number of voters in the draft-age range. This distribution would tend to increase the degree of restrictiveness in the range of voting rules that would pass the issue where $w_t > w_s$ prevails for the now expanded draft-age group.[8] Figure 3 depicts an "older" voting population where the opposite result holds. A larger number of voters lies outside draft-age, enlarging the range of voting rules that would pass the issue in the initial period. The central relationship, then, in this very simplified voting process is that between the number of voters in the draft-age group and the voting rule.

Once the draft issue is passed and put into operation, the effect of the ongoing draft system on the individual voter's present wealth can be used to show how the draft would tend to remain in operation over a conceivably long sequence of future generations.[9] Let it be assumed initially that the voting rule and voter-age distribution which prevailed when the issue passed in the initial period continue to prevail in all subsequent voting periods. Also, it is assumed that the draft has to be relegislated every two years. In this setting the viability of the draft depends on how the present draft-age group will choose on the issue once they have served their two years and assumed their roles as taxpayers-voters-beneficiaries (veterans) in the collective process. The voting behavior of veterans is critical since the requirement that all must serve means that at some future point the entire nondraft-age segment of the voting population will be veterans.

The veteran in the model faces a distinctly different choice situation than he faced in the initial voting period. The opportunity cost imposed on the veteran by the draft is a sunk cost which was subjectively capitalized in the initial period. In subsequent periods this cost is conceptually irrelevant to the veteran's voting decision on the draft issue. The subsidy involved in the draft process for the veteran is of a different character. Although the future veteran capitalizes the expected subsidy in the initial period, the continued re-

8. Where $w_t \leq w_s$ prevails, the distribution of voters by age does not matter. The issue would be passed under all combinations of voting rules and voter-age distributions.

9. To move beyond the initial voting period, it has been assumed that the issue passed under some configuration of voting rule, voter-age distribution, and draft-age group choice condition. Since it is clearly possible for the issue to fail under some sets of these conditions, the movement beyond the initial period is not guaranteed in any general sense. The analysis here must proceed on the view that plausible combinations of these conditions would pass the issue.

ceipt of the subsidy over time is dependent on the choice behavior of the individual in all future referenda on the draft. This is due to the requirement that the system must be relegislated every two years. In terms of a voting decision the veteran faces a $w_s > 0$ choice condition on the draft issue in all post-draft voting periods and will rationally choose for the process to be continued regardless of how he chose on the issue at draft-age.

As the voting process of the model proceeds over time under the postulated conditions, the draft will be relegislated in all future voting periods with the support of veterans. The draft basically creates its own continued existence in the model by channeling each generation of 18- to 20-year olds into their postdraft existence with a vested interest (of some form) in seeing that the process goes on.[10]

The model can be generalized over time as the voter-age distribution changes. If the distribution is becoming younger over time with the $w_t > w_s$ condition holding for all subsequent draft-age groups, the possibility that the issue will fail under a constitutionally fixed voting rule will be increased each period. If the distribution is becoming older, the converse will hold. Since the perpetual relegislation of the system is not guaranteed in any general sense, it is necessary to conjecture that plausible changes in the relevant variables will not be such as to stop the process.

11. Variations on the Model

It will be worth a brief digression to see how viable the choice process of the model is under more realistic assumptions.

First, the assumption of perfect discounting of the tax-in-kind and subsidy is central to the choice problem posed by the model. Without this condition the wealth effects of the draft issue can be distorted by imperfect, illusory, or uncertain perception on the part of individual voters. The choice problem would become more unpredictable under these circumstances. The most probable case is that where the tax-in-kind is accurately and confidently capitalized and the subsidy is not. The tax is a specific levy which the individual would have little difficulty in perceiving and capitalizing. The sub-

10. Pauly and Willett [10, pp. 60–61] clearly recognize the intergenerational aspects of the voting process described here. Their discussion, however, is framed in equity terms and deals with the differential tax burdens placed on succeeding generations when military manpower demand is not constant. Also, Willett has developed an intergenerational view of how the draft transfers real income from higher to lower utility time locations. See [13].

sidy, however, consists of a reduction in the military budget that is generally dispersed over the collectivity. It is quite possible under these conditions that individuals perceive (guess?) imperfectly their share of this reduction. If this condition held in extreme form where the subsidy created no impact on the present wealth positions of nondraft-age voters, the initial legislation of the draft issue would not be possible in the model. The initial voting period would be characterized by a draft-age group which would vote against the issue and all others who would be indifferent ($w_t = w_s = o$). The draft-age group would choose to defeat the issue for the whole collectivity. In a less extreme form, however, so long as the nondraft-age group in the model perceives the existence of the subsidy to any extent, the choice process described in the model will be operable. It does not seem unrealistic to think that this is the case.

Second, once other issues and political agreement costs are introduced to the model, the complexity of the choice problem facing the individual voter is increased. Logrolling processes can possibly emerge to defeat the draft issue in any period. Various models of political exchange could be developed, but each would be unique to given assumptions about the voting rule, size of the draft-age group, intensity of feeling on the issue by the draft and nondraft-age groups, and so on. The essential point is that coalitions to abolish the draft would tend to form around a set of issues which benefit the nondraft-age group as much as the draft-subsidy while at the same time damaging the draft-age group less than the draft-tax. To the extent that the draft issue represents an intense minority facing a non-intense majority, the probability of political trades to abolish the draft would be increased.

There are, however, some complications with logrolling the draft out of existence. Any political exchange to abolish the draft need not involve the whole collectivity. Only a set of voters large enough to surpass the given voting rule is required. This raises an interesting prospect. Since the increased budgetary costs of paying market wages will be distributed via the general income tax structure of the economy, it is possible that any exchange to abolish the draft will involve negative external effects for the set of voters which does not participate and does not benefit. These voters would simply face higher tax prices for military manpower. It seems possible, therefore, that alternative coalitions could form in the future in terms of the voting process described in the foregoing model to reinstate the draft.

Furthermore, the benefits to be derived from any exchange on the draft issue must be net of the costs of arranging the exchange.

These costs represent the organizational problem of political exchange. They could, however, be significant with the draft issue when institutional rigidities (such as the general absence of voting rights among the 18- to 20-year olds) are taken into account. Also, benefits to be derived from political exchange on the draft must be net of the additional income tax costs to the participants of defeating the draft issue (paying higher military wages). These problems, while of an organizational nature, make the voting process of the model potentially viable in the face of logrolling activity.

Third, it was assumed that voting rights were extended to the age group under consideration for the draft liability. The relaxation of this assumption in favor of a more realistic (in a literal sense) rule which precludes anyone under age 21 from voting makes it possible to legislate the draft issue under any voting rule and any voter-age distribution in the initial period and over time. The group for which $w_t > w_s$ could potentially prevail has no say in the process. Once each draft-age group has been subjected to the process, however, their opposition to the system should rationally cease, and the process would continue over time supported by the nondraft-age group in the collectivity.

Fourth, by modifying the condition that all those qualified must serve to allow some element of the draft-age group to escape the tax-in-kind, the issue could be legislated under less restricted sets of voting rules and voter-age distributions. The explanation for this is clear—there now exists an additional set of voters who escape the tax-in-kind and are purely subsidized. The immediate problem in this more realistic context is to choose those who will serve.

The inverse of the incidence problem is the case where manpower demand exceeds the capacity of the given draft-age group. The collectivity faces the problem of extending the draft-age range to meet the needs of the military for manpower. The extension process would proceed by voting to extend the age coverage of the system while not exceeding the point in the voter-age distribution where the issue would fail. If manpower demand exceeded the point in the voter-age distribution where the issue would not pass, the system could conceivably break down. In reality, however, it would seem reasonable to assume that the draft-age range could be varied up or down within substantial limits without impairing the continuance of the process.

Fifth, the model assumed that the draft-age group homogeneously faced various choice conditions on the draft issue. It is clear that there are many factors at work to create divergent attitudes toward the draft among draft-age individuals. Patriotism (however interpreted) is just one example of such a factor. The effect on the model of this more realistic assumption about the draft-age group is clear. To the extent that elements of the liable group face the $w_t \leqq w_s$ conditions, the draft can be started and perpetuated over time under a less restricted range of the relevant collective conditions.

The introduction of more realistic conditions to the analysis does little to question the conceptual validity of the choice process of the model. Indeed, in many cases the realistic conditions tend to reinforce the inference that something like this choice process explains the existence and stability of real world draft systems.

III. *Distributional Implications of Eliminating the Draft*

The main implication of the voting model is that the draft is a unique type of income transfer from draft-affected individuals (the young) to the rest of society. This means that correspondingly unique distributional changes in taxes would be required to eliminate the draft. Those who would otherwise have been drafted must be taxed while those beyond draft-age remain exempt.

The problem of arranging such changes would be a barrier to collective action aimed at eliminating the draft. This problem is particularly acute in the context of the individualistic voting model because there are no clear incentives for current taxpayers, draft or nondraft-age, to engage in tax adjustments to eliminate the system. This is because the primary beneficiaries of such an action would be future "generations" of taxpayers. Future taxpayers could possibly benefit in two senses. First, there is the distinct possibility that the budgetary costs (tax bills) for market-procured manpower would be lower than present and extrapolated future budgetary costs of draft-procured manpower after an initial transition period. This possibility exists because of the various manpower economies that the military would be forced to seek in the face of a higher price for its labor input. Second, future draft-age groups would potentially benefit from not having to bear the implicit tax associated with being drafted. This assumes, of course, that the differential tax on the draft-age group of this period needed to finance the immediate transition and higher budgetary costs of the change to market procurement is dropped once the transition is completed. At this time, the budgetary costs of military manpower would be distributed in accordance with the general income tax structure of the economy. It is clear, then, that current taxpayers would have a propensity to engage in individual adjustment to eliminate the draft only to the extent that they envision themselves as part of the future taxpaying public that benefits from the change. This represents the essential adjustment problem in the individualistic collective model, and it is perhaps the primary reason that widespread support to eliminate the draft through differential taxation has not emerged.

There would appear, however, to be a way out of this dilemma. The answer lies in the close analogy of the individual adjustment problem in eliminating the draft to the problems of eliminating monopoly or retiring deadweight public debt.[11] These problems are basically similar in that the benefits from current sacrifices to solve the problems lie in future periods and are captured by future consumers or taxpayers. In each case the appropriate solution would be to issue public debt instruments to finance the change in the present period. In this way the real cost of the present action is shifted to individuals living in the future.[12] As regards the draft, a special issue of public debt could be used to finance an initial transition period to market procurement of manpower with, perhaps, interest on the debt also borrowed for a period. The "burden" of the shift to market procurement would thus be transferred to future periods when the debt would have to be serviced and amortized. This is in essence a way of taxing those (today's young) who potentially benefit from the change. This manner of adjustment could perhaps generate enough support to eliminate the draft in any given period.

There is, however, a major drawback to the proposal. Implicit in its adjustment process is that at some point in the future *all* the budgetary costs of manpower procurement through the market will be transferred to the general income tax structure of the economy. The eventual abolition of the differential levy (the transitional debt issue) against today's young to pay the *additional* costs of market procurement over a transition period would be called for. This may not be possible. Such a change in tax distribution implies that nondraft-age individuals are possibly going to be confronted with higher tax prices for military manpower at some point in the future. If this should be the case, these individuals would have an incentive to rebel against the elimination of the draft and to reinstitute it at that time in terms of their choice behavior in the voting model. It is possible, however, that there are significant manpower economies to market procurement and that even when the differential levy is removed in the future, the nondraft-age group would face significantly lower tax prices for manpower than would have prevailed if the draft had been

11. As regards the latter two problems, see Buchanan and Tullock [3].

12. The theory of public debt on which this discussion is based appears in Buchanan [2]. Subsequent discussion appears in Ferguson [5].

maintained. In this case, the differential levy could probably be dropped without the nondraft-age group acting to reinstitute the draft. The viability of the debt issue proposal could thus hinge on the predicted existence of substantial manpower economies to market procurement.

Debt issue would appear, then, to be at least a conceptually attractive way to offset the strong collective bias toward perpetuating the draft. Whether such a proposal could be realistically viable is another question and would basically depend on how difficult such an adjustment would be to arrange in real world collective institutions.

iv. *Conclusion*

The model is at least suggestive of other hypotheses about voter behavior and attitudes regarding the draft. Perhaps the major implication is the predicted voting and lobbying behavior of veterans' groups. A preliminary sampling of the testimony of the leadership of veterans' organizations on the extension of the current draft law indicates that these groups lobby very strongly for extension and tend to view the draft as an "obligation" of today's young.[13] This activity and attitude are fully consistent with the voting process of the model in which veterans view the continuation of the draft (and veterans' programs) as repayment on their sunk tax burden. Indeed, the lobbying position of the veterans' groups on the continuation of the draft is possibly the pivotal link in an intergenerational voting process that "explains" the modern development of the collective activity of veterans' groups and more generally the origin of the whole array of veterans' programs that currently exist.[14] In the latter regard,

13. For a limited sample, see the statements by John E. Davis, National Commander of the American Legion, Leslie M. Fry, Commander-in-Chief of the Veterans of Foreign Wars of the United States, and John S. Stillman, National Chairman of the American Veterans Committee, that appear in the U.S., Congress, Senate, Committee on Armed Forces [12].

14. Olson calls veterans' groups noneconomic in the sense that their political power is derivative from the social benefits (camaraderie) provided to members and not from any economic benefits provided. This is because all veterans, members and nonmembers of veterans' groups, benefit alike in the economic benefits generated by the lobbying activity of these organizations. This is correct, but it addresses the phenomenon of veterans' groups in a static context. These groups have an intergenerational character that is related in an important way to the continuation of the draft. The draft is the institution which insures that future veterans will

the model would qualify as an individualistic explanation of the origin and growth of a major component of the Federal budgetary process.[15]

As previously indicated, economists have traditionally shown that the draft is inefficient relative to voluntarism. This is correct, but this view has never impressed the legislator who well recognizes the changes in tax distribution implied by the higher budgetary costs (at least in the short-run) of shifting to an all-volunteer policy. The model presented here supplements the traditional economic analysis by explaining the political origin and stability of the draft. Draft reform is, after all, a political process. If this paper has been able to lay bare the political elements that underlie a draft system in a democracy, the substantive issues of draft reform can perhaps be better understood.

References

1. Altman, S. H. and Fechter, A. E. "The Supply of Military Personnel in the Absence of a Draft," *Am. Econ. Rev.* 57 (May 1967), 19–31.
2. Buchanan, James M. *Public Principles of Public Debt.* Homewood, Illinois, 1958.
3. Buchanan, James M. and Tullock, Gordon. "The 'Dead' Hand of Monopoly," *Antitrust Law and Economics Review* 1 (Summer 1968), 85–96.
4. Davis, J. Ronnie and Palomba, Neil A. "On the Shifting of the Military Draft as a Progressive Tax-in-Kind," *West. Econ. Jour.* 6 (Mar. 1968), 150–53.
5. Ferguson, James, ed. *Public Debt and Future Generations.* Chapel Hill, 1964.
6. Fisher, A. C. "The Cost of the Draft and the Cost of Ending the Draft," *Am. Econ. Rev.* 59 (June 1969), 239–54.
7. Hansen, W. L. and Weisbrod, B. A. "Economics of the Military Draft," *Quar. Jour. Econ.* 81 (Aug. 1967), 395–421.
8. Oi, Walter Y. "The Economic Cost of the Draft," *Am. Econ Rev.* 57 (May 1967), 39–62.

---

exist (probably in large numbers) and that gives a clear rationale for the lobbying activity by veterans' groups for a continued and maybe increasing flow of economic benefits to veterans. In this context, part of the explanation of the opposition of veterans' groups to the volunteer army proposal would be predicted to reside in the feeling that less veterans would be created by such a manpower procurement system. For the discussion of Olson, see [9, pp. 159–60].

15. In the 1968 Federal budget, spending on veterans' benefits and services was estimated at $6.7 billion or roughly 4 percent of all expenditures.

9. Olson, Mancur. *The Logic of Collective Action.* Cambridge, Mass., 1965.
10. Pauly, M. V. and Willett, T. D. "Who Bears the Burden of National Defense?" *Why the Draft? The Case for a Volunteer Army,* ed. by James C. Miller III. Baltimore, 1968, pp. 53–57.
11. —————————. "Who 'Should' Bear the Burden of National Defense?" *Ibid.,* pp. 58–68.
12. U.S., Congress, Senate, Committee on Armed Services, *The Selective Service Act of 1967: Hearing on S. 1432,* 90th Cong., 1st Sess., 1967.
13. Willett, T. D. "Another Cost of Conscription," *West Econ. Jour.* 6 (Dec. 1968), 425–26.

V

CONCLUSION

23

Economic Imperialism[1]

Gordon Tullock

If we define "economics" as "what economists do," then a vast expansion of that field is one of the more interesting intellectual developments of this generation. There is now a sizable literature by economists and using recognizable economic methods in the field normally described as political science. Since Von Neumann and Morgenstern's book was published, economists have been working in the field of military strategy. Recently this interest has expanded to take in problems in the field of diplomacy and international relations. These developments are in addition to economic interest in problems of management and efficiency in all branches of the government. Indeed, although I suppose that applications of economics such as cost-benefit analysis can hardly be regarded as outside the theoretical sphere of traditional economic interests, until recently almost all work on such matters was left to the students of public administration, a branch of political science.

Economists are not only doing research in "public administration," they have also invaded the field of business administration, with the result that a number of leading members of the profession now draw more of their income from consulting contracts than from their academic work. To continue, economists are now producing work on criminology, where, as usual, their approach appears unorthodox to the point of eccentricity to the traditional practitioners.

1. The "economic theory of democracy indeed as developed by Anthony Downs and others is a very good example of what I have sometimes called 'economics imperialism,' which is an attempt on the part of economics to take over all the other social sciences," Kenneth Boulding, "Economics as a Moral Science," *American Economic Review*, LIX, No. 1, March 1969, 1–12.

After generations of repeating that economics could say nothing about income distribution, economists are now working on the economics of charity and income redistribution. Here they are, in a way, inventing a new field rather than invading an existing one, although I suspect many Ph.D.'s in social welfare administration would deny it. The recent upsurge of economic interest in the operation of non-profit organizations, however, is clearly the creation of a new field rather than an imperialistic invasion of an existing one.

But we are not finished. Economists have devoted much time recently to educational problems. Admittedly, their interest has been mainly confined to education as a form of investment, a subject which educationists have normally neglected, but they are showing some interest in teaching techniques, so far mostly in connection with the teaching of economics as a subject. Problems of the organization of science have also attracted some economic interest recently. Here they directly compete only with a few sociologists, but most natural scientists have strong views on the subject and tend to be annoyed by the economists' tendency to calculate instead of emote. The economic historians have recently produced information on such matters as the actual cost to the thirteen colonies of the British restrictions on trade which are of great importance to standard history, although the historians do not seem conscious of this fact. Lastly, at least one economist, myself, is interested in economic applications in the field of biology. So far, the biologists have ignored me, but in view of the impact of Malthus on an earlier generation of biologists, I still have hope.

But all of this intellectual activity, important as I think it is, has attracted remarkably little attention. The readers of this book are certainly more interested in these new fields of economics than the overwhelming majority of the academic community who will not read it, yet I doubt that many of them will have even heard of much of the work I have listed above. The average economist is even less informed. If we consider academic specialists in the fields now being invaded by economists, the overwhelming majority will not have even heard of the movement. Among those few who have become vaguely aware of this threat to their disciplinary sovereignity, only a small proportion will know anything about the actual work done by the economists. In most cases, the number who have actually familiarized themselves with the new approach is still smaller.

Why this lack of attention to what appears to be an important development? One obvious answer would be that the economists engaged in applying their tools to new fields are simply wrong: that their work is wasted and not worth studying. I do not believe that this is so, but I shall not devote any time here to refuting it. If the other essays in this volume have not already convinced the reader that economists are doing important work outside the traditional field of economics, it is unlikely that I could do so in a few pages. There are other explanations than the possible lack of real worth to these studies, and it is to these other explanations I shall now turn.

The fact that only a minority of economists are interested in these forays of economists outside their traditional field arises, I think, mainly from the rapid growth of specialization within economics. Only a minority of economists are interested in almost any given specialty within the general area of economics. Economics has now become such a broad and complex subject that a detailed knowledge of all of its branches would be beyond the intellectual capacity of most, probably all, economists. The human brain, after all, is finite and the steady increase in the total of scientific knowledge carries with it the corollary that any individual human being must reduce the percentage of that total which he learns. Thus disciplines were originally established, and thus specialties and subspecialties are now developing.

It is notable that economists who are specialists in public finance will normally be interested in the new developments, such as those in this volume, which fall in the traditional field of political science simply because they are obviously closely related to problems of public finance. Similarly, economists interested in economic development normally are concerned with the economics of education which is closely related to their subdiscipline, and in fact was largely developed by people interested in the backward countries and their problems. The lack of an active body of economists interested in some of the other new fields is largely the result of the fact that there is no obviously closely related subdiscipline in the existing organization of economics. As these fields develop it is likely that only a fraction of the economics profession will be interested in them simply because only a fraction of the economics profession is interested in any subdiscipline.

The reasons why academic specialists in the fields being invaded by the economists are relatively uninformed about this development are, in my opinion, quite different. In the first place, some of these fields, the social organization of science or nonprofit organizations are not within the ambit of any well defined discipline. It is true that a few sociologists have done work in these general areas, but they are not major interests for any recognized subdiscipline of sociology. The total number of sociologists interested in either field is small, and most of them have other interests.

320 Theory of Public Choice

In such fields as political science, however, a great many scholars are directly concerned with the problems dealt with in such an "economic" book as *An Economic Theory of Democracy*.[2] The fact that most political scientists have not read it (although the situation is rapidly changing) can be put down to another result of the finite nature of the human brain. Learning a discipline is a capital investment process in which the individual invests time, energy, and some direct physical resources in acquiring knowledge. If a man has made such an investment and a book is produced which purports to deal with his subject but which requires a totally different set of intellectual capital to understand and evaluate its message, he is understandably reluctant to read it. To an economist, Downs' book is relatively easy to read. To a political scientist who has had the traditional training, it is an extremely difficult book. Not only is reading it hard, he is likely to misunderstand it. This is not because economists are smarter than political scientists; there are books which political scientists regard as easy which would raise great difficulties for economists. It is true, however, that a political scientist who wanted to become familiar with the economic approach to his field would probably find it necessary to devote six months to a year to acquiring the necessary intellectual capital in the form of a good background in economics.

Clearly the political scientist is not going to make this sizable investment unless he feels considerable assurance that it will be worthwhile. Indeed, he may fear that the intellectual capital he has already accumulated will be rendered obsolescent.[3] Under the circumstances, we should not be surprised if political scientists do not rush into this sort of speculative investment. On the contrary, we may be surprised that so many of them have shown serious interest.

2. Anthony Downs, *An Economic Theory of Democracy* (New York, 1958).

3. I cannot forebear giving an example of this sort of Ludditism which affected me personally. I left the University of Virginia in somewhat tense circumstances. Sometime thereafter, there was an exchange of correspondence on the subject in the pages of the student newspaper (*The Virginia Weekly*, Vol. II, No. 11, January 15, 1968). The editor of the paper, clearly reflecting the views, and probably the language, of at least one member of the Department of Political Science editorialized: "Admittedly Mr. Tullock published a good deal, but the quantity of his writing easily exceeded their quality. Mr. Tullock, who had pretentions to competence as a political scientist as well as an economist, was looked on by professionals in the field very much as George Plimpton was looked on by members of the Detroit Lions."

Most political scientists, however, are working with their traditional methods and ignoring the new developments. With time, this will probably change (the younger members of the profession are much less conservative, probably because they have less accumulated capital in danger of obsolescence) and the example of Vincent Ostrom, William Riker, and L. L. Wade will be followed.

The fact, then, that the new drive to apply economic methods in fields far from traditional economics has so far had relatively little impact on the average scholar is not surprising. Neither is it particularly unfortunate. Almost by definition the scholars now working in these fields have been self-selected for originality and interdisciplinary interests. They are building a solid body of work which will provide a foundation for future expansion. A gradual spread of the new approach, with research solidly backing each new advance, is healthier than a sudden fad based on preliminary findings. We can anticipate that our influence will grow somewhat slower than our knowledge. On the whole this is healthy, if sometimes frustrating.

The restrictions on the development of economic approaches in other fields of the social sciences, however, are clearly temporary. The boundaries between the disciplines are mere traditions and they are automatically eroded by the passage of time. We can confidently expect that twenty years from now the problems of specialization and conserving of intellectual capital which today still restrict the influence of the new methods will no longer constitute serious barriers. What will be (or should be) the shape of the social sciences then? I should like to devote the remainder of this essay to attempting an answer to this question. Since prophecy is notably difficult, I can hardly ask the reader to give much weight to my guesses as to the future, but if he will regard what I have to say as a proposal for the reorganization of the social sciences, I think he will agree that it is at least worth serious consideration. It would not only eliminate some artificial barriers between closely related disciplines, it would provide a framework for specialization which should make cooperation between fields easier and less subject to disciplinary jealousy than at present.

Let me begin my proposal for the future with a brief survey of the past. The Enlightenment was, in my opinion, one of the high points of human intellectual development. In the latter part of those halcyon days, economics was founded by two friends, David Hume and Adam Smith. Although we can clearly see in their work, particularly, of course, Smith's *The Wealth of Nations,* the origins of scientific economics, it does not appear that they felt that the distinction between economics and the rest of the social studies was of any great importance. *The Wealth of Nations,* after all, contains chapters on military affairs, administration of justice, public works, and education.[4] Hume also normally discusses both economics and politics in a manner which we now normally associate with economics.

With Hume and Smith, then, we see an "economic" approach to a very large part of social behavior. They called their discipline "political economy" and certainly thought of it as as much political as economic. It happened, of course, to be easier to analyze economics (in the modern meaning) than politics with these tools and they made more progress there, but they would probably have been both surprised and disappointed if told that their work would, for nearly 200 years, be regarded as the foundation of economics, but largely ignored by scholars in other areas such as the study of politics. It is probably the influence of David Ricardo which led to the reduction in the scope of the area studied with the methods of Smith and Hume to what we now call economics. Brilliant though Ricardo undoubtedly was, however, there seems no inherent reason why his tastes in the fields he wished to study should mold the present day structure of the disciplines. The differences between politics and economics are real, but they are readily bridged, as witness the number of economists who have written in political science.

For a more fundamental organizing principle for the social sciences let us return to a distinction that Hume and Smith thought vital: the difference between "reason and the passions." That Hume thought this distinction important is, I suppose, not in doubt, but it deserves further emphasis. To Hume, the role of reason was simply that of a servant of the passions. Putting the same thought in modern terms, we have a set of preferences, and we use our intellectual capacities for the purpose of achieving as much of the things preferred as possible. Thus the "rational model" dealt with the means men would adopt to achieve goals determined upon by nonrational means. Smith, on the other hand, wrote two books, not one. *The Wealth of Nations,* I think, can be taken as a working out of the slave-reason role in society, particularly in that portion of social action which we call economics; and the other, *The Theory of Moral Sentiments,* an effort to explain why human beings have certain of the "passions." It should not be forgotten that it was *The Theory of Moral Sentiments* which originally made Smith's

4. Modern Library edition, pp. 653–764. All of these subjects are discussed under the general title "of the expenses of the sovereign of commonwealth," but the text goes much farther afield.

reputation, and guaranteed that *The Wealth of Nations* would receive serious consideration.

Let me put the distinction between reason and the passions into a more extensive modern form. Any individual has a collection of preferences. We may equate this preference structure to Hume's "passions." The individual, in attempting to achieve his preferences as much as possible, makes use of his rational faculties and makes choices of various sorts between the alternatives available to him. Traditionally, the study of these choices and their interaction with the choices of other individuals within the sphere that we call economics has been the basic field studied by those members of the academic community who are called economists. What has happened in recent years is that the economists have begun to study such choices and their interaction with the choices of other individuals in areas which are not traditionally economics. Fortunately, it turns out to be possible to bring into these areas a very large part of the apparatus already developed in economics, but a good deal of new invention is also necessary. It also turns out, as this book has demonstrated, that much of the work in at least one of these new branches, public choice or the theory of governmental decision, is applicable to areas which, I think, would previously have been called a subsection of economics—public finance.

Economists in general have been relatively little interested in the preferences that individuals have. They assume the preferences and then deduce what the outcome is but do not pay much attention to investigation of these preferences. Traditionally, an economist will tell you that this is a problem for the psychologists rather than for economists. In practice, however, it is not only the problem of the psychologist, it has to a very large extent been the problem of the sociologist and of the behavioralist political scientist. A great deal of the research of the sociologists, behavioralists, and political scientists concerns the type of person who is apt to be involved in some particular activity. This can be thought of as an effort to determine which people have certain sets of tastes and preferences. The economist, for example, if asked about why people are lawyers or garbage collectors, will point out that there is a positive return to these activities and state that people of suitable degree of talent would enter these fields until the returns of labor effort invested in these fields is equivalent[5] to that in other fields for persons with the same amount of talent. He would probably add the statement that

5. With a large number of modifying factors which need not be discussed here.

individuals may have particular tastes for certain particular activities and are more likely to be found in those activities than in those for which they have a personal dislike. The sociologist, considering the same problem, will turn to the question of what particular type of people are apt to be lawyers or garbage collectors. He may determine, for example, that lawyers are brighter, more likely to come from upper class backgrounds, more likely to be of somewhat studious bent, etc. than garbage collectors.

Traditionally, these two approaches to the same problem have led to a good deal of conflict. This conflict is unfortunate because the two approaches are perfectly consistent. They simply are aimed at different objectives. It has turned out that the examination of the outcome of preferences which the economists have undertaken permits much more elaborate, precise, and testable statements about the real world than does the examination of the tastes themselves by the other social scientists. The reasons for this greater advance of economics are probably that it is older and more developed, and also probably because it is dealing with somewhat easier problems. In the present state of knowledge of psychology, determining why people have some particular set of preferences is an extraordinarily difficult problem, and it is even extremely difficult to find out what preferences they have unless they "reveal" their preferences by some type of interaction which the economist would logically study.

As the reader will no doubt already have deduced, my proposal for the future organization of social sciences is that they be divided into two grand domains, the sciences of choice and the sciences of preferences. The sciences of choice would essentially be an outgrowth of economics and would be devoted to determining the likely outcome of the interaction of individuals attempting to maximize their preference functions in a society where it is not possible for everyone to have everything he wants. It would no longer be confined to what is traditionally known as economics, but could deal with any institution. No doubt subdisciplines within this major field would rapidly develop because of the finite nature of the human mind. Still, it would be recognized that these subdisciplines were defined solely by the particular institutional structure they happen to be dealing with and not through any difference of approach or method.

On the other hand, there would be the sciences of preferences, tastes, or passions. They would be devoted to attempting to determine what the preferences of various people in society are, to examining individual preferences, to trying to find out how the preferences in society can be summarized conveniently, and, what is perhaps more important than all these things, the factors which mold preferences.

With this division of labor between two general areas, it would seem that we would have a basis for cooperation, rather than conflict. Presently most economists tend to regard sociologists and the political scientists as among the unwashed. They look down on their methods and point out, quite correctly, that they do not have anything in the way of elaborate theories and that their empirical research is usually an effort to find specific fact instead of an effort to validate a general theory.

This feeling on the part of economists is, to put the matter mildly, fully reciprocated by the sociologists, political scientists, etc. One of the major points that they will make again and again and again is that man is not rational, and hence the economists' assumption that he is, is false. In discussion with people of this persuasion, I've always found that they define rational in a way which is not characteristic of the economist. They have as their idea of a rational man, a person who is perfectly informed, cold-blooded, takes very long views, gives a great deal of consideration for all decisions, and invariably aims at direct, selfish aims. Needless to say, with this view of the word rational, it is easy to demonstrate that men are not rational. Still, the fact that people I have talked to who propose this view are, generally speaking, unwilling to accept my assurance that I do not think that people are rational in their meaning of the term is indicative of deeper drives. When I attempt to present the economist's meaning of rationality and point out that it is reasonably immune to the criticism that men are not rational, I normally find an unwillingness on their part to admit that such use of the word rational is legitimate or that it is possible for me to justify the "rational models" of economics by alleging that the word rational means something different from what it means to the sociologist, etc.

It seems to me that much of this clash comes from the fact that the borders of the two disciplines are not so located that cooperative activity is easy. In general, if an economist and a sociologist, say, deal with the same problem, each will find that the other's research is of very little value to him, and they regard each other as opponents. Coming from different intellectual backgrounds, they also find a good deal of difficulty understanding each other. An explicit division of labor in which the economists consider the consequences of people making choices in efforts to maximize their preferences, and the psychologist-sociologist-behavioralist study those preferences themselves, would permit a relaxation of the current tension in the social sciences.

326 Theory of Public Choice

This division of labor would not be radically different from the actual present organization of the social sciences. There are some differences, of course. The economists have, of necessity, some rather primitive ideas as to the preferences people have because this is necessary to test their theories. The political scientist and sociologist on the other hand have some rather primitive theories of the effect of differing individual choices in social interaction. Nevertheless, it seems to me that an explicit division of the field in these terms would be an improvement on the present situation. It will require relatively little change in the things that are actually being done by people in different parts of the social sciences.

Speaking as a man who has gradually over the years tended to become an economist, I should like here to suggest certain mild reorientations in the research now undertaken by the social scientists who are not economists. Since the principal point of this mild reorientation, other than improving the nature of that research itself, is to make it more usable by economists in the division of labor which I have suggested, it may be that noneconomists will resent my advice. Nevertheless, as will be seen, it does not reduce the scope or importance of the work of noneconomists.

Let me begin by pointing briefly to a sort of general theory which underlines much of noneconomic work in the social sciences. I can do no better than quote John Harsanyi, "The implicit assumption usually has been that 'all good things come together,' all desirable factors have positive correlation with one another. Greater popular participation can only make the political system 'more democratic' in all respects; greater democracy can only increase the rate of economic development; more freedom and more permissiveness for the child can only improve its academic progress, etc.

"We shall call this implicit assumption the positive correlation fallacy; it has been one of the main obstacles to clear thinking among social scientists and is probably responsible for a high proportion of the bad policy recommendations we have made."[6]

That this criticism is, at least in part, well founded, I think would be hard to deny. But, it seems to me that the political scientists, sociologists, and psychologists are not really totally wrong in taking this attitude if we assume that they are attempting to reconstruct peoples' preference structures. If we look at the typical "behavioralist" article in a political science journal or a sociology journal, we will find that it involves some such question as what

6. "Rational Choice Models of Political Behavior vs. Functionalist and Conformist Theories," *World Politics*, July 1969, pp. 537–38.

type of people are apt to be in some occupation or what preferences do people in some occupations apparently have. In both cases, this is a matter which economists would call taste, although I'm not at all certain the political scientist and sociologist would recognize it under that title. It happens to be so that, to the best of our current knowledge, there is no intrinsic reason why an individual who has a taste for one "good" thing under the specification of some particular value system may not have taste for other "good" things as specified by the same value system. In many ways, the purpose of education *is* to produce people all of whose values are "good" in the terms of the appropriate general value system.

Thus, it is very commonly so that, if we look at individuals who have been trained in any particular society, "all good things come together." They will be indoctrinated in the values of that society. Hence, there will be a distinct correlation between the degree to which they accept the values which they have been indoctrinated into one field, and the degree to which they accept them in another. Further, much activity of politically interested people is directed towards attempting to indoctrinate particular value sets in people, and, in general, this is done in a way which once again produces this type of correlation.

Looking at it from the standpoint of the economist, we might say that there is no particular conflict, at least as far as our present knowledge exists, between a person having a "good" set of preferences in one area and his having a "good" set of preferences in another. The education of an individual produces a set of preferences, and giving a preference for A in one field and B in another field is, on the whole, as easy as giving a set of preferences for A in one field and A in another field.

Thus, the behavioralist "positive correlation fallacy" is not, if we are thinking about preferences only, necessarily a fallacy. It is only when we look to policy and interaction that we find this a fallacy. In certain areas it isn't even a fallacy there. In general, if we have something or other which is desirable in all ways, i.e., meets all the requirements of all individuals, we will rapidly carry it out. It is only the fact that we've already normally exhausted all *easy* possibilities for such quasi-Paretian moves, that leads to the "scarcity" of resources which economics studies. No economist would deny that if a positive correlation between all good things *did* exist, we should move out along the ray indicated. What we, in fact, say is that we have already reached the end of the possible changes which have this favorable outcome, and must now pick and choose among possible courses of action which have both advantages and disadvantages. To put the matter differently, we must now choose between policies which some people favor and other people do not.

Thus, a theoretical "positive correlation" among preferences and tastes may well exist. It is among the interactions of the real world that the assumption of this positive correlation leads to fallacious outcomes. "Greater democracy" *may* "increase the rate of economic development," but the fact that both of these things are, in certain value systems, desirable is irrelevant in discussing whether it will or will not. If it turns out that these two desirable characteristics are not interrelated in such a way that one can increase the rate of growth by increasing the rate of democracy, then we must make choices between things that we desire. This is a characteristic situation for economic investigation. A great deal of the noneconomic discussion of these problems has, in essence, foreclosed this type of problem by carrying over the "positive correlation" assumption from the area of taste to the area of interaction.

Having criticized the noneconomists, it is perhaps only sensible that I close this essay by offering a somewhat similar criticism of the economists themselves. There are pure theories of human interaction which will fit any possible set of human tastes. These theories are, of course, not testable by operational means, since any conceivable outcome in the real world could be explained by some particular taste. In order to make their theories testable, economists implicitly, not always explicitly, *do* make assumptions about the tastes that people do have. These assumptions, which I call the 90 per cent selfish hypothesis, normally take the form of assuming that the people under study have a set of desires for their own personal well-being which are rather similar to those of the economist himself, although not identical. Further, they are rarely specified in any detail.

This set of rather primitive assumptions about human behavior, which is implicit in empirical testing of economic theory, works out rather well in practice because it is not thought by the economist who is *implying* the theory that he can exactly specify the tastes of the group of people under test. He assumes that his assumption is, at best, a reasonable approximation of their tastes. Thus, the deviation between the tastes of the individuals and the tastes which the economist is ascribing to them becomes a random variable in the statistical testing routine and is dealt with in the normal manner in which noise is cut out in statistics.

The end product is to provide a mechanism for testing economic theory which works out rather well. It should be realized, however, that it works very much less well than a more specific and exacting view of human preferences would. Economists have always ignored this problem, and it seems to me this is a real defect in current economics. I do not propose that economists begin to investigate human preferences, but that they recognize that it is a problem for people in another field of the social sciences and pay attention to discoveries in these fields. It does not seem to be likely that great progress will be made in the "science of taste" in the near future simply because it seems to me these are extremely difficult areas; but they are also areas which will repay extensive research.

The reader may not regard my proposal for reorganization of the social sciences as desirable. Certainly he is unlikely to regard the prophecy that this may happen in the next twenty years as having a high degree of probability. I think he will have to admit, however, that my proposed reorientation would make only a small difference in the actual research being undertaken by people in the two different grand divisions which I have specified. There would be minor changes in what they study and their methods of study, and there would be a possibility of cooperation and understanding between them to replace the present antagonism and interdisciplinary warfare. In a sense, my proposal is that the other social sciences accept the recent sharp expansion of economics. That they recognize that the objectives of the economic research are basically different from the objectives of the researchers now in these fields. In return, I suggest that the economists welcome sociologists, psychologists, etc. who are attempting to determine the nature of human preferences in the economic or political area. Whether the net effect of this is an expansion of the economic profession or an expansion of the non-economic disciplines I cannot now say. Further, although this is important in terms of our personal ambitions to be members of rapidly growing disciplines, it has no significance for the progress of science.

Contributors

JAMES M. BUCHANAN, Department of Economics and Center for the Study of Public Choice, Virginia Polytechnic Institute and State University

J. RONNIE DAVIS, Department of Economics, University of Florida

CHARLES J. GOETZ, Department of Economics and Center for the Study of Public Choice, Virginia Polytechnic Institute and State University

KENNETH V. GREENE, Department of Economics, State University of New York at Binghamton

DAVID B. JOHNSON, Department of Economics, Louisiana State University

COTTON M. LINDSAY, Department of Economics, University of California at Los Angeles

CHARLES R. McKNEW, JR., Department of Economics, California State College at Haywood

CHARLES W. MEYER, Department of Economics, Iowa State University

MARK V. PAULY, Department of Economics, Northwestern University

WILLIAM CRAIG STUBBLEBINE, Department of Economics, Claremont College

ROBERT D. TOLLISON, Graduate School of Business and Public Administration, Cornell University

GORDON TULLOCK, Department of Economics and Center for the Study of Public Choice, Virginia Polytechnic Institute and State University

RICHARD E. WAGNER, Department of Economics, Tulane University